The aims and objectives of business

PROFIT Profit is the difference between how much a business sells its goods or services for and how much it costs to produce them. For example, MLC Bikes sells 1000 mountain bikes at £500 each and therefore receives £500,000 from its customers (1000 x £500). The cost of making 1000 bikes, including materials, wages, the rent of the workshop, etc comes to £400,000. MLC Bikes, therefore, makes a profit of £100,000 (£500,000–£400,000).

The profit and non-profit making sectors

Businesses can be grouped into those that aim to make a profit by providing goods and services, such as car manufacturers, supermarkets and banks, and those that are non-profit making such as the police or charitable organisations. The aim of General Motors, Sainsbury's or Barclays is to make the largest possible profit. The aim of the police is to use the resources provided by the Government to keep law and order as effectively as possible. The aim of the RSPCA is to raise as much money as possible to support animal welfare. Most of this book is concerned with the profit making sector of the economy. Unit 16 looks at central and local government business which provides most of the non-profit making sector.

Business objectives

Businesses in the profit making sector of the economy will have a number of objectives designed to help them achieve their overall aim of making profits. These might include:

- INCREASING THE SHARE OF THE MARKET (Tesco might set an objective to increase its share of grocery sales by 5% in the next five years.)
- BREAKING INTO A NEW MARKET (A firm might sell a product at or below what it costs to make it in order to get a 'foothold' in the market. Having established itself, the firm would then raise the price in order to increase profits.)
- SURVIVAL (In times of economic difficulty a firm may need to take measures in order to stay in business at all. This may mean it cuts the number of workers it employs, or sells off parts of the business.)
- ENVIRONMENTAL AND COMMUNITY SUPPORT (The Body Shop seeks to produce 'environmentally friendly' products and donates considerable sums of money to support community projects. This all helps to improve the 'image' of the company which in the long term may help to improve profits.)

x

See Unit 18

Case study

The Times Newspaper In September 1993 The Times newspaper cut its price from 45p to 30p.

Sales of 'Quality' Daily Newspapers

	September 1993 (daily sales)	May 1994 (daily sales)
The Times	442,000	517,000
The Daily Telegraph	1008,000	993,000
Financial Times	287,000	300,000
The Guardian	404,000	402,000
The Independent	332,000	277,000

- Why do you think The Times reduced its price?
- What appears to have been the effect of this on sales of **a** The Times **b** other 'quality' papers?
- Which paper was affected **a** the most **b** the least by the reduction in the price of The Times? Why do you think papers were affected differently? What do you think the effect would be on sales of the Sun newspaper?
- Calculate the total amount of money collected through the sale of The Times in **a** September 1993 **b** May 1994. What conclusion do you draw? Why might the strategy help to increase profits of The Times in the long term? (Clue; most of the cost of newspapers is paid through advertising).
- The Daily Telegraph responded in June 1994 by reducing its price to 30p. Shortly afterwards The Times cut its price by a further 10p to 20p. The other newspapers did not change their prices. What would you expect would happen to the circulation of
  - **a** The Times
  - **b** The Daily Telegraph
  - **c** the other papers as a result of these further price changes?

The chain of production

The production of goods starts with raw materials and ends with sales to consumers. The chain of production shows the stages a product passes through from start to finish. Different products will have different chains of production but each stage will **add value** to the materials.

The chain of production for a bar of chocolate

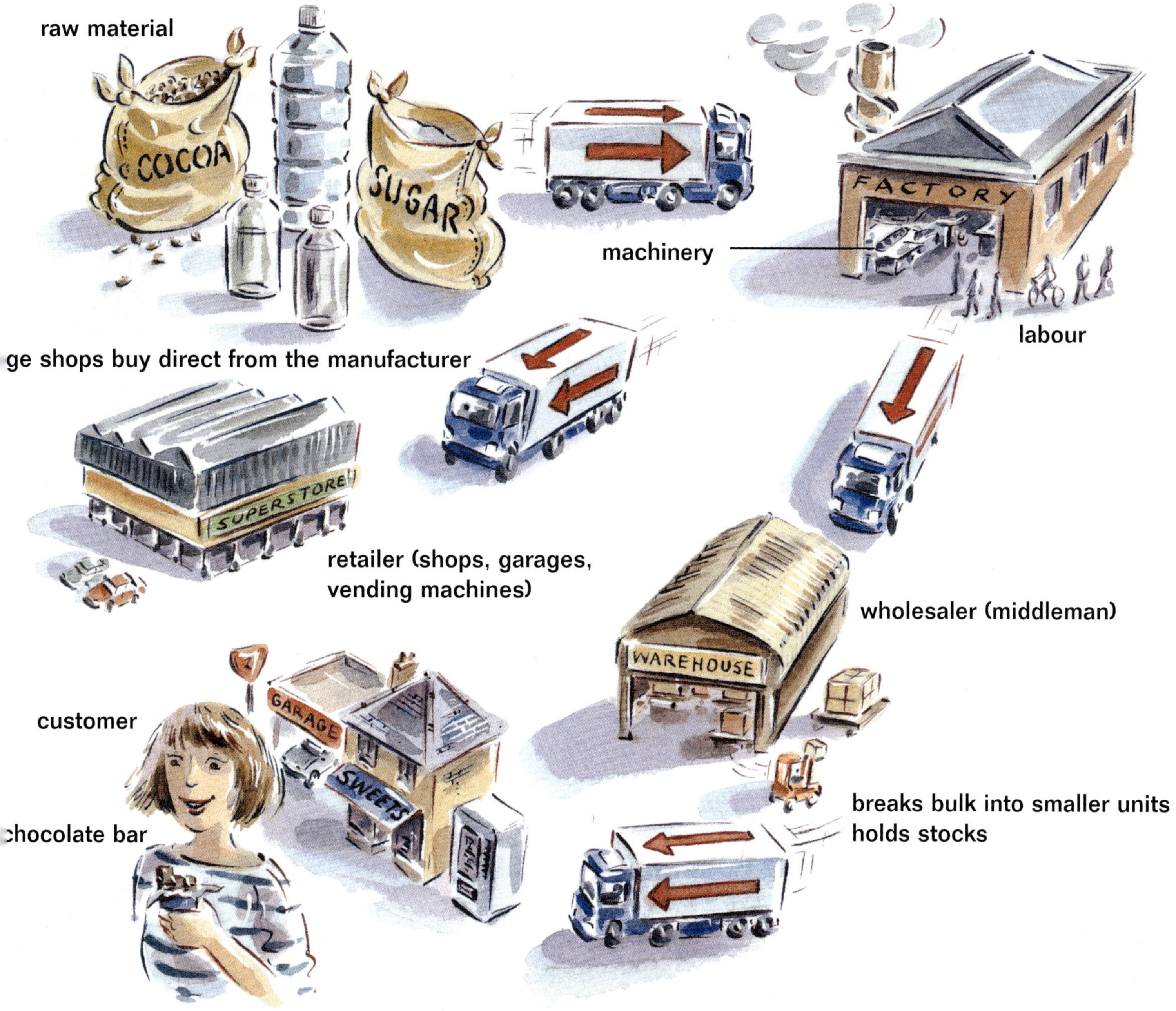

Exercise

Draw chain of production diagrams for
a a bottle of milk,
b a pair of jeans.

Types of economic activity

Primary
(Extraction of raw materials)

farming
forestry
fishing
mining
quarrying

Secondary
(Manufacturing - turning raw materials into products)

building
making machines
making products for the consumer

Tertiary
(Services)

trade, commerce
(banking, insurance, communications, transport, retailing, advertising)
direct services (teachers, doctors, hairdressers)

Exercise

1 Write down the three types of economic activity: Primary, Secondary and Tertiary. List each of the following activities under the correct heading: Lloyds Bank, dentist, British Coal, Ford Motor Company, British Steel Corporation, Marks and Spencer, London Brick Company, British Gas, British Telecom, Shell Oil, Hilton Hotels, Heinz.

2 Explain why some of the activities listed above could be considered under more than one heading.

Case study

Changes in the proportion of the working population employed in different sectors of the economy

	1964	1974	1984	1994
	%	%	%	%
Primary	6	3	3	2
Secondary	46	39	33	30
Tertiary	48	58	64	68

1 Represent the above figures by bar charts.

2 Describe how the working population has changed in the last 30 years.

3 Why do you think these changes have occurred?

De-industrialisation

Extension section

In the last 30 years there has been a decline in the number of jobs in manufacturing in the UK, both in actual numbers and in the percentage of the total workforce. Between 1974 and 1994 there was a loss of two million jobs in manufacturing. This has been called de-industrialisation. Why has this occurred? Economists disagree as to the exact cause. Suggested reasons include:

- New technology has meant less need for workers in manufacturing as machines have been taking over more and more jobs.
- A modern economy requires more services, such as banking, insurance and leisure industries.
- Foreign competition has made it more difficult to sell UK manufactured goods abroad. At the same time, the UK is buying more manufactured goods from other countries.
- There has been a growth in services provided by the Government and local government in the last 30 years, including health, social services and education.

Although there has been a decline in the total number of jobs in manufacturing, some manufacturing industries have been expanding and employing more people. These growth industries include the making of electronic components and computers, as well as food processing.

There have also been changes within the service industries, with some types of employment expanding and others declining. There has been a growth of employment in such industries as information technology, finance and leisure pursuits, and a decline in employment in transport and domestic service.

An important trend has been the increasing proportion of women in employment. There is now almost an equal number of male and female workers. However, there has also been a growth in part-time employment and this accounts for much of the increase in female employees.

The factors of production

The resources required to produce goods and services can be divided into three groups:

- **Raw materials** such as minerals, crops, wood etc.
- **Labour** including manual workers (people working with their hands), office workers and managers.
- **Capital** the buildings, machinery and equipment used to produce the goods and services.

x

(*Note*: The word 'capital' is also used to describe finance such as loans and shares. See Units 5 and 9)

Different goods and services require different combinations of the factors of production. A hotel will require relatively large amounts of capital and labour and little in the way of raw materials. It may also be possible to substitute one factor of production for another. A modern farm will employ more machinery (capital) and less labour than was the case in the 19th century.

How the factors of production are employed to produce a pair of jeans

Exercise

Choose any simple product and construct a diagram similar to the one above to show how the factors of production are used to produce it.

Types of economy

Extension section

All countries throughout the world are faced with the same basic economic problem – how to use their scarce resources and how to share out the goods and services produced by these resources.

Case study

You and a group of friends are shipwrecked on a desert island. Because of your charm, high intelligence and leadership qualities, you are elected as the supreme ruler of the island.

a What basic needs would you try to meet first in order to survive the first week?

A month has gone by and you have all survived – well done!

b What 'luxury' goods or services would you now try to produce?

After 6 months on the island only one person has died (as a result of a falling coconut) but you and your friends are getting bored with a diet of fish and coconuts. One day there is great excitement: a case of tins of baked beans is washed ashore. You immediately order them to be put in your hut until you are able to decide how to share them out. You are now faced with the basic economic problem. You have scarce resources (the tins of baked beans) and you need to decide how to share them out amongst competing wants (your friends). You jot down the following ideas in the sand:

- Share them out equally.
- Share them out according to each person's needs, eg big people get more than small people.
- Put a price on each tin in terms of so many hours work to be done.
- Keep most of them yourself and give the rest to the strongest people to protect you from the likely uprising.

What are the advantages and disadvantages of each method of sharing out the tins?

Planned economies

The desert island case study on the previous page is an example of a planned, or centrally controlled, economy. The central authority (you in this case) controlled the sharing out of resources and decided what goods and services would be produced. In Cuba the State controls the factors of production and decides what goods and services will be produced and how they will be allocated amongst consumers. In the past many countries, including Russia and China, were organised as planned economies. Most of these have now moved away from being strictly centrally planned.

Advantages of planned economies

- The State can decide upon an order of priorities for the whole community and try to provide benefit for all the population. It may, for example, decide that resources are better used to provide health care and education than luxury consumer items.
- Wasteful competition may be avoided and factors of production can be fully used. Unemployment, for example, can be avoided because the State owns and controls all the means of production.
- There are no private monopolies which might use their power to exploit the consumer. (A monopoly is where one firm controls most of the output.)
- Firms are not producing for profit and may therefore be able to take account of such problems as pollution and the effects on the local community.

Disadvantages of planned economies

- The lack of competition caused by the State owning all means of production may lead to a lack of efficiency and inventiveness.
- Because the main aim is not profit, there may be a lack of incentive to improve both as an individual and as a firm.
- It is very difficult to calculate the needs of the population and this may result in either under or over production.
- Central planning may restrict the economic freedom of the individual.

Free-market economies

A pure free market economy is one where there is no State ownership of the means of production. The State does not determine what is produced and how resources are allocated. This is done through the price system. Prices reflect the demand for a good or service in relation to its supply. Increased demand for a product will result in its price rising. The higher price will encourage more firms to produce the good because they can make more profit. If there is a surplus of a product the price will have to fall in order to sell the good.

Advantages of free-market economies

- Competition and the opportunity to make large profits may result in greater efficiency and more innovations.
- The price system helps to match demand and supply so that shortages and surpluses may be avoided.
- People are free to take part in business activities for the purpose of profit.

Disadvantages of free-market economies

- Competition may be wasteful.
- The market may not produce essential services if they do not make a profit.
- Private monopolies may exploit the consumer by controlling output and sales.

Mixed economies

- In reality few economies are either purely free market or totally centrally controlled. In China there is a considerable amount of free enterprise. In the USA there is some State involvement in business. When we refer to free market or planned economies we usually mean that the way in which resources are allocated comes very close to being one of the two types.
- Mixed economies involve aspects of both free market and centrally planned economies. In the UK, for example, the State owns a considerable share of the enterprise, but most of it is in the hands of the private sector. Prices largely control the allocation of resources in the private sector.
- The balance between the public and private sectors depends upon Government policy. The Conservative Government elected in 1979 reduced and size of the public sector by 'privatising' industries such as British Telecom and British Gas.
- The remainder of this book is concerned mainly with the UK and is set in the context of the mixed economy.

Summary of key words and ideas

- A **consumer** is a buyer of goods and services.
- A **producer** is a firm making goods or supplying services.
- **Profit** is the difference between what a business sells its goods and services for and what it costs to produce them.
- **Aims** – different businesses will have different aims but the overall aim of firms in the profit making sector of the economy is to make the greatest possible profit.
- **Objectives** – businesses will have sets of short term objectives designed to help them meet their long term aims.
- The **chain of production** is the stages a good passes through during the course of production.
- **Added value** is the amount each stage in the production process adds to the value of the product.
- The **wholesaler** is the middleman between the manufacturer and the retailer (shop).
- **Primary activity** is concerned with the extraction of raw materials.
- **Secondary activity** is manufacturing – turning the raw materials into finished goods.
- **Tertiary activity** is concerned with providing services.
- The **factors of production** are the 'ingredients' needed to make a particular good. They include Raw Materials, Labour (workers) and Capital (machinery, tools, buildings and equipment).
- **Deindustrialisation** is the decline in the number of workers employed in manufacturing industry.
- A **planned** or **centrally controlled** economy is one where the State owns and controls the means of production.
- A **free-market economy** is one where the means of production are owned privately and resources are allocated through the price system.
- A **mixed economy** contains elements of both the free market and planned economies.

Test questions

1 Explain the terms **a**) goods **b**) services **c**) consumer **d**) producer **e**) profit **f**) primary, secondary, tertiary sectors **g**) factors of production.

2 If it costs a business £10,000 to make 100 machines and it sells each machine at £1,500, how much profit does it make on the machines?

3 Why might a business choose to sell a product at or below what it costs to make it even though its long term aim is to make the greatest possible profit?

4 How will the aims of Marks and Spencer be different from those of the National Health Service?

5 **a** Complete the following chain of production diagram for a tin of tomatoes:

Raw materials → **?** → **Wholesaler** → **Retailer** → **?**

b What is a wholesaler?
c What is a retailer?

Employment in Radshire 1974 - 1994

% of Employment in:	1974	1984	1994
Primary sector	5	3	3
Secondary sector	60	50	40
Tertiary sector	30	40	50
Unemployment	5	7	7
Working population (000's)	400	410	420

6 **a** Give two examples of jobs in each of the primary, secondary and tertiary sectors.
b Describe the main changes shown in the table above.
c To what extent are the changes shown in the table similar or different to the changes in the UK's working population in the last 20 years?
d Calculate the number of people in each sector in 1994 (show your working).
e Give two possible reasons why the working population has increased in size.

7 List the following resources under the correct factor of production (Raw materials, Labour and Capital):
cement mixer, secretary, sugar, coal, building land, factory, driver, manager, screwdriver, scissors.

Extension questions

1 There has been a considerable decline in the number of manufacturing jobs in the UK during the last 20 years.

a Suggest three reasons why this has occurred.
b Name one manufacturing industry that has not declined and suggest why this is the case.
c Which sector of the economy has seen an increase in jobs? Give two possible reasons why this has happened.

2 Describe two differences between a centrally planned economy and a free market economy.

3 The UK is described as a 'mixed economy'. Explain what is meant by this term.

4 Both free market and centrally planned economies are faced with the problem of how to allocate scarce resources between competing needs. Explain how each type of economy attempts to deal with this problem.

Suggestions for coursework

1 The annual reports and public statements of large companies will often contain a list of their objectives. Produce a comparison of five of these and say how they are attempting to achieve them.

2 Write a set of possible objectives for The Independent as a response to the price cutting by The Times and Daily Telegraph described in the case study on page 4. Alternatively, choose your own example of a business which needs to 'change direction' and write a set of objectives.

Section 2 The small business

unit 2 Setting up

Aims

At the end of this unit you should understand

- Why small businesses are set up.
- What we mean by a market.
- Why some small businesses are a success and others are a failure.
- The purpose and meaning of market research.
- The advantages and disadvantages of small businesses

Starting a small business

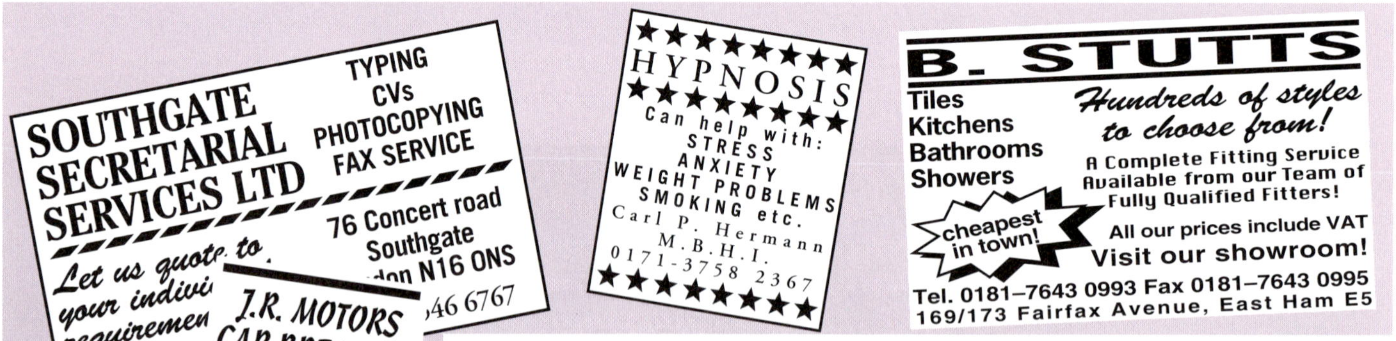

These are just a few examples of the estimated one and a quarter million small businesses in the UK. Firms with less than 200 employees account for about 25% of the total work force – although they only produce about 15% of total output in the UK.

A great number of these firms, like the ones in the examples, employ less than 20 people and many of them are 'one-man' businesses.

Each year a large number of new businesses are started. Some of these are successful and a few go on to become much larger organisations. Many new businesses, however, fail to survive and disappear after a few months.

Businesses are often started by people who have worked for others and now want the opportunity to 'go it alone'. They feel that they will gain more satisfaction from being their own boss and controlling their own affairs. There is always the chance too of making more money in the future than they might get from working for someone else. In the last few years many businesses have been started by people out of work, using redundancy money and help from the Government to set up. Some businesses have also been started by school and college leavers who have found difficulty in getting the types of jobs they want at the end of their education.

Be your own boss

What do you need to set up your own business?
The first thing is to start with a really good idea. You must think of a product or service that you can sell to other people. There must be consumers willing to buy whatever it is you are providing. We call this finding a **market** for the product or service. Your product might be something completely new – such as a new board game or toy. In this case you will need to create your own market for your invention. More probably you will choose something which is being done already. Here there will be an existing market and you will need to compete with firms producing the same or similar goods and services.

Exercise

Have another look at the advertisements on the previous page and ask yourself what the market is for each good or service being provided. Now think of a product or service which you could provide. You will get some more ideas by looking through your own local newspaper. Whatever you choose, it must not involve expensive equipment or premises. In this assignment you are limited to £1000 to start up with and the use of the garden shed if you need it.

1 Invent a name for your business.

2 Briefly describe your idea.

3 Describe the market for your product or service. (Say who you think your customers will be.)

4 Why do you think your business will be a success? What competition will you face?

Case study

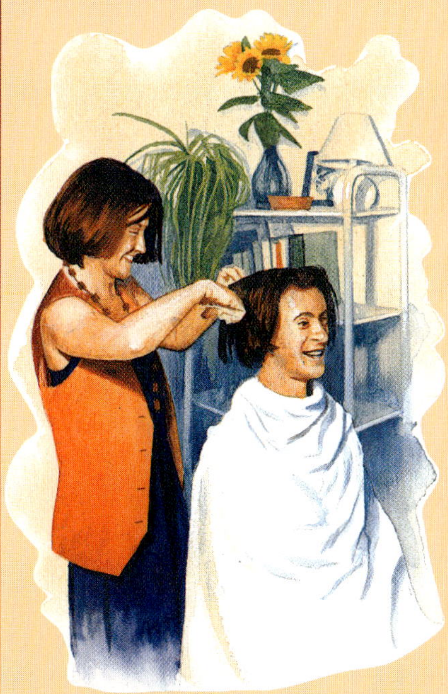

Klippers

Karen left school at sixteen and went to the local College of Further Education where she took a course in hairdressing. At the end of the course she was taken on part-time at a large hairdressers in the town. She gained some useful experience and eventually got a full-time job at a small shop near where she lived. After two years of working she was becoming bored and felt that there were few promotion prospects. She wanted to set up on her own but was unable to raise enough finance to buy or rent a shop. She then had the idea of cutting people's hair in their own house. Many old people in the area found it difficult getting to the hairdressers and other people, such as mothers with young children, found it hard to get out of the house during the day.

Karen had managed to save enough out of her wages to buy the basic equipment, such as razors and driers, as well as a small stock of shampoos, conditioners, colorants and other materials. She was also the proud owner of a small car which she had bought after passing her test.

She started off by working in the evenings cutting the hair of friends and relatives and worked full time at the shop during the day. After six months she had managed to build up enough business to give up her job at the shop and to work just for herself.

After a year Karen is still in business. She finds it very hard work because she needs to work the hours that suit her customers. Business also varies and some weeks she is left with less money than her earnings at the shop. Despite this, Karen likes working for herself and hopes that she can eventually make enough money to get her own shop.

1 Is Karen's business a service or a manufacturing business?
2 How did Karen raise enough money to start her business?
3 What was the market for Karen's business? (Who were her customers?)
4 Why do you think Karen has been successful in staying in business so far?
5 Karen often works longer hours and takes home less pay than she did working at the shop. Why do you think she wants to work for herself?
6 Suggest three ways in which Karen could possibly improve her business in the future.

Extension exercise

We saw in Unit 1 that businesses need to use combinations of the factors of production: raw materials, labour and capital. Klippers is no exception. Think of all the items Karen would need in her business and then divide them into materials and capital.

Materials	Capital
✓ Shampoo	✓ Scissors
✓	✓
✓	✓
✓	✓

Why do businesses fail?

Karen has already done better than many new businesses which fail in less than a year. Why do so many businesses fail?

- The idea is not good enough.
- The market is too small and there are not enough customers.
- There are insufficient funds to run the business, even though there are enough orders. This might be caused by customers being slow in paying for goods or services already provided (This is known as a 'cash flow problem'. See page 54.)
- The owner of the business lacks the right skills – they may not keep the accounts correctly or underestimate the cost of a job.
- Customers fail to pay for goods or services provided. (This is known as 'bad debts.' See page 61.)
- The business loses its market – other firms produce better or cheaper goods or services.

You might be able to add to this list by thinking of businesses that have failed in your area. In later units we will be looking in more detail at some of the problems that businesses face. The following case study shows several of the reasons for businesses failing.

Case study

PIPS

Simon and John left school at sixteen without jobs. After six months of being unemployed, and with little chance of finding suitable employment, they decided to have a go at setting up their own business. They had learnt a bit about printing at school and with the help of an interest-free loan from Simon's dad, they managed to buy a second-hand printing press, together with letters and plates. They called their business 'Personalised Ink Printing Services', or PIPS for short.

At first they did quite well with orders from friends and relatives for headed note paper, invitations and business cards. Before Christmas they had great difficulty keeping up with all the orders – they even had to turn some customers away because they knew they would be unable to complete orders, intended as Christmas presents.

Despite being very busy, Simon and John discovered that they had made very little money from their work before Christmas. Simon's dad suggested that they had not charged enough for their work and they needed a bigger 'mark up' in order to increase their profits. So Simon and John increased their prices. Things went from bad to worse. Now they had trouble getting orders. They were told that it was cheaper to get work done by Express Printers, a large organisation in the city. Simon and John knew that Express Printers handled a huge number of orders and had the most up-to-date printing equipment, but they were still puzzled by their low prices. Express Printers needed to rent a large building for their work and to pay a large number of workers. Then a friend of John's dad, who worked at Express Printers, told them that Express Printers managed to get their paper at almost half the price that John and Simon needed to pay.

1 List all the problems faced by Simon and John's business.

2 How were Simon and John caught in a trap over what prices to charge?

3 How were Express Printers able to 'undercut' PIPS?

4 Why do you think Express Printers were able to obtain their paper at almost half the price paid by Simon and John?

5 What advice could you offer to Simon and John to help their business survive?

Extension exercise

	PIPS	Express Printers
Cost of paper per 100 sheets	£3.00	£1.60
Other costs per 100 sheets		
(not including wages)	£2.00	£2.40
Selling price per 100 sheets	£7.00	£6.00
Mark up (selling price less costs)		
per 100 sheets	?	?
% Mark up $\left(\frac{\text{Mark up}}{\text{Costs}} \times \frac{100}{1}\right)$	?	?

a Complete the table

b What conclusions can you draw from the table?

Market research

- How do you know your product will sell?
- Who will buy your product?
- Have you got the right design?
- Is the price right?
- Why are you losing sales to your competitors?

A firm can find some of the answers to these questions through market research. Market research means finding out what people want in a product or service. Large firms will often spend very large sums of money on market research, but small firms may also find it useful. Some small firms fail because they have not carried out at least some basic market research.

One way of doing market research is through the use of a questionnaire. Because it is difficult and expensive to approach all your possible customers, the survey is usually carried out on a sample of people. This might be a random sample where, for example, you approach every tenth person regardless of whether they are male or female, young or old.

In general, the smaller the sample, the less reliable the market research will be. For this reason, it may be useful to 'target' the market research at the people most likely to buy your product. You might decide to just interview women or people under the age of 21. For example, there would be little point in interviewing senior citizens if you were doing market research on a teenage fashion product!

Much market research carried out by very small businesses is informal. Ideas might be discussed with friends and relatives. Personal knowledge of an area may reveal that there is a lack of a particular good or service available there. Visits to trade fairs might provide ideas for new products. Even the most sophisticated market research does not necessarily provide the right answers. Extensive market research showed that the Sony Walkman personal stereo would not sell but the company still decided to go ahead and produce it and it became a huge success!

x (Market research is dealt with in more detail in Unit 15.)

Case study

Exercise: **Sax Ltd**

The design

A Duffle Sax £10.99

Extra features -
Each bag has a zip pocket and one compartment

C Ruc Sax £12.99

D Barrel Sax £12.99

Possible extras -
Key Ring and name tag 50p
Removable zip pocket with pen/pencil holder £1
Removable waterproof compartment with space for notebooks,pens/pencils takes A4 size £1.50

B Shoulder Sax £11.99

Colours -
Each design available in purple, red, yellow and green background.

Sax Ltd are a small firm making different types of nylon bags. They want to launch a new bag which they hope will be used by school and college students. They have come up with four possible designs, each of which could be produced in four different colours. Firms find it very expensive to produce a large range, particularly if one particular design or colour does not sell well. Sax want to find out which two designs would be most popular and which two colours students would most want to see available. There are also a number of special features, such as zip pockets, separate compartments, name tags, etc, which can be added at extra cost.

Method

This exercise is best done working in a group of about four or five students. Each member of the group asks at least five students to complete the questionnaire on the next page. It is best if you are able to ask a range of students: males/females, and different ages. You may wish to design your own bags, colour range, and additional features. When you have each collected the information, put it all together to find out:

1. The top two designs.
2. The two colours these designs are most required in.
3. Which additional features are required (if any).
4. A customer 'profile' for each of the two designs picked. Who will be the most likely buyer? Male/female? Age range?

Market research sheet

		1	2	3	4	5	6	7	8
Age (Years)	11–13								
	14–16								
	17–18								
Male (M) Female (F)	M								
	F								
Design (A,B,C or D)									
Colour (P,R,Y or G)									
Additional features (tick) (more than one possible)									
Extra zip pocket (+£1)									
Extra waterproof compartment (+£1.50)									
Key ring and name tag (+50p)									

Extension exercise

1. Compare the group results with the rest of the class. Have other groups come up with the same two designs? If their results are different, can you discover why?
2. Carry out your own market research in the same way. It could be to decide on which flavour packets of crisps or chocolate bars to stock in a school or college shop, for example.
3. How would the type of market research vary according to the product or service in question? For example, how would market research for an industrial vacuum cleaner be different from a soap powder?

Designing a questionnaire for market research

- Decide what you are really trying to find out.
(Whether they would buy the product, which design/flavour/colour people prefer, what price they are prepared to pay, what rival products they buy etc.)
- Keep the questionnaire as short as possible.
(People are more likely to respond if you are able to say it will only take two minutes. Don't ask irrelevant questions.
- Make the questions as clear as possible.
(Keep them as short and as precise as possible. Avoid double questions such as 'How often do you use the local shops and which ones do you use most frequently?')
- Avoid using biased or leading questions.
(These are questions which point people in a particular direction such as 'Why do you think unleaded petrol is a good idea?' or 'Most people use a deodorant, which one do you use?')
- Think about how you are going to record the answers.
(You don't want to take up a lot of time writing lengthy answers – use tick boxes wherever possible.)
- Avoid asking personal questions.
(People may well be reluctant to tell you how much they earn but they may be prepared to state a range, for example within£10,000–£15,000.)
- Start with a general question before going into the detail.
(There is no point in asking what price people are prepared to pay for a new brand of cornflakes if they don't actually buy breakfast cereal.)
- Try the questionnaire out on a few friends and change any questions which do not work.

Using the Questionnaire

- Decide on your sample. You need to ask a sufficient number of people to obtain useful data.
- Decide on who you are going to ask. It is best to 'target' your market research according to the product. There is little point in asking local residents about whether they would use a new hotel in their town or asking 10 year olds which model of car they prefer.
- Work out your introduction carefully. You will need to explain why you are carrying out the market research and how long it will take. Example, 'Excuse me, would you be kind enough to help me by answering a few questions as part of a survey I am carrying out as part of my GCSE coursework in business studies. It will only take two minutes of your time'.
- Try to work through the questions quickly, but make sure the person you are interviewing understands what you are asking.
- At the end of the interview thank the person for their time.

Market research example

Unisex personalised T shirts

The brief

You have been asked to carry out research into the market for unisex personalised T shirts, which are available in one size only. The aim is to discover information about the customers' buying habits for T shirts. This will help the firm to make a product which will suit the needs of its customers. With this information the firm will be able to make better decisions about items such as the price to be charged, the quantities it could sell and the range of T shirt colours to be stocked. Having details of its potential customers will also help the firm to plan the launch and promotion of its new product more effectively.

The sample

It is expected that the target market for this product would be teenagers and younger adults. The sample would be taken equally from the 14-18 and 19 and over age groups. It is possible that some older adults will be purchasing for younger consumers.

The Questionnaire

Sex: Male ☐ Age: 14-18 ☐
Female ☐ 19+ ☐

1 Would you be interested in buying personalised one size T shirts?
a Yes
b No
If no go to Q7

2 Would you buy these T shirts for?
a Yourself
b For a friend of a similar age
c For a relative
d Other person (please state)

3 On what occasions would you buy a personalised T shirt?
a Birthday
b Christmas
c Other special occasion (please state when)
d For every day wear

4 How many do you think you might buy per year?
a 1
b 2 – 4
c 5 or more

5 What price would you be prepared to pay?
a Up to £6
b Up to £7
c Up to £8

6 What colour T shirt would you be likely to choose?
a Black b White c Blue d Green e Beige
f Other colour (please state which)

7 As you answered no to Q1 is there any particular reason why you would not be interested in buying this type of clothing?

Summary of key words and ideas

- **Small businesses** are those employing less than 200 people. Many of these employ less than 20 people.
- One out of every four workers is employed in a small firm.
- Small firms account for about 15% of all output in the UK.
- **The market** is the number of people willing to buy a particular product or service.
- In order to survive, firms must have a big enough market for their product or service.
- People who own their businesses and work for themselves get satisfactions from this apart from money.
- **Mark up** is the amount a firm adds on to its costs in order to fix its price.
- **Market research** is finding out what people want in the way of new or existing products and services.
- A **random sample** is when a certain number of people are asked about their wants regardless of their age, sex, income, etc.
- Different people have differing wants and requirements from goods and services.

Test questions

1 Name any two small businesses in your area. Describe what each business does. State whether each business is a service or manufacturing business.

2 What is meant by the *market* for a good or service? What is the market for a corner shop?

3 Tracey and Jon intend to set up a clothes shop in the town of Norton. They are advised by a friend to carry out some *market research* before starting the business.

a What is meant by market research?
b Describe four things they might hope to discover from their market research.
c Give two reasons why market research does not always provide the right answers.
d Give two reasons why they might want to set up their own business.

4 Many small businesses fail in their first two years. Give four reasons why so many small businesses fail to survive.

Focus on Business

Success story for Joiner Jim

Joiner Jim Smith from Huddersfield left working for a local firm of builders over a year ago and is now making a success of it on his own. Jim is making high quality, custom-built tables, chairs and cabinets. 'Many people are moving away from cheap stuff and back to really well built, solid wood – and they are prepared to pay for it'. Jim is not trying to compete with the large manufacturers – they are cheaper and better at producing standardised furniture.

Jim has a full order book for the next six months and has taken on extra help. But it wasn't always like that. Jim is the first to tell you that there were plenty of problems in the first few months and that he often works harder and takes home less pay than in his old job ...

5 a What is the market for Jim's firm?
b Why do you think that the large manufacturers are able to produce standardised furniture more cheaply than Jim?
c Give two reasons why Jim might gain satisfaction from being his own boss.
d Describe *three* problems that Jim might have faced in the first few months of his new business.

Extension questions

1 'Small businesses can sometimes find a *gap in the market* left by large firms'. Explain what this means and give an example of it.

2 A local bus company wishes to find out whether it would be profitable to set up a new route between a housing estate and a shopping centre. Explain in detail how the bus company could attempt to find out this information.

Comparison of prices between a 'corner shop' and large supermarket October 1994.

	Corner Shop (pence)	Supermarket (pence)
Tin of baked beans (420 grams)	38	29 (own brand)
Sugar (kilo)	82	61
Milk (pint)	35	27
Potatoes (lb)	15	20

3 a What do the above figures show?
b Explain the above figures.
c Give *two* possible reasons why people still use the 'corner shop' even though the supermarket is cheaper for most goods.

4 'The brewing industry is dominated by a few very large firms such as Grand Metropolitan or Whitbread, yet small firms such as Gales Ales still manage to survive.

a Why do you think the brewing industry is 'dominated by a few very large firms?'
b How do small firms in the brewing industry manage to survive?
c Name another industry with a large number of small firms and explain why you think they have survived.

Suggestions for coursework

1 Using local newspapers, pick out twenty small businesses.

- Group them into services or manufacturers.
- Say what market each one is trying to supply.
- For any *four* of them say whether or not you think they will be successful in the future, giving your reasons.

2 Interview the owners of at least *two* small businesses to try to find out:

- Why they set up their own businesses.
- What they did before they set up on their own.
- What satisfactions they get from running their own businesses.
- What problems they faced when they first started in business and what they consider to be their main problems now.

3 Imagine that you are going to set up a small business in your local area. Design a questionnaire and carry out market research to establish whether your business is likely to be a success. Include a description of the type of sample you used and the results of your research.

4 For the business identified in **3** above, draw up a basic business plan, including what the business will be doing, how you are going to organise it, who you will be selling to and any problems that you are likely to face.

unit 3 What type of business organisation?

Aims

At the end of this unit you should understand:

- What is meant by limited and unlimited liability.
- The need for different types of business organisations.
- How small businesses can be set up as sole owners, partnerships, private limited companies and co-operatives.
- The advantages and disadvantages of each type of business organisation.

Limited or unlimited?

x

Some businesses have the letters Ltd after their name. This stands for limited liability. (In Unit 9 we consider the PLC – public limited company, a form of business organisation used by large firms which also gives limited liability). Owners of firms having limited liability are only responsible for debts up to the value of the business. If a firm does not have limited liability, we say that it has unlimited liability. This means that the owner is personally responsible for all the debts of the firm. All sole owners and most partnerships have unlimited liability.

Case study

1 The sad story of builder Fred Jones

Fred Jones set up as a self-employed builder and decorator three years ago. Things went well for Fred at first and he started taking on other workers to help him. Unfortunately, whilst working on a property, one of Fred's workers punctured a water main and caused several thousand pounds damage. Fred hired most of his equipment and he did not have the necessary cash in the business to pay for the damage. The result was that Fred had to sell his most prized possession, his vintage sports car, in order to raise the cash.

Fred had unlimited liability so his personal property was at risk: in this case it was his car, but it could have included his house and savings.

2 The collapse of Jo Jeans Ltd

In July 1995 Jo Jeans Ltd, a small firm making high-fashion jeans, went bankrupt. At the time of going bankrupt Jo Jeans Ltd owed £2000 to their suppliers and had a loan from the bank of £5000.

A 'receiver' was called in to arrange for the debts to be settled by selling off all of the property belonging to Jo Jeans (known as the assets of the business). This included their stock, machinery, van, etc. All this amounted to only £6000. The bank had first claim on this money and the suppliers were left being owed £1000. Jo Jeans had limited liability, so only the value of the business was at risk.

1. Which business had limited liability and which was unlimited?
2. Name four local businesses which have Ltd after their name.
3. What problems did unlimited liability create?
4. Who lost out through limited liability?

Extension exercise

You will see later that getting limited liability costs money and involves the firm in keeping accurate records and accounts. For which types of businesses do you think it is desirable to have limited liability and for which types do you think it is not worth bothering with? Explain your answer.

Types of business organisation

There are a number of different types of business organisations, depending on how the firm is owned. In this unit we are going to look at:

- Sole owners
- Partnerships
- Private limited companies
- Co-operatives

A small business could use any of these forms of business organisation, but some firms are more suited to one particular type of organisation and some firms must be a particular type of organisation by law.

Sole owners

Many businesses start as sole owners. Klippers in Unit 2 and Fred Jones (Builders) were both examples of sole owners. They are easy to set up, there are few rules governing them, and they do not need to make their accounts public.

Key points about sole owners

- There is only one owner but s/he can employ as many other workers as s/he wishes.
- All of the profits go to the sole owner but s/he also bears any losses the firm makes.
- Sole owners have unlimited liability – their personal possessions are at risk if the business goes bankrupt. So this type of organisation is best suited to businesses which are unlikely to run into large amounts of debt.
- Like most small businesses, sole owners often find it difficult to raise large amounts of capital by obtaining loans.
- There is no one to share the responsibility of the business with.

Exercise

1 Name any four local sole owner businesses and state what each does.

2 List the advantages and disadvantages of being a sole owner (use the case studies on pages 17-26 to assist you).

3 Interview any sole owner to find out the benefits of being a sole owner as well as the problems.

Partnerships

Many professionals, such as doctors, solicitors, accountants, etc, form themselves into partnerships. Most professions are not allowed by law to be limited companies and they often involve little capital. There is nothing, of course, to stop businesses other than the professions from forming themselves into partnerships.

Key points about partnerships

- Partnerships are owned by between two and twenty partners (in some cases more partners are allowed).
- Partnerships can employ as many people as they wish.
- Most partnerships have unlimited liability.
- If one partner leaves the partnership, or dies, then the whole partnership comes to an end.
- A decision made by one partner is binding on all the other partners.
- Partnerships are easy and cheap to set up.
- Partnerships normally draw up a document called the *Deed of Partnership*: this sets out the details of the partnership, such as how the profits or losses are going to be shared out, how much holiday each partner is allowed, how much capital each partner is putting into the business and any interest they will receive, and how salaries will be paid.

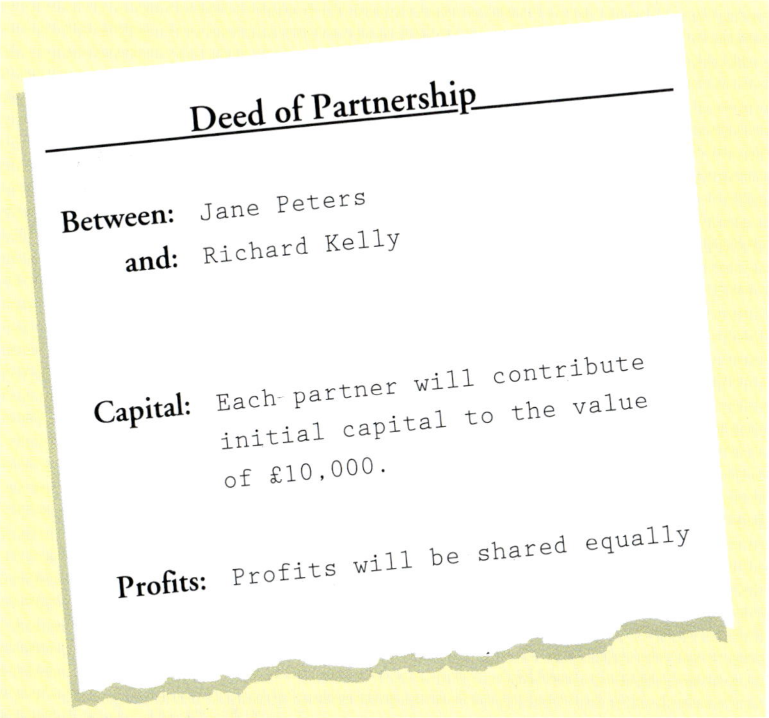
Deed of Partnership

Between: Jane Peters
and: Richard Kelly

Capital: Each partner will contribute initial capital to the value of £10,000.

Profits: Profits will be shared equally

(*Note* It is possible for a person to invest capital in a partnership and have limited liability. This partner is known as a 'sleeping partner'. For example, if a sleeping partner invested £5000 in a partnership and it went bankrupt owing £55,000, the sleeping partner would only lose a maximum of £5000 – the other partners would be required to pay the remaining sum of money owed.)

Case study

Peters and Kelly Medical Practitioners

Jane Peters and Richard Kelly qualified as doctors five years ago. They have both been working in other practices in order to gain experience but recently decided to set up their own practice together. They felt it was a good idea to work together because they could put their money together to rent premises, they could use the same receptionist, and they could cover for each other when either of them was away from the practice for any reason. They could also take turns in being on duty for emergency calls at night or at the weekend.

They contacted a solicitor and she advised them to become a partnership. She drew up a deed of partnership for them which stated:
exactly what each was contributing to the business, how much salary each was entitled to, how their bills were to be paid, what holidays each could take, and several other details. They paid the solicitor a small sum of money for drawing up the document which was done very quickly and simply.

If the practice does well in the future it is possible that Jane and Richard will take on more partners or possibly employ newly qualified doctors who will not be made partners immediately.

1 What advantages were there for Jane and Richard in combining to form a practice? (Can you think of any other advantages apart from those mentioned in the passage?)

2 Jane and Richard were good friends, so why do you think they were advised to set their practice up as a partnership with a legal document when they could have just agreed between themselves?

3 Apart from those things mentioned in the passage, what other details do you think they should have included in their deed of partnership?

4 Why do you think that Jane and Richard may wish to take on more partners in the future even though this will mean more people sharing in the profits of the practice?

Exercise

Try to find five examples of partnerships in your local area. Check each one carefully to make sure it is still a partnership, and briefly state what it does.

Private Limited Companies

Key points

- A private limited company can be set up by a minimum of two people (there is no maximum)
- The owners of a company are known as the shareholders – they each hold at least one share in the company.
- Each owner has limited liability: if the company goes bankrupt, they can only lose the value of their shares. Personal property is not at risk.
- The owners appoint directors to run the company. The owners may or may not take part in the actual running of the company.
- The company is separate from its owners, for example the company can sue and be sued.
- Each year the company must hold a general meeting of shareholders.
- Each year, shareholders must be sent a copy of the accounts and these must also be sent to the Registrar of Companies (see page 38) where they can be viewed by anyone.
- Shares cannot be sold to the general public on the Stock Exchange and they cannot be transferred to other people without the permission of the directors.
- Private limited companies have Ltd (Limited) after their name. This distinguishes them from public limited companies which are identified by having PLC after their name. (See public limited companies, page 99.)

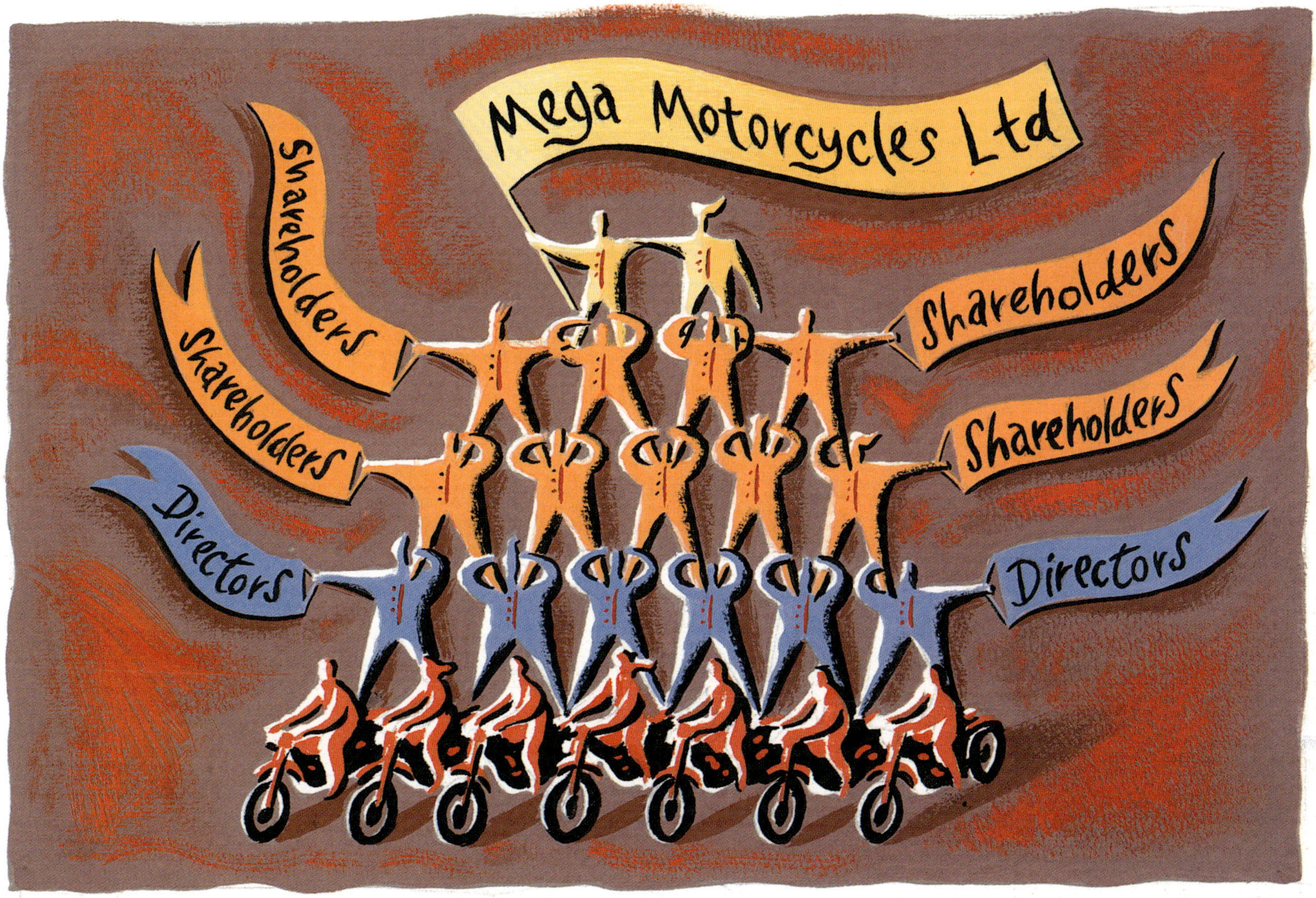

Case study Setting up a limited company: JJ's Nightclub

Scene Meeting between Julie Jason, sole owner of the successful JJ's Nightclub, and her accountant, Sally Watson.

Sally: So you're thinking about expanding JJ's and setting up elsewhere?

Julie: Yes, JJ's is going so well and there does seem to be the need for another one – I was thinking about using that old warehouse near the station in Castlebury.

Sally: Sounds like a good idea to me – perhaps I can give you some advice now you are heading for the big time. Have you thought about setting up a limited company?

Julie: Isn't that a bit complicated and expensive?

Sally: Not really. I can do the paper work and you can buy a ready-made company off the shelf for as little as £150 – or a bit more if you want to set up your own one.

Julie: Wouldn't it involve me in a lot of red tape? Keeping proper accounts and records. You know I've never been very good at that sort of thing!

Sally: Well, you do need to send a copy of your accounts each year to the Registrar of Companies. They keep a check on you to make sure you are operating your business properly. But don't worry, I'll handle your accounts for you. For a fee, of course!

Julie: All this is going to cost me money. What's in it for me?

Sally: For a start, you and any other owners will each have limited liability. That means that only the business is at risk. If you get into debt, you can't lose your personal possessions. You can invite other people to become shareholders in your business and raise more capital. Banks may also be keener to give you a loan and there may also be some tax savings too.

Julie: I can't form a company by myself, can I?

Sally: No, but you only need one other person to join you and you can have as many shareholders as you wish.

Julie: Why would anyone else want to be a shareholder in my business?

Sally: Well, they know how successful you've been already, and by becoming shareholders they would expect a share in the profits of the business. They're not going to invest money in your business for nothing.

Julie: What if I don't make any profits?

Sally: Then your shareholders won't get any dividend on their shares – that's a risk they take. But remember they can only lose the value of their shares if the worst happened and you went bankrupt.

Julie: Well, it's certainly worth thinking about. Can I let you know in a few days time?

Exercise

What would you do in Julie's position? Draw up two tables, one giving the advantages of becoming a private limited company, the other giving the disadvantages. Based on the evidence from your tables, make a decision and explain your thinking.

Case study

Julie forms a limited company

Julie decided to take Sally's advice and asked her to set up JJ's as a limited company. Julie invited her friend Tracey to join her as a director. These are the steps that Sally took to set the company up;

1
Legal Documents called Memorandum of Association & Articles of Association Drawn up by Sally and Julie

2
Registrar of Companies

3
Certificate of Incorporation

4
JJ's Nightclub Ltd formed

5
Shares sold

The Memorandum of Association states:

- The name of the business.
- The type of business it is engaged in.
- The names of one director and the company secretary.
- The address where the company is registered.
- How much share capital it intends to raise.
- It also guarantees the limited liability of all its shareholders.

(The Companies Act 1948, 1976 & 1981)

Memorandum of Association of:

JJ's Nightclub Ltd.

1. The name of the company is:
   JJ's Nightclub Ltd.
2. The registered office of the company is:
   18 Elm Grove, Peddlescombe,
   West Yorkshire, England.
3. The objects for which the company is established are:
   to run nightclubs and other forms of public entertainment in the U.K.
4. The liability of the members is limited.
5. The share capital of the company is:
   £5000 divided into 5000 shares of £1 each

Names, Addresses and Descriptions of Subscribers:	Number of Shares
Julie Jason 18 Elm Grove, Peddlescombe, West Yorkshire, England. Company Director	One
Tracey Smith 20 The Vale, Castlebury, West Yorkshire, England. Company Director	One

Exercise

Assignment

For the business you thought of in Unit 2 (page 17) draw up your own Memorandum of Association based on the one for JJ's.

The Articles of Association

These refer to:

- The internal running of the company.
- The powers of the managing director.
- Procedures to be followed at meetings, salaries of directors, etc.

The Certificate of Incorporation

This is issued once the Registrar of Companies is satisfied with all the details. This gives the company permission to start trading.

Shares

Julie invited a number of friends and relatives to become shareholders in JJ's Nightclub Ltd. The shares were sold at £1 each and Julie issued share certificates to everyone who agreed to become a part owner in her company.

No.
SHARES

J.J.'s NIGHTCLUB LIMITED
INCORPORATED UNDER THE COMPANIES ACTS OF 1948 1976 1981
Capital £5000
Divided into 5000 shares of £1 each

This is to certify that PAUL RICHARD JONES of 13 WESTERN ROAD, PEDDLESCOMBE, WEST YORKSHIRE is the holder of ONE HUNDRED Shares fully paid of £1 each Numbered 251 to 350 inclusive in the above named Company subject to the Memorandum and Articles of Association thereof.

Given under the Common Seal of the said Company.
the 3rd day of July 1995
Julie Jason Director
Tracey Smith Director
Peter Parker Secretary

NO TRANSFER OF THE WHOLE OR ANY PORTION OF THE ABOVE SHARES CAN BE REGISTERED WITHOUT THE PRODUCTION OF THIS CERTIFICATE

Exercise

Draw up a share certificate for your company and make it out to anyone who has agreed to become a shareholder.

Explain what the possible benefits are of being a shareholder in your business as well as the possible risks involved.

Co-operatives

Co-operatives have become increasingly common as a form of business organisation in the UK. Many new businesses have been set up as co-operatives and in some cases existing businesses have been bought out by the workers to form a co-operative. Co-operatives have been encouraged as a way of helping to reduce the problems of unemployment – especially in inner city areas.

Key points about co-operatives

- The workers are all owners in the firm, share in the profits of the business, and make decisions on the running of the business.
- Co-operatives may be registered as limited companies or they may be registered under the *Industrial and Provident Societies Act.*
- There are various forms of co-operatives. Workers are normally paid a salary by the firm as well as sharing in the profits of the business.
- Help and advice can be provided in the form of a *Co-operative Development Agency* (CDAs)
- There is no limit to the number of members in a co-operative.

Case study

Midland Gazette

Management and Worker buy-out at Haplows

It was confirmed yesterday evening that management and workers are buying the bankrupt Haplows Brewery from the existing owner. The new business will be known as 'Haplows Co-operative Brewery'. 'We decided to keep the old name because customers know and appreciate our products' said Sid Wright, the new managing director.

Most of the workers at the old Haplows Brewery have bought into the new co-operative. Asked whether he felt that the new co-operative would be more successful than the old brewery Sid Wright commented, 'We are working for ourselves now, we have to make a go of it. Industrial relations at Haplows have not been good in recent times. There were two really damaging disputes in the last year alone. That's one thing that should improve now that we are all working together'.

But Jim Longford, managing director of local rivals, Knutsford Brewery, questioned whether the new co-operative would have the necessary financial, technical, and management skills to turn Haplows into a profit-making business. Another major problem, he thought, could well be lack of capital...

1. Give two reasons why the new co-operative might be more successful than the old Haplows Brewery.
2. Why might the new co-operative lack the 'necessary financial, technical, and management skills'?
3. What benefits might there be for the workers in the new co-operative?
4. What disadvantages might there be for the workers in the new co-operative?
5. Why might there be a lack of capital in the new co-operative?

Summary of key words and ideas

- **Limited liability** – only the assets of the business are at risk.
- **Unlimited liability** – the owner's personal possessions are at risk in business in the case of bankruptcy.
- **Assets** – the value of the business, the buildings, machinery, stock, etc.
- **Receiver** – person called in to distribute the assets of the business to those people owed money.
- A limited liability company may not be able to settle all its debts even after all its assets are sold.
- Businesses which are likely to incur large debts normally become limited companies.
- Some professions are not allowed limited liability and many adopt the partnership as the form of business organisation.
- **Deed of partnership** – a legal document between the partners setting out how the partnership is to be operated.
- **Memorandum of Association** – a legal document required for limited liability companies which sets out the name, purpose, and amount of shares of the company.
- **Articles of Association** – also required by limited liability companies which sets out the rules by which the company will be run.
- **Registrar of Companies** – Government agency which approves new companies and keeps company records.
- **Certificate of Incorporation** – document giving companies the right to start trading.
- **Shareholders** – owners of a company.
- **Dividend** – interest paid on shares.

Test questions

1 Match the following businesses to a suitable form of business organisation:

a Peter Smith, self-employed window cleaner	Private limited company
b Hornby, Watts and Peters, Solicitors	Co-operative
c Barkers, Wholesalers Ltd	Sole owner
d BRS Cycles – a firm where all the workers are owners	Partnership

2 When you leave school, you are going to set up your own business. State what the business is, what form of business organisation you will use (sole trader, partnership, limited company, or co-operative) and give four reasons for your choice of business organisation.

3 Jane Parks is currently a sole owner making hand-made glass products. Suggest two reasons why she might want to become a limited company.

4 You are a shareholder in a limited liability company which has recently gone bankrupt owing large sums of money to its suppliers.
   a What is a shareholder?
   b What is meant by a company 'going bankrupt'?
   c What is the most that you can lose as a shareholder?

5 You are a worker at DRB Engineering Ltd. It is announced that the owners are selling the company. A group of your fellow workers suggest buying the company and making it a workers' co-operative.

   a How is a workers' co-operative different from other forms of business organisation?
   b Give one argument in favour and one argument against becoming part of a possible workers' co-operative.

6 'Despite the advantages enjoyed by limited companies, many businesses prefer to remain as sole owners.' Why do you think this is the case?

7 Karen is currently a sole owner fashion designer. She wants to form a partnership with her friend Nicki.
   a Give two reasons why this might be a good idea.
   b Explain briefly how Karen would go about becoming a partnership.
   Three years later Karen and Nicki are doing very well and want to form a limited company.
   c What would be the advantages of doing this?
   d Explain briefly how they would go about doing this.
   e They invite you as a friend, but with no previous experience of the fashion business, to become a shareholder in their new company. What benefits might you get from being a shareholder in their company?

Suggestions for coursework

1 Carry out a survey of businesses in your local area. (The Thomson and Yellow Pages directories will be a useful source of information.) List them under the headings: sole owner, partnerships, limited companies, co-operatives.

   a Add up the number of each type of business organisation.
   b Calculate each of these as a percentage of the total.
   c Can you make any conclusions as to which businesses use which types of business organisation?
   d Interview owners of a sole owner business, a partnership, and a limited company to find out why they chose each type of business organisation.

2 Make a study of one local private limited company. Try to find out:
   a Who the main officers of the company are (Managing Director, Company Secretary, etc.)
   b The number of shares and the number of shareholders.
   c What accounts they need to keep.
   d Whether they made a profit last year and how much dividend they paid on their shares.

3 Invent a private limited company. Draw up brief Memorandum and Articles of Association. Decide upon the amount of share capital you are going to issue and draw up a share for your company. Produce an agenda for your first general meeting of shareholders.

unit 4 Costs, revenues, and profits

Aims

At the end of this unit, you should understand:

- The difference between cost and price.
- The idea of fixed and variable costs.
- What is meant by revenue, profit, and loss.
- The idea of a break-even point.
- How costs and revenues vary with output and sales.
- The difference between gross and net profit in business.
- The idea of average and marginal costs and revenues.
- How firms may attempt to increase profits.

LJB textiles factory

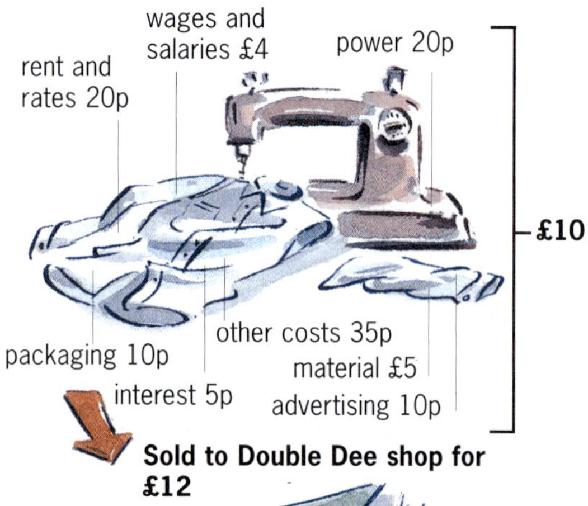

Cost and price

In everyday language you might say that the shirt you bought 'cost £15'. In business language you would say that 'the price was £15'. Cost in business means the cost of making the shirt.

Profit

LJB Textiles made £2 profit on each shirt they sold to the shop, Double Dee. It cost them £10 to make the shirt and they sold it to the shop at £12. *Profit* is the difference between *price* and *cost*.

1 What is the cost to the shop of each shirt it buys from LJB Textiles? What price does it charge to the customer?

2 How much profit does the shop make on each shirt in the example? (Give your answer both in £s and as a % of the price the shop purchases them at.)

3 How much profit will the shop make on the shirts, if it sells 100 in a week (assuming the same price and cost)?
(*Note* This would be called 'Gross Profit' as it does not take account of other costs to the shop, such as rent, wages, etc. See gross and net profit, page 44.)

x

Fixed and variable costs

Look again at LJB's costs of producing a shirt. We can divide these costs into two types: fixed and variable. Fixed costs remain the same regardless of how many are produced. (Rent is a fixed cost – the same amount needs to be paid out each week whether LJB produces 10 shirts or 1000). LJB will need to pay fixed costs even when the factory is closed for holidays.

Variable costs are those costs which increase with the amount produced (the cost of materials, for example, will rise as LJB produce more shirts).

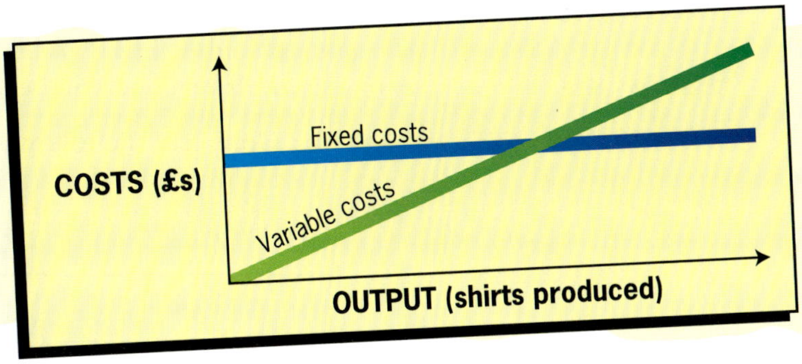

Total costs

Total costs = fixed costs *plus* variable costs

Average costs

Average costs are total costs divided by the number of things produced. The example given of LJB shows an average cost of £10 per shirt.

Exercise

1 Take LJB's costs and divide them into fixed and variable costs, depending on whether you think they would stay the same or increase as they produced more.

Note Some costs may be either fixed or variable, depending upon the length of time under consideration. In the short term, for example, the number of workers we employ may be fixed, so that we might regard wages as a fixed cost. In the long term, however, we might take on more workers, so wages become a variable cost.

In the very long term, all costs may be regarded as being variable. A firm might use a second factory, for example, and thus increase its rent.

2 Complete the following table for LJB Textiles, assuming that its fixed costs are £2000 each week and its variable costs are £6 for each shirt produced.

LJB Textiles production costs per week

Shirts produced	**0**	**100**	**200**	**300**	**400**	**500**	**600**	**700**	**800**
Fixed costs (£)									
Variable costs (£)									
Total costs (£)									

3 Draw a line graph to show the information in the table. Use a different colour for fixed costs, variable costs, and total costs.

Revenue

This is the amount of money a firm gets from selling a good or service. It is found by taking the price of the item and multiplying it by the number of units sold. If LJB Textiles sell 100 shirts to the shop Double Dee at £12 each, its revenue will be £1200.

1 Complete the following table for LJB Textiles assuming that each shirt is sold to the shops at £12.

Revenue from the sale of shirts

	Number of shirts sold per week								
	0	100	200	300	400	500	600	700	800
Revenue (£)									

2 Using the information from your costs graph, show total costs on a graph similar to the one shown here.

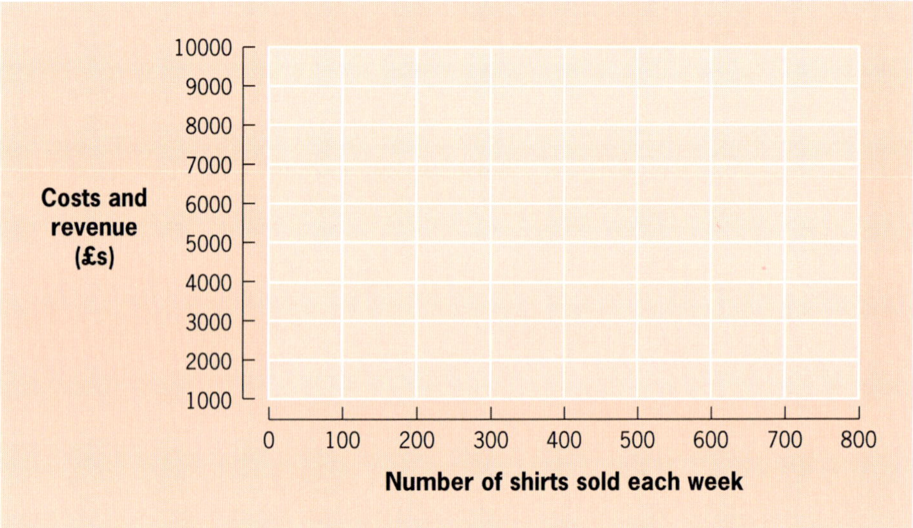

Now mark on the graph your revenue figures from the table above using a different colour.

Note A reminder about profit. We saw earlier that profit is the difference between what it costs to produce something and what it is sold for. Another way of saying this is that profit is the difference between total cost and total revenue.

Break-even point

3 Look at your graph showing total cost and total revenue again. Find the point where the revenue and cost lines cross. This is known as the break-even point. How much is being produced here? How much profit is made here? Why do you think that this is called the break-even point? Would LJB Textiles go bankrupt if it continued to produce at the break-even point?

Loss

A loss is made if a firm sells its goods or services for less than it costs to make them. In other words, it makes a loss when total cost is greater than total revenue.

4 Using your graph, complete the following table:

Number of shirts made and sold per week	0	100	200	300	400	500	600	700	800
Profit (+) Loss (-) (£)									

Extension section

Average and marginal costs and revenues

We have seen already that average costs are found by taking total costs and dividing them by the number of units produced. Average revenue is found by taking total revenue and dividing by the number of items sold. If price does not vary, then average revenue will be the same as the price. (Because revenue = price x number of units sold.)

Marginal cost is the cost of producing one extra item. For example, if 100 shirts cost £800 to make, and 101 shirts cost £807, we say that the marginal cost of the 101st shirt is £7 (£807 – £800). Because fixed costs do not vary with production, the marginal cost will be equal to the variable cost of producing an extra unit.

Marginal revenue is the revenue gained from selling one more unit of a product or service. For example, the revenue from the sale of 100 shirts = £1500, and the revenue from 101 shirts = £1515. The marginal revenue from the sale of the 101st shirt = £15 (£1515 – £1500). If the price does not change with sales then the marginal revenue will be the same as the price. (Because the addition to revenue of selling one extra item will be the same each time.)

Extension exercise

1 Complete the following table of LJB Textiles production and sale of T–Shirts per week.

No. produced and sold	1000	1001	1002	1003	1004	1005
Total cost (£s)	2800	2802	2804	2805	2806	2807
Marginal cost (£s)	–	2	?	?	?	?
Total revenue (£s)	3000	3003	3006	3009	3012	3015
Marginal revenue (£s)	–	3	?	?	?	?

2 What is the average cost of producing 1000 units?
3 What price was charged when 1000 units were sold?
4 Where was the largest profit made and how much was it?

Gross and net profit

A distinction is sometimes made in business between profits made before *overheads*, such as rent, rates, and interest have been paid, and profits after all expenses have been paid out. Profits before overhead payments have been made are called *gross profits*, and *net profits* are what is left when all costs have been met. You will see that in our examples we have used net profit in the case of LJB Textiles and gross profit in the case of the shop Double Dee. Net profit is what is available to the owners of the firm to use as they wish.

Double Dee Shop

Gross Profit =	**Net Profit =**
Selling price	Gross Profit (£3)
less	less costs (£2)
Buying price	(wages, rent, lighting, etc.)
(£15 - £12 = £3)	(£3 - £2 = £1)

Do profits mean success?

Profits are certainly one guide to how successful a firm is, but we must remember that profits are only one aim of the firm and in some cases they may not be an aim at all. Many small businessmen are often happy just to survive in business and to make a reasonable living. Making larger profits may mean a great deal more hard work and responsibility. Some organisations, such as clubs, charities, and state-owned businesses may exist in order to provide a service rather than to make a profit.

Do large profits mean that a firm is efficient?

Not necessarily – a firm may be very good at producing something, but because of a great deal of competition it may not be able to charge a price high enough to make large profits. On the other hand, a firm may be able to charge very high prices for something and make large profits without being very efficient.

Exercise

1 Name a good or service where there is a great deal of competition (ie there are a large number of different producers).
2 Name a good or service where there is very little competition (ie there are very few different producers).
3 Name two non-profit-making organisations.

Profit margin

Even if we take profits as a guide to success, total profits by themselves mean very little – large firms would be expected to make bigger profits than small firms. A better guide is to look at profits as a % of revenue (sometimes referred to as *turnover*). This gives us an idea of what our return is on sales, and is called the *profit margin*.

For example, the shop Double Dee pays £2400 for 200 shirts and sells them for £3000. Its gross profit is therefore £600. Its *profit margin* is calculated as
£600 ÷ £3000 x 100 = 20%
But remember, out of this, Double Dee would also have to pay its overhead expenses, so this might not be a very good return on its sales.

Exercise

1 Calculate LJB's *profit margin* from the table you constructed when it makes and sells, ***a*** 100 shirts, ***b*** 500 shirts. What does this tell you about LJB's performance?

Note Increasing the profit. Remember, profit is the difference between revenue and costs – so if we want to try and increase profits we can either try to increase revenue or reduce costs.

2 As accountant for LJB Textiles you are given the following figures:

	1991	1992	1993	1994
Sales revenue *(£000)*	50	65	80	85
Total net profit *(£000)*	10	12	14	15

a Calculate LJB's profit margin.
b What comments would you make about LJB's performance 1991-1994?
c What advice would you give to LJB Textiles to help them increase their profits? (For example, change prices, advertise more, reduce the workforce, use better machines, improve the product, etc.) Explain how you would expect your ideas to work in terms of either reducing costs or increasing revenue.

Opportunity cost

The idea of opportunity cost is very important in business and arises whenever individuals, firms or countries have to make choices. Opportunity cost is what is given up in order to obtain something.

- We might have £5 to spend on leisure activities in a week. We like going ten pin bowling and to nightclubs but have to make a choice because each costs £5. If we chose to go to the disco the opportunity cost is not going ten pin bowling.

- A firm can either buy a new machine or employ 10 more workers to increase production. The opportunity cost of buying the machine is not employing 10 workers.
- The opportunity cost for a government of spending more money on armaments may be spending less money on education.

Summary of key words and ideas

- **Costs** are how much it costs to make a product or supply a service.
- **Price** is what the supplier charges for a product or service.
- **Fixed costs** are those costs which do not vary with the amount produced.
- **Variable costs** rise as the amount produced increases.
- **Revenue** is the amount obtained from selling a good or service.
- **Profit** is the difference between revenue and costs (net profit takes account of all costs, gross profit simply looks at the difference between the buying and selling price of goods and does not take account of other costs).
- **Break-even point** is where a firm's revenue is equal to its costs and its net profit will be zero.
- **Losses** occur if costs exceed revenue.
- To increase profits a firm must either try to increase its revenue (by advertising, changing prices, improving the product, etc.) or reduce its costs (by being more efficient, using better machinery, getting cheaper supplies, etc.)
- **Profit margin** is calculated by profit divided by sales revenue x 100 and is one measure of the success of a firm.
- Some firms may have aims other than making the largest possible profits.
- **Average cost** = total costs divided by number of units produced.
- **Average revenue** = total revenue divided by number of units sold.
- **Marginal cost** is the cost of producing one extra unit.
- **Marginal revenue** is the revenue gained from selling one extra unit.
- **Opportunity cost** is what needs to be given up in order to obtain something.

Test questions

Read the following passage carefully and then answer the questions which follow:

John Stevens runs a greengrocer's business in a small village. Every morning he gets up very early and drives his van to the main town to buy fruit and vegetables at the wholesale market. At busy times of the year John employs a lad to help him. John does not own the shop but pays rent each week to a landlord. In addition to this, John has to pay for any lighting and heating he uses.

1 Make a list of all the costs mentioned in the passage that John pays out for each week.

2 Put a letter F next to any cost which is fixed (i.e. those costs which John has to pay for no matter how much he sells) and a letter V against those costs which vary with the amount he sells.

3 Name three other costs not mentioned in the passage which John might need to meet in his business. In each case say whether they are fixed or variable.
4 Last week John sold 50lbs of tomatoes at 40 pence per pound. What was his revenue on tomatoes?
5 If John increased the price of his tomatoes to 50 pence per pound, do you think his revenue would go up, down or remain the same – explain your answer. (There is no one correct answer to this question.)
6 Explain how John would go about calculating his 'take-home' profit each month.

Extension questions

1 Last week John bought 100lbs of apples at 20 pence per pound. He sold the first 50lbs at 40 pence and then reduced the price to 30 pence for the remaining 50lbs.
   a What was his total revenue on apples?
   b What was his total profit on apples?
   c What was his profit margin on sales?
   d What was his marginal revenue on the 21st pound of apples?
2 A customer at Stevens needs to choose between buying apples and grapes. Apples are half the cost of grapes. What is the opportunity cost to the customer of buying one pound of grapes?
3 John makes a reasonable living but he is ambitious and wants to do better. As an adviser for small businesses, suggest a plan for John in order to assist him in making larger profits in the future. Explain the various parts of your plan, saying why you feel that this would help to improve his business. Use the following statistics on John's business to assist you in deciding upon the plan:

Stevens the Greengrocers

	1992	1993	1994
Sales Revenue *(£000s)*	104	110	120
Gross Profit *(£000s)*	51	52	54
Net Profit *(£000s)*	10	11	12

Suggestions for coursework

1 Invent a small manufacturing firm. Make two lists – one for fixed costs, one for variable costs. Try and put actual values to these costs. Decide on a selling price for your product. Show on a graph costs and revenues, and mark clearly the break-even point. Suggest ways in which you might try and go about increasing profits in the future.
2 For a real life small business (for example a shop) try and find out the approximate running costs (the fixed costs) and the cost of goods bought each month. Try and work out net and gross profit, and the break-even point.
3 Interview owners of small businesses to try to find out what their aims are (do they try to make the largest possible profits, or sell as much as possible, or try to survive, or what?)
4 Look at the costs and revenues involved in the running of a school or college function, such as a disco or a play. What is the break-even point? How are prices established? Why are prices not higher/lower?

unit 5 Financing the small business

Aims

At the end of this unit you should understand:

- The need for finance.
- The difference between fixed capital and working capital.
- The types of finance available for small businesses.
- How to draw up a simple business plan.
- What is meant by SWOT analysis.
- How a business calculates how much finance it requires.
- How to draw up a cash flow forecast.

Why do we need finance?

The case of Ling's Pottery

Ling Lau wants to develop her hobby of pottery into a small business. She lives in a small market town in an area which attracts lots of tourists. There are some suitable small premises which can be rented for £200 a month. She will need to spend about £2000 converting these to a Pottery. She has the offer of a second-hand wheel, kiln and other necessary equipment for a further £3000. She will need another £500 for clay, glazes and other materials. Then there will be the running costs of the business, such as lighting and heating – she calculates these at about £100 a month. She has set £10 a week aside for advertising in local papers and the tourist office.

Although Ling has already made a selection of items for sale, she feels that she will need to make a bigger range of pottery before she is able to really open the business. She doesn't expect to make any sales until a month after she has set up.

Ling has managed to save up £5000. Part of this was from a redundancy payment when she lost her job at a local firm last year.

Fixed capital and working capital

Some of the items Ling requires money for are things which will remain permanently in the business – the kiln, for example. These items are called *fixed assets* and the money used to buy them is *fixed capital*. Ling also requires money for things which will be used up in the business, for example the clay. For these items she will need *working capital*.

Exercise

Make two lists, one for Ling's fixed capital and one for her working capital (include any additional items you can think of which are not mentioned).

How can the small business raise capital?

Ling has managed to raise £5000 of capital by using her own savings and a redundancy payment from her previous job. Many small businesses get their initial capital in this way. Other people would be very reluctant to lend money to Ling if she was not prepared to make a financial commitment herself by putting some of her own money into the business.

Getting Advice

A local Business Link office

However, despite her £5000, Ling still needs a great deal more capital to start her business. Where could she go for advice on obtaining loans? Ling remembered seeing an advert about a local *Business Link* centre and decided to give it a try. Business Links were set up by the Government in 1992. Each *Business Link* is an independent company run by the local Training and Enterprise Council (TEC), local authorities and Chambers of Commerce.

Ling found her visit very useful. She received lots of helpful advice on where to go for loans and how to raise capital. They also gave her advice about training courses at the local college of further education on starting up and running small businesses. She decided to take a course which covered how to keep the accounts and other financial aspects of the business.

The local bank where Ling kept her personal bank account was another useful source of advice. The bank's adviser for small businesses explained the need for *a business plan* and a *cash flow forecast*. (See pages 52 and 54.)

Borrowing from a bank

The adviser talked about two different ways of borrowing money:

Overdrafts

These are for short-term borrowing. They are particularly useful for cash flow problems when the business might temporarily run short of cash even though it has plenty of orders. (See pages 54 and 55.)

For example, before the main holiday season Ling would have to buy materials and produce her pottery. She would hope to sell most of the pottery in the holiday season but might well need an overdraft to assist her finances until then. An overdraft would enable Ling to write out cheques for more than was in her account. In other words, she could officially overdraw on her account up to an amount agreed by her bank. She would pay interest only on the amount by which she was overdrawn and the bank had the right to withdraw the overdraft facility at any time.

(*Note* An alternative to the overdraft which is becoming increasingly popular with medium and large sized businesses is Factoring. See page 106.)

Loans

The adviser explained to Ling that a loan was for longer-term finance. It was a fixed sum of money to be paid back with interest over an agreed number of years and had to be used for a particular purpose in the business – normally for fixed assets, such as the purchase of the kiln.

The adviser told Ling that the bank normally required some guarantee that the loan would be paid back. The loan might be secured on your house. (The item the loan is secured on is known as *collateral*). This would mean that, if you failed to pay back the loan, the bank would have the right to sell your house and keep the amount you still owed. Ling did not own property and even if she did, she would be unhappy about giving the bank the right to it. However, the adviser explained that it was possible that she could get at least part of the loan secured by the Government under its *Loan Guarantee Scheme.*

Other sources of finance

The Government

Ling lives in an area of high unemployment and there are a number of types of assistance she could apply for:

- Grants for setting up
- Reductions in rent or rates
- Allowances against tax for buying equipment

The European Community also provides a variety of different types of assistance in areas of high unemployment.

Ling will also be able to apply for an *Enterprise Allowance* which gives her a small regular income for up to a year in place of the unemployment benefit she would otherwise be entitled to.

Charities

Organisations such as the Prince's Youth Business Trust and Livewire give grants to young people attempting to set up businesses.

Trade credit, hire purchase, and leasing

It is possible that Ling will not need to pay for all her materials immediately. Her suppliers may allow her a few weeks to pay – known as trade credit. However, the supplier may charge more than if the materials are paid for when they are delivered.

Instead of buying the equipment she needs with cash or a loan, Ling may choose to use hire purchase. Under this arrangement she pays for the equipment over a period of time. This may cost substantially more than the cash price. Alternatively, she may decide to lease the equipment. This is similar to renting it over a period of time.

x

(Different types of credit and leasing are dealt with in detail in Unit 7. Private and public limited companies can raise capital by selling shares and debentures. These are dealt with in Unit 9).

Which type of finance to choose?

Ling discovered many financial organisations who might consider loaning her money. Several of these require some type of collateral but this still leaves a number of possibilities. In choosing the type of finance that best suits her, Ling needs to take account of:

- *The cost of the finance*. All loans from commercial organisations will require interest to be paid. The law now requires all lenders to state exactly how much a loan is going to cost the borrower.
- *What the finance is for*. Ling might use different types of finance for different purposes. For short term needs, such as buying materials, she should use short term finance such as overdrafts. For longer term needs, such as buying a kiln, she needs long term finance such as a bank loan or hire purchase.
- *How much finance is needed*. The more finance Ling requires the less will be her choice. Some organisations, such as the Government and charities, will only be prepared to loan or give small amounts of money. It is also important for Ling to calculate as accurately as possible how much finance she will need and when it will be required in order to avoid unnecessary interest charges.

Calculating the finance required and applying for loans

SWOT

Ling was advised to draw up a business plan and a cash flow forecast to help her decide how much finance she requires and to help her apply for a loan. The plan also requires her to consider the *strengths*, and *weaknesses* of her idea for a business and the *opportunities* and *threats* in the market place. This is known as carrying out a *SWOT analysis*.

The business plan

The business plan helps Ling decide how much finance she needs and sets out her ideas for developing the business. It is also useful to organisations considering loaning money or giving grants to Ling. The small business adviser at the bank showed Ling some examples of business plans and gave her a form to help her.

Business plan

The nature of the proposed business:

The business is to be located in Newminster-upon-Sea and will produce hand crafted pottery, mainly for the tourist market. Customers will be able to view the pottery being made as well as a range of finished items. The business will be a sole ownership and the owner will be the only employee.

The market for the proposed goods or services:
Most customers will be tourists but there will also be some sales to local people. All sales will initially be from the Pottery but consideration will be given in the future to supplying local gift shops. My market research suggests that sales during the main tourist season (June-September) might be £500 a week. Sales during the remainder of the year might average £100 a week. Time will be devoted to building up stocks during the 'low' months of January and February. Tourism is growing in the area and there has been an increase in 'short break' holidays outside of the main season.

Competitors:
There are no other potteries within a ten mile radius. Some of the gift shops stock hand crafted pottery but this is not produced locally. Much of what is on sale is either of inferior quality or very expensive. There is a very limited range of pottery because the gift shops stock a wide variety of goods.

Market research:
A questionnaire survey has been carried out at different times during the past 6 months. The survey concentrated on tourists but included a small sample of local residents. The results were very encouraging and suggested that a high proportion of visitors would be interested in buying hand crafted pottery at reasonable prices.

Advertising:
The Pottery will be advertised in the local tourist offices, in the tourist guides, and in local papers. There will be advertising outside the Pottery itself to attract tourists in.

Pricing:
Overhead costs will be low. Even with 100% mark up on materials, prices can be kept below other quality pottery available locally.

Break-even:
Total costs in the first year are estimated at about £10,000. This does not include wages which will be paid from the Enterprise Allowance. It is

Exercise

1. Using the information on page 48 and in the business plan, calculate Ling's total costs and sales revenue.
2. Ling expects to break even by the end of the first year. How realistic is this?
3. Why might she make a profit in the second year of running the business?
4. Write a business plan using the same headings as in Ling's plan for a business of your choice.

anticipated that sales revenue will just about cover costs (including setting up costs) in the first year.

Premises:
A small shop is available for rent in Newminster Terrace. This is close to the centre of town and other tourist attractions. It is suitable for conversion to a Pottery and there should not be any problems over obtaining planning permission.

Start up capital required:

Advance rent for 6 months	£1200
Conversion of premises	£2000
Equipment (wheel, kiln etc.)	£3000
Materials	£ 500
Advertising for 6 months	£ 240
Heating and lighting for 6 months	£ 600
total	£7540
Amount of capital contributed by owner	£5000
Capital required	£2540

Strengths, Weaknesses, Opportunities and Threats (SWOT analysis):

Strengths of the business idea: Good quality, hand crafted pottery at reasonable prices. Customers will be attracted into the Pottery to see it in action. In time, the Pottery may be seen as a tourist attraction by Newminster District Council and it will receive free advertising and sign posting.

Weaknesses of the business idea: Tourists may be attracted to the Pottery to see it in action but not necessarily to buy. They may not appreciate the quality of the pottery and buy cheaper, lower quality products from the gift shops.

Opportunities in the market place: There are no other potteries within a 10 mile radius of Newminster. Local people might buy personalised pottery either for themselves or for friends and relatives. Gift shops in Newminster and elsewhere might be persuaded to sell the pottery.

Threats in the market place: The tourist trade is seasonal. Tourism might decline in the future. A rival Pottery might be set up nearby. The current fashion for hand crafted pottery may change.

Extension section

Cash flow

Ling now has a good idea of how much capital she needs to set up the business. Her next concern is calculating how much finance she will require once the business is running. She knows that many small businesses run into trouble even when their goods are selling well because they run short of cash.

The small business adviser was helpful again here – he showed her how to draw up a cash flow forecast. This is a table estimating her income and expenditure on a monthly basis for the first six months after she sets up the Pottery. The table they came up with for the first three months using the standard bank form is shown below. The Budget column shows the estimates and the Actual column will be completed by Ling at the end of each month to check on the accuracy of the forecast amounts. The bottom line indicates the size of the overdraft Ling would require each month.

Cash Flow Forecast from *March* **19** *94* **to** *August* **19** *95*

Branch *Newminster* **Account** *Ling Lau* **Business** *Ling's Pottery*

Period			March		April		May								Total	
e.g. Four weeks/month/Quarter			Budget	Actual	Budget	Actual	Budget	Actual	Budget	Actual	Budget	Actual	Budget	Actual	Budget	Actual
Receipts																
Cash sales			50		200		300									
From debtors			0		20		40									
Other revenue sources			160		160		160									
TOTAL A			210		380		500									
Purchases																
Payments																
Cash purchases			60		60		80									
To creditors			20		40		50									
Wages/Salaries/PAYE			160		160		160									
Rent/Rates/Insurance			30		30		30									
Light/Heat/Power			50		50		40									
Transport/Packaging																
Repairs/Renewals																
HP Payments/Leasing Charges			40		40		40									
Bank/Finance charge & interest			50		50		50									
Sundry Expenses			20		40		60									
TOTAL B			430		470		510									
A–B (net inflow) or B–A (net outflow)	C	Cr														
		or Dr	220		90		10									
Bank Balance at end of previous period brought forward	D	Cr	100													
		or Dr			120		210									
Bank Balance at end of period carried forward Aggregate of C and D		Cr														
		or Dr	120		210		220									

Exercise

1 Why are receipts low in the first month?
2 In which month does Ling estimate that she will require the largest overdraft?
3 Give two reasons why Ling's budget column may be different from the actual column.
4 Why would Ling expect to reduce the size of her overdraft in the future?
5 Either continue Ling's cash flow forecast for a further three months or draw up a similar table for your own business.

Summary of key words and ideas

- **Fixed capital** is finance used for purchasing **fixed assets** – equipment which remains permanently in the business.
- **Working capital** is finance for items which will be used up in the business, eg raw materials.
- Finance for small businesses comes from a variety of sources. These include:
  1 the owner's own savings,
  2 redundancy payments,
  3 bank loans and overdrafts,
  4 partnership capital,
  5 shares, in the case of limited companies,
  6 central government, the European Commission,
  7 local government,
  8 charities (eg the Prince's Trust).
- Additional finance is available to firms in areas where there is high unemployment.
- A **bank loan** is a fixed sum of money given for a particular purpose and paid back with interest over an agreed period of time.
- A **bank overdraft** allows the business to overspend on its account up to an agreed maximum. Interest is only charged on the amount by which the account is overdrawn. Often used for expenditure which is irregular or unexpected.
- A **cash flow problem** is when the business runs short of cash because its money is tied up in stocks or other assets, including debtors (people who owe the business money).
- A **business plan** sets out the details of the business, considers its strengths and weaknesses and estimates the amount of initial finance required.
- **SWOT analysis** involves comparing the strengths and weaknesses of the business and the likely opportunities and threats in the market place.
- A **cash flow forecast** is an estimate of how much cash a business will have at the end of each month during the next year.

Test questions

1 John Jenkins owns a small garage which sells petrol and carries out repairs. John is the only owner at present. John is interested in selling his business and buying a larger garage which has recently become available. The new business would cost £100,000. John has calculated that his fixed assets are worth £40,000 and his current assets are worth

£20,000. He is paying back a bank loan of £20,000 and he has reached the limit of his overdraft facility of £10,000. His bank manager is not willing to increase his loan at the current time. He is currently owed £2000 by customers.

a How much extra finance does John require to purchase the new business?
b What type of business organisation is John's garage?
c Describe two ways in which John might be able to raise extra finance.
d What is the difference between fixed assets and current assets?
e Give an example of a fixed asset and an example of a current asset that John is likely to have in his business.
f Explain the difference between a bank loan and an overdraft, giving an example of how John might use each in his business.

2 Marcia Jones is considering setting up a firm specialising in knitwear in her home town of Newcastle-upon-Tyne. She has been unemployed for the last six months but has £5000 in savings and redundancy payments.

a Describe three ways in which Marcia could get financial help from the Government, bearing in mind that Newcastle-upon-Tyne is an area of high unemployment.
b Describe two ways in which Marcia's bank could assist her financially.
c What are the advantages and disadvantages of the types of finance you listed in (a) and (b)?

3 Steve Bailey Cycles Ltd. is a small manufacturer of specialised racing bikes. They have been doing well and have plenty of new orders but their accountant has told them they are facing a 'cash flow problem'.

a What is meant by a 'cash flow problem'?
b How might this have come about in the case of Steve Bailey Cycles Ltd?
c How might Steve Bailey Cycles Ltd. try to overcome their cash flow problem?

4 a What would be regarded as the fixed assets and the current assets of the firm shown in the picture opposite?
b What types of finance might the business use for each set of assets?

5 a What is the purpose of a business plan?
b What types of information might be included in a business plan?

6 What is SWOT analysis?

7 What is the purpose of a cash flow forecast?

Suggestions for coursework

1 Set up an imaginary business. Find out as much as you can about different forms of finance available. Show how you might use these to finance different aspects of your business. Try to include information on the rates of interest that would be charged to you. Explain why you might use some forms of finance rather than others. Distinguish between fixed and working capital.

2 For any four small local businesses try to find out how they:
   a raised their initial capital,
   b what forms of finance they continue to use in the business,
   c why they chose those particular forms of finance.

3 For an area of high unemployment, find out about all the forms of finance available to firms wishing to set themselves up in the area. Prepare a publicity document to attract small firms to the area.

4 Devise a computer spreadsheet for a cash flow forecast. Demonstrate how this might be used by entering different sales figures.

unit 6

Keeping the books

Aims

At the end of this unit you should understand:

- The need for businesses to keep accurate financial records.
- The main types of accounts kept by businesses and their purposes; income and expenditure, profit and loss, and balance sheets.

Keeping track of income and expenditure

Ling, who we met in Unit 5, has been operating her business for a year, and she now needs to produce some simple accounts. Accounts show how the business is doing by recording how it has spent its money, its income from sales, and the value of its assets. Ling found her course at the college in basic bookkeeping and accounts for small businesses to be extremely helpful.

From the day the business started, Ling kept a simple record of what she received from sales (her income) and everything she spent out on the business (her expenditure). Each week she recorded this income and expenditure in two separate columns in the accounts book for her business. At the end of each month she compared the total income with the total expenditure. This gave her an indication of how the business was doing:

INCOME	
Cash Sales Wk 1	300
P Partridge	7
C Lovett	16
J Smith	20
B Trevithick	5
Cash Sales Wk 2	200
A Teasdale	6
Cash Sales Wk 3	150
B Carlton	14
M Wong	25
Cash Sales Wk 4	270
O Comper	10
B Bradley	6
B Jones	9
Total	**1038**

EXPENDITURE	
Tools	50
Apron	10
Electricity	300
Wages	400
Clay	70
Advert	15
Total	**845**

How was business in May for Ling's Pottery?

Ling has sold pottery to the value of £1038 in May. This is her income, which came from a mixture of sales by cheque, credit and cash. From this Ling must deduct her total expenditure of £845 to find out if she has made a profit.

Total Income - Total expenditure = Profit
£1038 - £845 = £193

Ling's profit is £193, which is lower than she has made in other months. Generally, most businesses aim to make as high a profit as possible, but trade often varies throughout the year. Ling expects June, July, and August to be better because there will be more tourists in town.

Types of account

At the end of her first year in business the bank asked Ling to draw up a trading, profit and loss account, and a balance sheet. These would give Ling and the bank a summary of how well the business had done in its first full year of trading. The accounts would also be useful to the Inland Revenue when they came to work out how much income tax Ling owed.

x (See page 232.)

Ling was fortunate in getting some help in drawing up the accounts from one of the lecturers on her college course who was an accountant.

Trading, profit and loss accounts

Note Only limited companies are required to produce profit and loss accounts and balance sheets. However, many sole owners and partnerships find they are useful.

LING'S POTTERY

27 THE LANE, UPPER THEIKSTON,
CORNWALL, EX13 4GF
TEL: (01730) 12378

Trading and Profit and Loss Account for the Year to 31 March 1994

		£
Sales		18000
Less:		
Cost of Sales		
Opening Stock	2250	
Add: Purchases	1800	
Less: Closing Stock	750	
Cost of goods sold		3300
Gross Profit		**14700**

	£	£
Brought forward		14700
Less: Expenses		
Rent	2400	
Wages	2000	
Heating/Light	1200	
Advertising	600	
Depreciation	1000	
Bank charges	400	
Small tools	250	
Moulds	150	
Sundries	350	
Bad Debt	50	
		8400
Net Profit		**6300**
Appropriation		
Drawings	3990	
Retained Profit	2310	
Total		**6300**

Notes on trading, profit and loss account:

- Depreciation – Equipment used in a business, such as Ling's pottery wheel, will be worth a bit less each year because it will start to wear out. This is known as depreciation. Ling believes that her present equipment will last around 5 years and needs to show this wear and tear in her accounts as a cost. To calculate the amount to be shown she divided the total cost of the equipment by five which amounts to £1000 per year. This is known as the straight line method of calculating depreciation.

- **Bad Debt** – Ling supplied some stock for £50 on credit to a gift shop in another town which has not been paid for. This shop has now gone out of business and Ling is unlikely to get the money back. Ling can treat this as an expense and it is shown in her accounts as a bad debt.
- **Appropriation** – This section in the accounts shows how the net profit is used. In the example given Ling has drawn out £3990 for her own use (Drawings) and kept £2310 in the business (Retained Profit).

Balance sheet

A balance sheet is a statement of the financial position of a business at a certain point in time. It shows all that it owes (its liabilities) and owns (its assets).

LING'S POTTERY
27 THE LANE, UPPER THEIKSTON,
CORNWALL, EX13 4GF
TEL: (01730) 12378

Balance Sheet

	Cost £	Depreciation £	Net £	Total £
Fixed assets				
Equipment	3000	600	2400	
Fixtures and Fittings	2000	400	1600	
	5000	1000	4000	4000
Current Assets				
Debtors	300			
less Bad Debt	50	250		
Stock		750		
Cash		350		
Bank		5000		
		6350		
less:				
Current Liabilities				
Creditors		500		
Working Capital				5850
Total Net Assets				9850
Financed by:				
Capital Account				
Owners Capital	5000			
Net Profit	6300			
	11300			
less:				
Drawings	3990			7310
Long Term Liabilities				
Bank Loan				2540
Capital Employed				9850

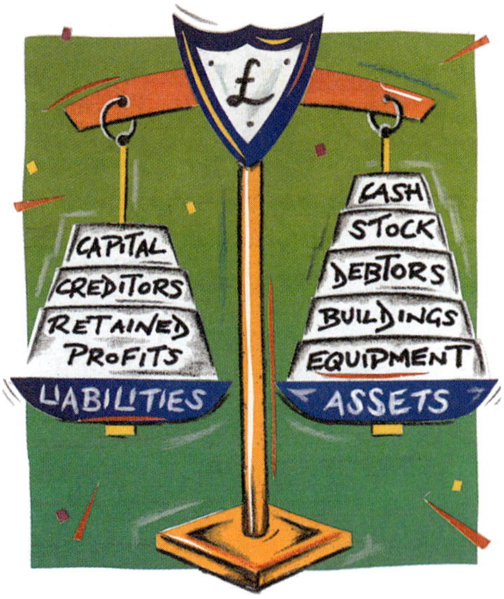

Notes on Balance Sheet

- Fixed Assets – items such as buildings, equipment and fittings owned by the business and not used up in production. (*Note* Depreciation of £1000 is subtracted to arrive at net fixed assets).
- Current Assets – money owed to the business (debtors), cash, stock. (*Note* The bad debt of £50 is 'written off' by subtracting it from the debtors because it is money owed which she will not get back).
- Working Capital – Current assets *less* current liabilities
- Total Net Assets – Working capital *plus* fixed assets
- Owner's Capital – the money that the owner has put into the business
- Drawings – What the owner has taken out of the business
- Capital employed – Owners capital *plus* net profit *less* drawings

x

(See Public Limited Company Balance Sheet page 110.)

Summary of key words and ideas

- Businesses keep accounts in order to provide a financial summary of the business.
- The **trading, profit and loss account** shows the sales, costs, and expenses of a business over a period of time.
- The **balance sheet** is a statement of the full financial situation of a business at a particular moment in time.
- **Gross profit** is the profit made before running costs are deducted.
- **Net profit** is gross profit less running costs.
- **Debtors** are people who owe the business money.
- A **bad debt** is an amount owed to the business which is not going to be paid. The business writes this off as a loss and it is therefore recorded as an expense in the accounts.
- **Creditors** are people the business owes money to.
- **Assets** are anything owned by the business. These are made up of **fixed assets** such as buildings, equipment and machinery and **current assets** such as stock, cash and money owed to the business.
- **Liabilities** are anything the business owes.
- **Depreciation** is the amount by which fixed assets such as machinery and equipment are reduced in value over time.

Test questions

1 T.R. Evans is a small private limited company making kitchen cupboards. What types of accounts are they likely to keep? What is the purpose of keeping these accounts?

2 What is a balance sheet? How is it different from a trading, profit and loss account?

3 'The fixed assets of a business often depreciate over time and this needs to be shown in the balance sheet.' Explain what this statement means and how depreciation might be shown in the balance sheet.

4 Explain, giving examples, what is meant by **a** the creditors and **b** the debtors of a business.

5 What is meant by 'a bad debt'? How are bad debts shown in the trading, profit and loss accounts?

6 A market trader buys 200 pounds (lbs) of strawberries from a farm at 30p a lb and sells them at 50p a lb. The cost of transport, renting the stall and other expenses comes to £20 in total.
- a What was the trader's gross profit?
- b What was the trader's net profit?

Extension questions

1 A business buys a machine for £10,000 and expects it to last for 5 years before needing replacement.
- a What value will be put on the machine in the balance sheet after two years if the straight line method of depreciation is used?
- b In reality depreciation is likely to be greater in years four and five. Why is this?

2 a Draw up a simple trading, profit and loss account for Quantock, a partnership, for the year ending 31 December 1995 based on the following information: Opening stock at 1 January 1995 £80,000. Purchases during the year £300,000. Stock at 31 December 1995 £100,000. Sales during the year were £550,000. Wages were £50,000, rent was £10,000 and other expenses came to £30,000.

b Draw up a balance sheet for Quantock on 31 December 1995. Equipment, machinery and fittings as at 31 December 1994 were valued at £200,000. Depreciation is £20,000. Quantock is owed £10,000 by debtors. Bad debts are estimated at £5,000. Cash in hand and at the bank comes to £50,000. The business owes £5,000 to creditors. The owners have contributed capital of £100,000. Drawings for owners are £50,000. There are no long term liabilities.

Suggestions for coursework

1 Businesses keep their accounts in different ways. Collect accounts from two businesses. For each business explain what the accounts show. Compare how the two businesses present their accounts and discuss the advantages and disadvantages of each approach.

2 Develop a simple computer spreadsheet for a trading, profit and loss account for a small business. Explain how this might be useful to the small business.

unit 7

Obtaining equipment and supplies

Aims

At the end of this unit you should understand:

- How firms purchase or rent materials and equipment.
- What is meant by credit
- What is meant by the Annual Percentage Rate of Interest.
- The use of business documents when purchasing goods.
- The purpose and methods of stock control.

Methods of obtaining goods and equipment

There are four main ways open to the small business wishing to obtain goods and equipment:

1 Cash (including cheques)

This is the most straightforward method of purchasing. In some cases this may be the only method available to the small business because the seller does not offer any alternative. Some sellers may require cash with the order whilst others may accept cash on delivery (COD). It is to the advantage of the seller to be paid immediately because s/he then has the use of the money. In order to encourage buyers to pay quickly, the seller may offer a cash discount – this is a certain percentage reduction in the selling price given for prompt payment.

2 Credit

If goods are bought on credit it means that the purchaser is given a certain period of time to pay for the goods after receiving them. It is quite common for businesses to be allowed several weeks to pay for goods.

Sometimes the seller will allow credit without making any extra charge: this is known as *interest-free credit.* This is true of the supply of gas and electricity – the customer pays the bill every three months after using the gas or electricity and is not charged any extra.

Sometimes the buyer will be charged interest if the goods are bought on credit. In this case the purchaser must be told,

a the cash price,
b how much interest s/he is actually paying.

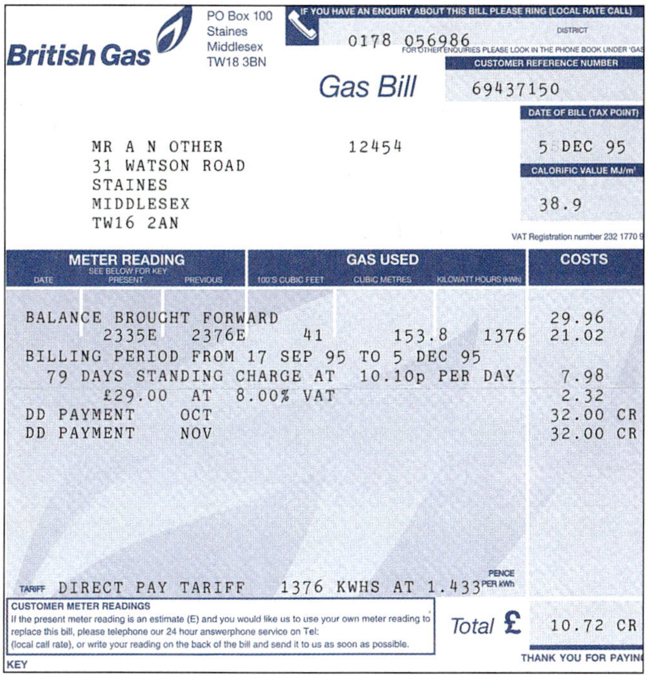
British Gas
PO Box 100
Staines
Middlesex
TW18 3BN
IF YOU HAVE AN ENQUIRY ABOUT THIS BILL PLEASE RING (LOCAL RATE CALL)
DISTRICT
0178 056986
FOR OTHER ENQUIRIES PLEASE LOOK IN THE PHONE BOOK UNDER 'GAS
Gas Bill
CUSTOMER REFERENCE NUMBER
69437150
DATE OF BILL (TAX POINT)
5 DEC 95
MR A N OTHER
31 WATSON ROAD
STAINES
MIDDLESEX
TW16 2AN
12454
CALORIFIC VALUE MJ/m³
38.9
VAT Registration number 232 1770 9

METER READING (SEE BELOW FOR KEY) DATE / PRESENT / PREVIOUS	GAS USED 100'S CUBIC FEET / CUBIC METRES / KILOWATT HOURS (kWh)	COSTS
BALANCE BROUGHT FORWARD		29.96
2335E 2376E	41 153.8 1376	21.02
BILLING PERIOD FROM 17 SEP 95 TO 5 DEC 95		
79 DAYS STANDING CHARGE AT 10.10p PER DAY		7.98
£29.00 AT 8.00% VAT		2.32
DD PAYMENT OCT		32.00 CR
DD PAYMENT NOV		32.00 CR

TARIFF DIRECT PAY TARIFF 1376 KWHS AT 1.433 PENCE PER kWh
CUSTOMER METER READINGS
If the present meter reading is an estimate (E) and you would like us to use your own meter reading to replace this bill, please telephone our 24 hour answerphone service on Tel:
(local call rate), or write your reading on the back of the bill and send it to us as soon as possible.
KEY
Total £ 10.72 CR
THANK YOU FOR PAYING

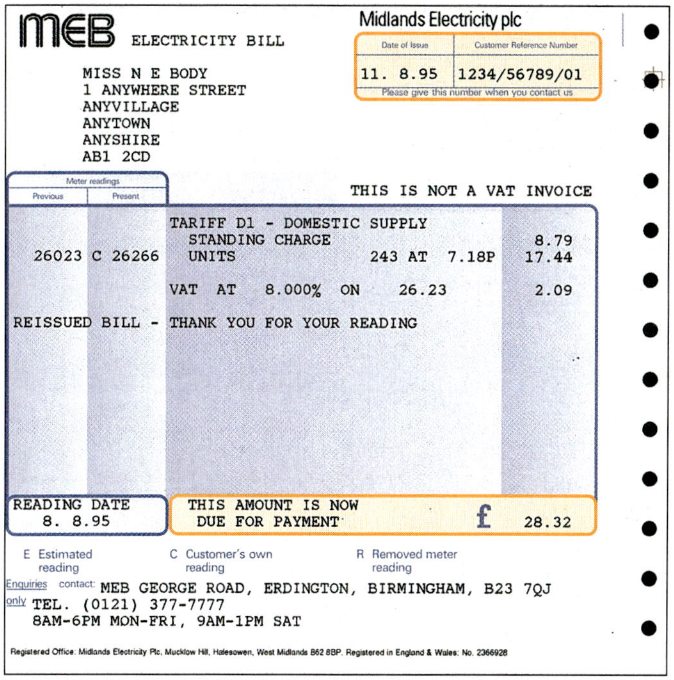
MEB ELECTRICITY BILL
Midlands Electricity plc
Date of Issue: 11. 8.95
Customer Reference Number: 1234/56789/01
Please give this number when you contact us
MISS N E BODY
1 ANYWHERE STREET
ANYVILLAGE
ANYTOWN
ANYSHIRE
AB1 2CD
THIS IS NOT A VAT INVOICE

Meter readings Previous	Present		
		TARIFF D1 - DOMESTIC SUPPLY	
		STANDING CHARGE	8.79
26023 C	26266	UNITS 243 AT 7.18P	17.44
		VAT AT 8.000% ON 26.23	2.09
REISSUED BILL -		THANK YOU FOR YOUR READING	

READING DATE 8. 8.95
THIS AMOUNT IS NOW DUE FOR PAYMENT £ 28.32
E Estimated reading C Customer's own reading R Removed meter reading
Enquiries only contact: MEB GEORGE ROAD, ERDINGTON, BIRMINGHAM, B23 7QJ
TEL. (0121) 377-7777
8AM-6PM MON-FRI, 9AM-1PM SAT
Registered Office: Midlands Electricity Plc, Mucklow Hill, Halesowen, West Midlands B62 8BP. Registered in England & Wales: No. 2366928

3 Hire purchase (HP)

Businesses sometimes buy equipment on hire purchase.
This is exactly what it sounds like: the business rents (hires) the goods whilst it is paying for the goods by instalments. The business will normally be required to make a % down payment as a deposit on the purchase. The business will then pay the remaining amount over a period of time by regular instalments. The items will not become the property of the business until it has completed all the payments.

The total repayments will normally be considerably more than the cash price but the advantage to the business is that it has the use of the equipment straight away. Hire purchase is usually arranged through a finance company which pays the seller and has the power to take back the goods from the buyer if s/he has not paid more than one third of the value of the goods.

4 Renting and leasing

In some cases businesses may find it better to rent equipment rather than purchase it themselves. Businesses may lack the finance to purchase the equipment or property. In other cases, they may only need to use an expensive piece of equipment very occasionally, so it does not pay them to purchase it and tie up their money unnecessarily. Another benefit of renting rather than purchasing is that usually the business hiring the equipment is responsible for repairs and maintenance. However, the business does not end up owning the equipment or property.

A special form of renting is known as leasing. This is when a business rents assets over a long period of time from a leasing company. The leasing company is again responsible for maintaining and repairing the item on lease. Many businesses now lease cars and other vehicles rather than purchase them. Some businesses will also lease machinery and other equipment.

Extension section

Interest

Interest is the cost of borrowing money and is usually shown as a % *(the rate of interest)*. The Consumer Credit Act of 1974 states that borrowers must be given the *Annual Percentage Rate (APR)* of interest. This is the true rate of interest paid over a year and is usually about twice the amount of the *Nominal or Flat Rate* interest. The nominal or flat rate interest is calculated by: amount paid on credit divided by cash price x 100.

For example, if the cash price of a piece of equipment was £1000 and the credit price was £1100 when it was bought over a year, the nominal rate of interest would be £10%. The purchaser would pay 12 monthly instalments of £91.66 (£1100/12 assuming there was no deposit). However, the nominal rate does not give a true picture because the borrower is not really borrowing £1000 for a whole year. After 6 months half of the loan would have been paid back but the interest paid each month remains the same.

Question

Why does the APR give a truer picture and allow the borrower to make better comparisons than the nominal or flat rate of interest?

(See Consumer Credit Act, page 213.)

Case study

The Corner Shop

Ramesh Patel owns a newsagent and confectioners called The Corner Shop. Each week he purchases stock from a cash-and-carry wholesaler. The newspapers are delivered every day by a distributor and he pays for the ones he sells at the end of the month. Ramesh runs a newspaper delivery service for his customers who normally pay him each week.

The Corner Shop also offers a photocopying service. Ramesh does not own the photocopier but pays a certain amount each month to a company which maintains the machine and carries out any necessary repairs.

Ramesh has recently put a deposit down on a van and is paying instalments each month to a finance company. He uses the van to collect his stock from the wholesaler but it will not actually belong to him until he has completed paying all the instalments.

1 The Corner Shop case study gives an example of a cash purchase, leasing, hire purchase and two examples of credit. Make a list of these methods of obtaining material and equipment and write next to each one an example of it from the Corner Shop business.

2 For each method suggest one advantage and one disadvantage of using it for Ramesh.

Ramesh is buying his van on hire purchase from Central Motors. Ramesh has signed the agreement with a finance company who have paid Central Motors. The van is second-hand and costs £4000. Ramesh was required to put a deposit of 25% down and to pay the rest in instalments. The table on the next page shows how much he would pay each month at various rates of interest over different periods of time.

3 Calculate how much it will cost him on HP if he pays for the van over two years at 8% interest. (Remember, he pays a deposit first.)

4 How much more would it cost if the interest was 10% and he paid over four years?

HIRE PURCHASE MONTHLY REPAYMENT TABLE

SUM BORROWED

FLAT RATE	6%			8%			10%			12%		
PERIOD	2yrs	3yrs	4yrs	2yrs	3yrs	4yrs	2yrs	3yrs	4yrs	2yrs	3yrs	4yrs
£50	£2.33	£1.64	£1.29	£2.42	£1.73	£1.38	£2.50	£1.81	£1.46	£2.59	£1.89	£1.55
£100	£4.67	£3.28	£2.58	£4.84	£3.45	£2.75	£5.00	£3.62	£2.92	£5.17	£3.78	£3.09
£200	£9.33	£6.56	£5.17	£9.67	£6.89	£5.50	£10.00	£7.23	£5.84	£10.34	£7.56	£6.17
£500	£23.33	£16.39	£12.92	£24.17	£17.23	£13.75	£25.00	£18.06	£14.59	£25.84	£18.89	£15.42
£600	£28.00	£19.67	£15.50	£29.00	£20.67	£16.50	£30.00	£21.67	£17.50	£31.00	£22.67	£18.50
£800	£37.33	£26.22	£20.67	£38.67	£27.56	£22.00	£40.00	£28.89	£23.34	£41.34	£30.23	£24.67
£1000	£46.67	£32.78	£25.83	£48.34	£34.45	£27.50	£50.00	£36.12	£29.17	£51.67	£37.78	£30.84
£2000	£93.34	£65.56	£51.66	£96.68	£68.90	£55.00	£100.00	£72.24	£58.34	£103.34	£75.56	£61.68
£3000	£140.01	£98.34	£77.49	£145.02	£103.35	£82.50	£150.00	£108.36	£87.51	£155.01	£113.34	£92.52
£4000	£186.68	£131.12	£103.32	£193.36	£137.80	£110.00	£200.00	£144.48	£116.68	£206.68	£151.12	£123.36
£5000	£233.35	£163.90	£129.15	£241.70	£172.25	£137.50	£250.00	£180.60	£145.85	£258.35	£188.90	£154.20

Documents used in purchasing

When goods are purchased by a firm, certain documents pass between the buyer and the supplier. The most important of these are the order form, the delivery note, the invoice, receipts, credit and debit notes, and monthly statements. A firm may not use all of these, but the following example of The Village Stores illustrates the purpose of each document.

Case study

The Village Stores

Sally Johnston is the owner of The Village Stores, a general grocers in the village of Lastwaite. She obtains her stock from a wholesaler in Carlisle who makes a delivery each week to Lastwaite.

The order

1 Sally has a price list and details of the stock available from Carlisle Wholesalers. Each week she completes an order form and sends it to the wholesaler to let them know her requirements for the following week. This is done on a computerised form which uses code numbers for the various goods which Sally is ordering.

Carlisle Wholesalers process the order form from The Village Stores and pack the goods ready for delivery the following week.

The delivery note

2 Carlisle Wholesalers deliver the goods to The Village Stores. The driver gives Sally a delivery note which lists all the items being delivered and shows any items unavailable. Sally checks this off against her own copy of the order.

ORDER FORM

CARLISLE WHOLESALERS
CARLISLE
CUMBRIA

Order No. 3/2
Date 30/5/95
Ref. VS/L

Please supply THE VILLAGE STORE
LASTWAITE
CUMBRIA
(Name and Address of BUYER)

with the following goods

Quantity	Description of Goods (Please quote Stock Number)	Unit Price £	Total Value £
4 DOZ	032172 BAKED BEANS	0·24	11·52
5 DOZ	032189 TOMATOES	0·20	12·00

Carlisle Wholesalers

Carlisle, Cumbria

DELIVERY NOTE

Delivery Note No. 499
Order No. 312
Date: 7/6/95

Goods supplied to: (Name and Address of Buyer)
The Village Store
Lastwaite
Cumbria

Our Ref. CW/396
Your Ref. VS/L

Quantity	Description of Goods
4 DOZ	032172 BAKED BEANS
5 DOZ	032189 TOMATOES

Date ---------- Signed ----------

The invoice

3 Carlisle Wholesalers send an invoice to The Village Stores. This is also done on a computer. The invoice gives all the details of the goods ordered and delivered, including the quantity and the price. The invoice also shows any VAT being charged by the wholesaler and any discounts being allowed.

You may also find some of these terms on invoices:
Carr. paid means that the cost of the transport is already included in the price of the goods.
Carr. fwd means that the buyer must pay for the transport.
FOR = free on rail.
FOB = free on board ship.
E & OE = errors and omissions excepted. This allows the seller the right to correct any errors at a later date.
Terms These are the various discounts allowed; trade discounts for recognised traders, cash discount for immediate payment in cash, seven days 2 1/2% for bills settled within a week.

Credit and debit notes

4 Carlisle Wholesalers will send The Village Stores a credit note for any amount that it may have overcharged Sally on the invoice or for damaged stock returned. A debit note is sent if Sally has been undercharged.

Carlisle Wholesalers Carlisle, Cumbria

INVOICE

Invoice No. 219 V.A.T. Reg. No. SR/3

To: The Village Store
Lastwaite
Cumbria

Date: 20/6/95

Our Ref. CW/394
Your Ref. VS/L

Quantity	Description	Recommended Retail Price £	Amount £
4 DOZ.	032172 BAKED BEANS	0.24	11.52
5 DOZ.	032189 TOMATOES	0.20	12.00
6 DOZ.	092864 PEAS	0.18	12.96
3 DOZ.	092865 SOUP	0.30	10.80

Total £ 47.28
Less 20% Trade Discount 9.46
£ 37.82
Add 17.5% V.A.T. N/A
Total £ 37.82

Terms: 2½% Discount 7 days
E&OE CARR.PAID

Carlisle Wholesalers Carlisle, Cumbria

V.A.T. Reg. No. SR/384/21

CREDIT NOTE

Date: 30/6/95

Credit Note No. 312

To: The Village Store
Lastwaite
Cumbria

Our Ref. CW/396
Your Ref. VS/L

Quantity	Description	Invoice Price £	Amount £
4 TINS	BAKED BEANS	0.24	0.96

Total £ 0.96

Reason for return DAMAGED STOCK

E&OE

Monthly statements

5 Each month Carlisle Wholesalers send Sally a statement of how much is currently owed. This lists all the invoices she has been sent and records any payment made by Sally since the last statement. The statement will also show any credit and debit notes that may have been issued during the previous month.

Receipts

6 Sally pays her bill to Carlisle Wholesalers each month and they send her a receipt to show that payment has been made.

Carlisle Wholesalers

Carlisle, Cumbria

V.A.T. Reg. No. SR/384/21

STATEMENT OF ACCOUNT

Date: 31/6/95

Statement No. 28/87

To: The Village Store
Lastwaite
Cumbria

Date	Details	Debits £	Credits £	Balance £
	Balance b/f			28.61
13/6/95	CHEQUE		16.51	12.10
20/6/95	INVOICE NO.219	37.82		49.92
25/6/95	CHEQUE		10.16	39.76
28/6/95	INVOICE NO.312		0.96	38.80

The last amount is the amount due.

E&OE

Terms: 2½% Discount 7 days

Exercise

1 You are the owner of Sweetway – a small confectioners which buys from CRT Wholesalers Ltd. This week you order the following items: 2 boxes of Mars Bars at £8.50 a box, 3 boxes of Bounty Bars at £8.30 a box, 5 boxes of plain crisps, 4 boxes of salt and vinegar crisps and 3 boxes of beef flavour crisps – all at £5.20 a box.

a Prepare an order form and an invoice for the items shown above.

b It is later discovered that the price charged on Mars Bars should have been £8.10 a box. Prepare an appropriate document to correct the error on the invoice.

Case study (continued)

Knowing how much to purchase

How does Sally Johnston at The Village Stores (page 69) know what to order each week from the wholesaler? Although The Village Stores is a small shop, it still stocks a large range of goods and it would be very easy for Sally to run out of an item. Sally has neither the finance nor the space for a large stock so it is particularly important that she keeps a careful check on the goods she has in the shop. She does this by using stock record cards on which she records the amount of stock coming into the shop and the amount of stock which has been sold. She regularly updates the cards by checking the items on the shelves. The stock record cards tell Sally which items are selling well and which are not so popular. Sally can also tell which items are nearing their sell by date.

Sally is considering investing in a small personal computer which has a program for stock control. Sally would need to input the data each week and the computer will remind her which goods she needs to order. Many firms now use computerised stock control methods. We will see later how important it is to maintain the correct levels of stock in a large manufacturing company in order to produce a steady flow of finished goods.

Stock record

item

date	stock purchased	stock in hand	stock sold
1 Oct '95		20 lge. 40 sml.	
8 Oct '95	50 lge. 30 sml.		
1 Dec '95		10 lge. 20 sml.	60 lge. 50 sml.

Notes On 1 October Sally checked her stock and found she had 20 large and 40 small tins of beans. she took delivery of 50 large and 30 small tins of beans on 8 October. She checked her stock again on 1 December and found she had 10 large and 20 small tins left. She could therefore work out that she had sold 60 large tins and 50 small tins of baked beans between 1 October and 1 December.

Summary of key words and ideas

Methods of purchasing

- **Cash on delivery (COD)** The purchaser must pay for the goods at the time of delivery.
- **Cash discount** A reduction in the price of the goods given for prompt payment.
- **Credit** When the purchaser pays for the goods over a period of time.
- **Interest** A charge made on top of the cash price for buying on credit.
- **Interest-free credit** When the purchaser is given credit and no extra charge is made above the cash price. It is to the advantage of the purchasers if they are offered interest-free credit because they retain the use of their money for an extra period of time.
- **APR** is the annual percentage rate of interest and is the true rate of interest. It must be stated in any credit purchase.
- **Nominal or Flat Rate interest** is credit price divided by cash price x 100.
- **Hire purchase** The purchaser makes a deposit and pays for the goods over a period of time in instalments. The goods do not belong to the purchaser until s/he has completed paying for them.
- **Finance company** An organisation that arranges HP.
- **Leasing** A form of long-term renting of assets, such as vehicles and machines. The leasing firm is responsible for their repair and maintenance.
- It often pays small firms to hire equipment rather than purchase it if the equipment is very expensive or not used often.

Documents used in purchasing

- **The order** Form on which the purchaser lists requirements.
- **Delivery note** Document containing details of the goods being delivered.
- **The invoice** Document giving all the details of the order including price, quantity, VAT, etc.
- **Credit note** Sent by the seller if the purchaser has been overcharged.
- **Debit note** Sent by the seller if the purchaser has been undercharged.
- **Monthly statement** Shows on their account how much the purchaser owes.
- **Receipt** Sent by the seller when the purchaser has paid for the goods.
- **Stock control** A check on the level of stock needed in the business.
- **Stock record cards** Method of recording information on how much stock is in the business at any one time.

Test questions

1 John Draper, self-employed electrician, has been offered some equipment on '3 months interest-free credit'.
  a What does '3 months interest-free credit' mean.
  b What would John need to check before taking on the credit?
  c What are the advantages of interest-free credit for John?

2 You are the owner of a small bakery which makes deliveries to shops and cafes in the locality. You need to use two vans. List the advantages and disadvantages of
  a buying the vans by cash,
  b buying them on HP,
  c leasing them.

3 Suggest an appropriate method of purchasing the following items giving reasons for your choice:
  a cars for sales representatives,
  b stocks of raw materials,
  c extension to existing buildings,
  d payment of wages without enough cash in your bank account to cover them.

4 Marcia Lloyd manages a knitwear shop. She orders her supplies from a wholesaler called Scottish Woolmasters. List and describe any four documents that would pass between Marcia and Scottish Woolmasters after she places an order.

5 How would a supplier correct an error on an invoice if s/he had overcharged a customer on an invoice?

6 Explain how Quickbuild, a small firm of builders, might make use of three different methods of purchasing for obtaining items for their business.

7 What is the purpose of stock control? Explain how a small manufacturing firm might keep a record of its stock.

Extension questions

1 a Explain the difference between the annual percentage rate of interest (APR) and the nominal (flat) rate of interest.
  b Why is the APR said to be 'the true rate of interest'?
  c A business wishes to buy a machine with a cash price of £10,000. The business decides to pay on credit by making a deposit of 20% and 12 monthly payments of £700. What is the nominal (flat) rate of interest paid by the firm?

2 a 'Too much stock is as bad as too little'. Why might this be true for a small shop?
  b How might a small garage which sells petrol and undertakes car repairs and servicing make use of a simple computerised system of stock control?

3 Study the invoice shown and answer the following questions:

JMB SUPPLIES LTD.

Wingate, Norwich, Norfolk

INVOICE

Invoice No. 1826

Date: 10 March 1995

Your Order No. 967

To: Arcadia Nurseries
The Avenue
Bromley
Kent

Qty.	Description	Unit prices	Total
5 doz.	Grow Bags	2.30	138.00
3 doz.	Peat Pots	0.50	18.00

Terms :
Cash 5%
One Month 2½% **Carr. Paid**

a What is the supplier?
b Who is the purchaser?
c What has been supplied?
d At what stage would an invoice be sent?
e What is the purpose of the invoice?
f What does 'Carr. paid' mean?
g What does 'Terms: cash 5%, One month 2.5%' mean?
h What is a trade discount given for?

Suggestions for coursework

1 Choose two items which are normally available on HP or rental terms (e.g. televisions, video recorders, etc). Compare the cost of buying by cash with HP or renting for a year. List the possible advantages and disadvantages of each method.

2 For either a real or an imaginary business, draw up the appropriate documents used in purchasing, showing how a particular order is processed.

3 Develop a simple stock control system for a shop using a computer spreadsheet.

unit 8

Marketing the product

Aims

At the end of this unit you should understand:

- What is meant by the marketing mix.
- The purposes and methods of advertising.
- The idea of product differentiation.
- How firms decide upon a price.
- The different channels of distribution.

The marketing mix

Marketing is everything involved in selling and promoting a product or service. There are four main factors to consider in marketing:

Product the design of the product or service, packaging, after sales service, etc.

Promotion advertising, publicity, display, etc.

Price the price of the product or service, discounts, etc.

Place where the product or service will be sold; shops, mail order, direct selling, etc.

The marketing mix is how the four P's of marketing (**Product**, **Promotion**, **Price**, and **Place**) are combined to sell the product or service.

The marketing mix will vary between different types of products. The mix will be very different for a fashionable watch than for a heavy industrial machine to be sold to a manufacturer. Colour, style, and packaging will be important in marketing the watch but will be less so for the machine where after sales service might be crucial.

x

(Market research for the small business is covered in Unit 2 and returned to in Unit 15 along with other aspects of marketing in a large business)

A business might well draw up a *marketing plan* to show how it intends to sell and promote a product or service.

The Wooden Toy Company Ltd

You are the Marketing Manager for The Wooden Toy Company Ltd. The firm makes hand-crafted specialist wooden toys. Currently its three main products are:

1 a railway engine which can be assembled by a three-year-old,
2 a clown which balances and rotates between parallel rails,
3 a miniature rocking horse and rider.

A new managing director has just taken over at The Wooden Toy Company and you receive the following memo:

MEMO

From: Managing Director   To: Marketing Manager
Date: 29-9-95
Ref: Sales figs. 1993-5 (attached)

You will notice from the enclosed figures that total sales have been virtually static for the past three years despite a growing toy market. I am very keen to improve upon our sales in the next financial year and to show improved profits to our shareholders. Please prepare a new marketing plan setting out three alternative strategies for Wooden Toys, giving your views on the suitability of each strategy.

SALES FIGURES 1993-5

	1993	**1994**	**1995**
Railway Engine	4025	5982	6745
Clown	5673	4031	4021
Rocking Horse	6514	5821	4954
Other toys	2384	2518	2427
Total sales	18596	18352	18147

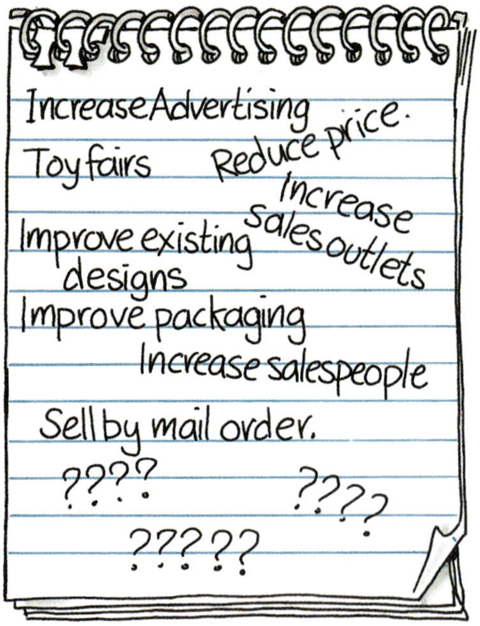

Exercise

Your task as marketing manager is to carry out the instruction in the memo from the managing director. In the time given (one year) it will be very difficult for the firm to switch into a completely new product outside the wooden toy range. It may well be possible, however, to develop a new type of wooden toy. The first thing you do is to jot down all the possible ways of improving your firm's sales in the next year.

From your jottings you construct different plans. Against each plan you list the possible disadvantages. At the end of your report you recommend one particular strategy.

The exercise on The Wooden Toy Company should have given you some idea of the range of factors which can help to increase sales. Using the example of The Wooden Toy Company we will now look at some of these influences in turn.

Promotion

Advertising

Purpose

Advertising is a very large industry in the UK. Each year firms in the UK spend approximately £10,000m on advertising. Much of this is spent by large firms but even quite small firms often spend a considerable proportion of their budget on advertising.

Advertising by firms is a way of increasing sales of their products or services. Advertising is also used to launch a new product and to keep the name of a product in the public's mind. It attempts to do this in two ways:

a by informing them about the product and making the consumer aware that the product exists.

b by trying to persuade the consumer that they need a particular product or service and that their product or service is the best on the market.

Exercise

Look at the following example of an advertisement for The Wooden Toy Company that appeared in a local newspaper.

a List all the facts given which inform the consumer about the firm's products.
b List the statements that attempt to persuade the consumer that they need Wooden Toy products.
c Carry out the same exercise for advertisements of your choice from a newspaper or magazine.
d Design an advertisement for a new soft drink which contains both factual information about the product and also attempts to persuade the consumer to buy it.

Types of advertising for the small business

Exercise

Using the pictures below to assist you, list all the places where advertisements appear.

Advertising costs

Here are some examples of the costs of different types of advertising.

Postcard in a newsagent's window 50p per week
Small ad in 'free' newspaper 14p per word
Local newspaper (circulation 33,000) £800 full page
Local newspaper (circulation 110,000) £2,225 full page
The Times (circulation 500,000) £12,000 full page
The Sun (circulation 4,000,000) £28,000 full page
30 second advert on local radio Monday-Sunday 12.00-16.00 £50
30 second advert on local radio Monday-Friday 0600-0900 £85
30 second advert on local TV off-peak £200
30 second advert on local TV peak £400

Exercise

a Of the methods of advertising you listed in the previous exercise, which do you consider to be appropriate for the small business?

b Why is the cost of an advert in the Sun more than the same one in the Times?

c Why is the cost of an advert on local radio at 3pm less than the same one at 8am?

Apart from the cost, firms must consider the likely market for their product or service. It would be unwise, for example, for a village store to go to the expense of advertising in a national newspaper when most of the readers are not going to be living near the shop. Firms which do not sell direct to the public often advertise in trade journals which are read by people specialising in a particular product or service, e.g. the grocery trade, electrical services, etc.

Exercise

Suggest appropriate forms of advertising for,

a a small hair salon,

b a window cleaner,

c a chain of 12 bakeries located in one region of the country,

d a food wholesaler selling only to shops,

e a small manufacturer of clothing kits sold directly to the public by mail order.

Other methods of promotion

Display Attractive displays of goods in shops help to promote them. The Wooden Toy Company might negotiate with shops to mount a special display of their products.

Sponsorship Many small businesses support local organisations and events. In return, the name of the business gets mentioned. A business might sponsor a local football team by buying their kit and having their logo on the shirts. The Wooden Toy Company might donate some toys as prizes at a school Christmas fair in return for having their name in the programme.

Trade Fairs These give businesses the chance to display their goods for viewing by shops and other customers. The Wooden Toy Company hires a stall at a large craft fair each year. The fair is attended by buyers who come from toy shops all over the country and abroad.

Below: A trade fair

Price

How do firms go about deciding upon the price of their product? Choosing the correct price will be crucial to selling the product. One way of fixing the price is to take the average cost of making the product (see page 41) and to add on a profit. This method is known as mark-up pricing. This is the approach adopted by Wooden Toys. The average cost of making and selling their railway engine is £4.00. They add on 25%, which would give a selling price of £5. They actually sell it at £4.99. (Why do you suppose they reduce the price by 1 penny?)

How do firms decide upon how much to mark up their products by? Why do Wooden Toys add on 25% and not 50% or 10%? An important factor here will be how much any rival firms are charging for similar products. If Wooden Toys charge a great deal more for their railway engine than similar products on the market they are clearly not going to sell many. At the same time, they must ask themselves whether they will sell many more if they greatly reduce the price. If they make the price too low, people may think that there is something wrong with the product. (See Pricing strategies, page 201.)

Exercise

Wooden Toys currently sells its railway engine at £4.99. At this price it has been selling an average of 130 engines a week. A rival firm has cut the price of its similar engine to £4.75 and this has reduced sales of Wooden Toys' engine to an average of 100 a week. As Marketing Manager of Wooden Toys, you are considering reducing the price of your engine. You have estimated the following sales figures:

Price	*Expected sales* (weekly average)
£4.99	100
£4.80	103
£4.75	120
£4.70	130
£4.60	132

a Why is a large increase in sales expected if the price is reduced from £4.80 to £4.75?

b What price would you recommend for Wooden Toys' engine, assuming that production costs remain the same?

c At the new price would Wooden Toys be better or worse off than they were before their rivals cut their price?

d What might the rival's reaction be to Wooden Toys' new price?

e What other options might be open to Wooden Toys, apart from changing price?

f What might happen to Wooden Toys' prices and sales if the rival firm went out of business?

Product

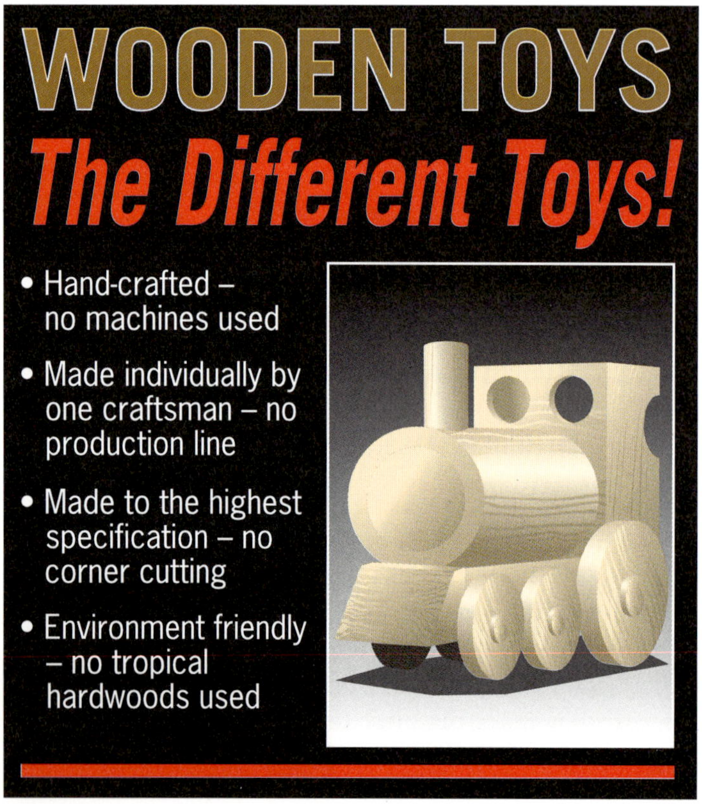

Apart from advertising and reducing their price, what other methods could Wooden Toys adopt to gain a larger share of the market?

Product differentiation

One possibility is for them to stress the differences between their products and their rivals'. This is known as product differentiation. The differences may be real or the consumer may be persuaded by advertising that there are differences.

Exercise

How are Wooden Toys trying to differentiate their products from other toys?

Packaging

Products can also be made to look different or more attractive by clever packaging. Wooden Toys might adopt more eye-catching colours and better looking boxes for the packaging of their products. Alternatively, they might use very simple packaging and stress that it is made out of recycled materials.

Case study

Fullerton's Fudge

Fullerton's, a small sweet manufacturer, have been making fudge for the past 50 years. It is packaged in rather boring and unattractive plastic bags. It is only sold in shops within a radius of 30 miles from the factory. It is not surprising that Fullerton's Fudge has a rather small and, recently, declining market.

a As the recently appointed Marketing Manager you have been asked to come up with a new image for Fullerton's Fudge. The basic product will remain the same but you will need to design new packaging and a new poster advertisement for it.

b Suggest other ways of improving the marketing of Fullerton's Fudge, paying particular attention to the marketing mix.

c Write a memo to your sales representatives, indicating the new image you wish them to try to create for Fullerton's Fudge when they visit retailers who have not previously stocked the product.

Place

The ways in which Wooden Toys sells its products to the consumer are important. The more retail outlets it has, the better its chances of selling its products. Wooden Toys currently employs two sales representatives who visit toy shops in order to try to persuade them to stock its products. Each year a number of toy fairs are held where toy manufacturers display their products to buyers from shops. Wooden Toys could certainly consider the possibility of attending more of these in order to try to increase the number of shops where their products are sold.

The channels of distribution

The ways in which a business gets its products to the customer are known as the channels of distribution:

Direct selling

Many small manufacturing firms sell direct to the consumer. Ling's Pottery in Unit 6 is a good example of direct selling to the public. She was both the *manufacturer* and the *retailer* (the place where goods are sold to the public).

For some manufacturers the consumer may be another manufacturing firm. A small firm may make components for a larger firm. In this case the small firm will often sell direct to the large manufacturer.

Door-to-door salespeople

Some small firms may employ door-to-door salespeople, who carry a stock of goods or advertising information about the goods and call on selected houses in an area. A very small firm, such as a one-person business, might employ this method of selling. It is also used by large organisations such as Avon Cosmetics.

Mail order

Mail order is another method of direct selling used by both small and large firms. Large firms may produce expensive catalogues which can be used by the consumer to order the goods of their choice. Small firms may simply place an advertisement in the local paper inviting customers to buy direct from the firm through the post. This was one method of selling used by The Wooden Toy Company earlier in this unit.

Telephone selling

A recent development in the UK, has been telephone selling. The firm employs staff who telephone members of the public and try to persuade them to purchase goods. This has tended to be used by larger firms, but some small firms use a telephone selling agency as a way of selling their goods.

Selling through a middleman

It is often very expensive for manufacturing firms to sell in small quantities to a large range of consumers. These firms will often sell through a middleman. The middleman buys in bulk from the manufacturer and breaks this into smaller quantities to be sold to the final customer. A wholesaler is a type of middleman. You may remember that Ramesh Patel in Unit 7 bought the goods he required for his corner shop from a cash-and-carry wholesaler. This is where retailers visit the wholesaler and transport their own goods. Other wholesalers, like that used by Sally Johnston in Unit 7, operate a delivery service for retailers.

Some manufacturers may use selling agencies to distribute their goods for them. The selling agent acts for a number of manufacturers who find it cheaper to operate through a specialist in selling. This is particularly the case when small firms wish to sell overseas (see Unit 7).

Exercise

1 What advantages are there for
  a the manufacturer,
  b the retailer
  in using a wholesaler?

2 Why does the use of a wholesaler normally result in higher prices for the customer?

3 What is meant by a 'cash-and-carry' wholesaler?

Types of retail outlets

Exercise

Match the following definitions of types of retail outlets to the pictures and titles on the next page:

Definitions

1 A collection of rented stalls selling a range of goods. Often held outdoors in the centre of a town either daily or once a week.

2 A coin-operated machine supplying items like drinks, sandwiches and sweets. Often found on railway stations and in other public places.

3 A vehicle that sells goods in a variety of places. Most common in rural areas where there is a lack of shops. Often sells food such as fish, fruit and bread.

4 A small shop, often a sole-owner business. Very often a corner shop, general stores or newsagents.

5 One of ten or more shops under the same ownership. Examples include Marks and Spencer, Boots, Dixons.

6 Normally large shops in the centre of towns selling a very wide variety of goods. There are normally a large number of shop assistants in each section. There are often several floors in these shops. Harrods is a famous example.

7 These are large shops on one level with a floor area of more than 2000 square feet. They sell food but are increasingly stocking other household items. Self-service for most items is usual and they are often located outside town centres with large car parking facilities. Leading examples include Asda and Tesco.

8 A collection of shops under one roof, often outside of towns. They have very large car parking facilities and sell a wide range of goods. The Brent Cross Centre in North London is an example.

9 Located on the outskirts of towns, often in industrial estates. Customers select items, such as furniture, which are collected from a large store. Examples include B&Q and Texas. Prices are often lower than those in town-centre shops.

Retail outlets

Case study

The continuing story of Fullerton's

At present Fullerton's sell their sweets direct to local shops without using a wholesaler. As Marketing Manager you wish to increase the number of retail outlets stocking Fullerton's products. Selling outside of the present locality will either involve employing more salespeople to visit new shops, or using wholesalers to distribute the sweets for them. Using more salespeople will be costly as they need to be equipped with vehicles. Using wholesalers will require fewer salespeople and has the added advantage of supplying easy access to a large number of retailers who already visit the wholesalers. The main drawback of using the wholesalers is that, because the wholesalers need to make a profit, the price to the consumer will be higher, unless Fullerton's are prepared to make less profit on each packet of sweets they sell.

1 What advantages will there be for Fullerton's using wholesalers rather than selling direct to retailers?

2 What costs will be reduced by using wholesalers?

3 Explain why using a wholesaler will mean either higher prices for the consumer or less profit per packet of sweets for Fullerton's.

4 Can you think of any other disadvantages for Fullerton's of using wholesalers rather than direct selling by salespeople?

5 Fullerton's might also consider using mail order as a method of selling. What is mail order? What advantages are there for Fullerton's of this method of selling? Which costs would be saved by this method of selling compared to using salespeople or wholesalers? What extra costs would there be if mail order selling was used?

The small firm and retail outlets

Most small firms making products to be sold to the public will either sell direct, use wholesalers or sell to small shops. The large chain stores and supermarkets need to buy in bulk and the small manufacturer is often unable to produce in sufficient quantity or at low enough prices to compete with the larger manufacturers. Some small specialist manufacturers do manage to win contracts to supply the large retailers. This has been the case with Betta Pies, a small bakery, which has supplied fresh meat pies and quiches to leading supermarkets.

There are three ways, however, in which small retail businesses can appeal to a wider range of customers.

Franchising

This is when a business buys a licence or franchise to operate as a well-known firm. This is often the case in the fast food trade where businesses buy franchises to operate as Domino's Pizza, Kentucky Fried Chicken, etc.

Voluntary trading groups

The best-known example is SPAR shops. The shops are owned privately, often as sole-owner businesses, and they join the SPAR organisation. SPAR buys products from the manufacturers, often obtaining a bulk discount similar to the large supermarkets, and sells to the member shops often under their own label. This means that the small retailer benefits from using a well-known name and from lower prices from the manufacturer.

In-store boutiques

Some large department stores rent floor space to other businesses wishing to display their products. This is sometimes the case for cosmetics, household products and food. The in-store boutique benefits from being in a large shop which attracts many customers. Although they need to pay rent to the department store, the boutique does not have to pay all the overhead costs of a large shop in a town centre.

Cosmetics companies often rent specialist counters in large department stores

Summary of key words and ideas

- **Marketing** Finding and developing the right product, getting the product from the manufacturer to the consumer using advertising, packaging, pricing, salesmen and other methods of sales promotion.
- **Advertising** attempts both to inform customers of a product or service and to persuade them to purchase it.
- There are many different types of advertising appearing in a wide range of places. The cost of advertising varies directly with the expected sizeof audience. Firms will take account of costs and the type of audience they are trying to reach when selecting methods of advertising.
- **Mark-up pricing** is calculated by taking average costs and adding a profit % to it. The % mark-up will depend upon such factors as the prices competitors are charging and the amount people are prepared to pay for the good or service.
- **Product differentiation** is an attempt by a firm to distinguish its product or service from that of its rivals.
- **Retail outlet** The place where goods are sold to the public as consumers.
- **The marketing mix** The way in which the various aspects of sales promotion are combined in marketing a product. The mix will vary depending upon the nature of the product and the market it is intended for. The factors making up the marketing mix are promotion, price, product, and place.
- **Sales representatives** People employed by the firm to sell its products or services to customers.
- **Direct selling** When the firm sells its products to the final consumer without going through any middlemen. Methods include door-to-door salespeople, mail order, and telephone selling. This may reduce costs for the firm but it may not reach such a wide market.
- **Wholesalers** Middlemen between the manufacturer and the customers. They buy in bulk from the firm and break this into smaller units for the customer. The wholesaler may save the firm transport costs and help it to reach a wider market.
- **Channels of distribution** The ways in which goods reach the final consumer from the manufacturer.
- Small firms can become better known by using franchising, voluntary trading organisations and by renting accommodation from large stores.

Test questions

1 The Standard Pen Company Ltd is a small manufacturer of writing implements (fountain pens, propelling pencils, etc.). Its products tend to be rather traditional in design. Recently sales have been falling as a result of increased competition.

Suggest four different ways in which the Standard Pen Company could regain its share of the market, explaining how each method might attract extra customers.

2 'Advertising attempts both to inform and to persuade.'

a Explain how advertising attempts to sell more goods and services.

b Explain how the following advertisement attempts both to inform and to persuade the consumer.

The Standard Ink Master Pen

A traditional pen made to the highest quality by our skilled craftsmen. Each pen is individually produced in our own workshops using only the finest materials.

Make sure that your writing is at its best by buying the best.

Available at quality retailers **£6.50**

c How is the Standard Pen Company trying to differentiate its product?

3 Alek has recently started a small hairdressing business in the suburbs of a large town. He has allowed himself £500 a year for advertising and promotion. Advise him on how best to use the money. Include three different methods of advertising and sales promotion in your advice.

4 You are the owner of a greengrocers.

a Describe two things you might take into account when deciding on the price of oranges in your shop.

b The price of a large orange is currently 15p. You calculate that if you were to reduce the price to 10p you would sell 20% more oranges. Should you reduce the price? Explain your answer.

5 a Describe two ways in which a firm could sell direct to the customer without using any middlemen.

b Give two advantages and two disadvantages of this selling method.

6 Some firms sell by mail order.

a What does this mean?

b What cost does the firm save by using mail order?

c What extra costs does this method of selling involve for the firm?

7 'A wholesaler is a middleman'.

a Explain what this means.

b Describe two advantages of a firm selling through a wholesaler rather than selling direct.

8 'The Corner Shop' is a small independent general store located in the suburbs of a large city. The owner purchases stock at a local cash-and-carry wholesalers. In general its prices are higher by about 10% than the nearest supermarket which is two miles away.

a What is meant by an independent shop?

b What is a cash-and-carry wholesaler?

c Give two reasons why prices in The Corner Shop are 10% higher than those in the supermarket.

d Give two reasons why people still shop at The Corner Shop rather than go to the cheaper supermarket.

9 a Give an example of a multiple chain store.

b Why is it often difficult for a small manufacturer to get its goods sold in a large multiple?

c What advantages are there for a firm selling its goods through a multiple?

Extension questions

1 D H Philips is a large department store in the centre of a major town. MID is a cash-and-carry discount warehouse on the outskirts of the same town. Both retail outlets sell furniture but MID is considerably cheaper.
   a What is a department store?
   b What is a cash-and-carry discount warehouse?
   c Why is MID cheaper for furniture?
   d Why will people still buy at D H Philips?

2 Recently a company has applied for planning permission to build a new hypermarket on the outskirts of a market town.
   a What is a hypermarket?
   b Why are hypermarkets normally located on the outskirts of towns?
   c What arguments are there for and against the building of the hypermarket?

3 Describe how the marketing mix of a new board game might be different from that of an industrial carpet-cleaning service.

Suggestions for coursework

1 Show how you would go about marketing a product of your choice including the product design, the advertising, packaging, channels of distribution and any other relevant aspects of marketing.

2 Carry out a survey of advertising to show,
   a the range of advertising,
   b how different types of firms use different forms of advertising,
   c the methods employed by advertisers,
   d how television advertising varies with the time of day and the likely audience.

3 Conduct a survey to test reactions to advertising:
   a List five catch phrases or names of well-known personalities from advertisements and find out how many people connect them with the right product.
   b Find out which brands of various common household products people use and why they use them in order to check the influence of advertising.
   c Find out how people regard advertising. Does advertising entertain, spoil good programmes, put up prices, inform, persuade you to buy things you do not require, mislead, etc?

4 Make a comparison of shops in a town centre with those in a village or suburb of a town. Compare types of shops and what they sell.
   Carry out a survey to see,
   a how frequently people shop,
   b where they shop for particular goods,
   c why they use particular shops.

Section

3 The large firm

unit 9

Expanding the business

Aims

At the end of this unit you should understand:

- The importance of large firms in the UK economy.
- Why firms wish to expand.
- The advantages and disadvantages of firms becoming larger.
- How firms expand.
- How public limited companies are formed and operate.
- How large companies are financed.
- The purpose and function of the Stock Exchange.

The importance of the large firm

In Section II we have been looking at small firms employing less than 50 people. Small firms are very important in the UK economy, particularly for employment. 60% of people working in the private sector of the UK economy work for firms employing less than 50 people. At the same time, large firms produce 60% of the UK's manufacturing output. The importance of large companies is also growing. The top 100 companies in the UK produce 70% of total manufacturing output compared to 60% 10 years ago. In some industries, a very small number of firms produce most of the output.

The case of the UK washing powder industry

All of these examples of washing powders are produced by just two companies: Proctor and Gamble and Unilever, who together make over 90% of all washing powders, as well as many other soap products.

Exercise

1 What disadvantages could there be for the consumer of only having two major producers of washing powders?

2 What advantages are there for Proctor and Gamble and Unilever of being the only two major producers of washing powders?

Extension exercise

1 How do the two washing powder firms compete with each other when they advertise? Do they compete on price or mainly in other ways?

2 Why do you think competition takes this form?

Why do firms wish to expand?

Richard Branson

Many firms are content to remain as small businesses, while for others expansion seems to be the main aim of the firm. There are many good examples today of large firms which started in a very small way in the past.

Richard Branson, multi-million pound founder of Virgin Records and Virgin Atlantic Airways, started by trading second-hand records and producing a school newspaper.

Alan Sugar, multi-million pound founder of Amstrad, started by selling aerials from the boot of his car.

Marks and Spencer started life as a market stall, and Boots the Chemist developed from one shop in Nottingham.

What motivated the owners of these businesses to grow larger?

- **Greater profits** Normally, as a firm grows larger, it increases its turnover and adds to its profits. Most large companies are owned by shareholders and they benefit from the company making increased profits. Increased profits often encourage more people to buy shares in the company and this gives the firm more money for expansion.
- **The desire to dominate the market** The larger the share of total output a firm has of a particular product, the more it can control prices. When there is only one major producer of a particular product, the firm is called a monopoly. (We will see in Unit 17 that the Government attempts to control monopolies because they are obviously in a very powerful position and could exploit the consumer).
- **The personal satisfaction gained** Apart from increasing their profits, owners may gain satisfaction from seeing their company grow larger.
- **Diversification** When some firms expand they diversify. This means that they start producing a range of products or services different from the one they started with. This spreads the risk involved in concentrating on one product which might suffer from declining sales.

Exercise

Why have the Imperial Group and United Biscuits diversified into a wider range of products?

- **The economies of large-scale production** Some firms expand in order to gain what are known as the economies of scale. These are the advantages to the firm of increasing its size. A firm gaining economies of scale will see its average costs fall as it increases production. For example, 100 units may cost £400 (average cost = £4) while 1000 units may cost £3000 (average cost = £3).

What are the economies of scale?

Case study

The example of Taylor's fuel service

Ten years ago, Taylor's was a small firm delivering fuel oil to homes in its local area. Taylor's is now a company with a nationwide network of fuel delivery services which include coal and butane gas in addition to fuel oil. The expansion of Taylor's illustrates many of the economies of scale. They now buy their fuels in larger amounts from the suppliers. Buying in bulk normally means lower prices. In addition to this, Taylor's now have greater bargaining power when dealing with their suppliers.

Taylor's now use much larger oil tankers for delivery. An oil tanker which is capable of carrying 20,000 gallons does not cost twice as much as one which will only carry 10,000 gallons. An oil tanker of 20,000 gallons will cost more per mile to run than one of 10,000 gallons, but will not cost twice as much.

Taylor's now advertise in the national press and on television. This is much more expensive than when they only advertised locally, but they now reach a much wider audience. Taylor's can now afford to employ specialists to help run the business more efficiently. They now have their own experts in purchasing, marketing and finance.

1. List all the benefits Taylor's have gained as a result of expanding.
2. What do you think is meant by 'greater bargaining power'?
3. Why will an oil tanker of 20,000 gallons not cost twice as much to purchase or to run as one of 10,000 gallons?
4. How has Taylor's diversified its service? What benefits might this bring to Taylor's?

Other examples of economies of scale

- Large firms find it easier to raise finance.
- Large firms can afford to employ scientists and researchers to develop new and better products.
- Large firms can employ expensive equipment because the size of their output means that they can use it to its maximum capacity.
- Large firms can divide work up more easily into specialist departments.

Diseconomies of scale: the disadvantages of size

Although there are many advantages of large-scale production, there may also be some disadvantages caused by a firm expanding.

- Firms may become very complicated in their organisation and find it difficult to make decisions quickly.
- The management may lose contact with workers in the factory and this may lead to poor working relationships, which may in turn lead to less efficient work.
- Large firms are often less flexible than small firms. Small firms may find it easier to switch production to meet a new fashion than large firms.
- Communications between people in large firms often become more difficult and involve more paperwork and meetings. All this requires more in the way of administrators and secretarial staff.

How do firms expand?

There are basically two ways in which a firm can grow larger:

a By expanding on its own, taking an increasing share of a market, or entering new ones, by diversification of products or services. Firms do this by being more competitive than their rivals or by offering a better product or service. This has been true of firms such as Sainsbury's – which now accounts for 17.1% of all grocery trade in the UK.

b By buying up other companies through take-overs and mergers. A take-over is when one company buys enough shares in another firm to gain control of it. A merger is when companies agree to join together under one board of management. Where a firm has acquired a number of other companies which retain their original names, it is known as a holding company. Imperial Group are an example of a holding company.

Extension section

Types of integration (joining together of firms)

There are two types of integration

- **Horizontal** Firms at the same stage of production join together, e.g. two manufacturing firms join together or two service industries amalgamate.
- **Vertical** Firms at different stages of production join together, e.g. a manufacturer buys up a supplier of raw materials, or a manufacturer buys up a chain of shops. Vertical integration can be further divided into

forwards vertical (where a firm joins together with one in a later stage of production) and *backwards vertical* (where a firm joins together with one in a previous stage of production).

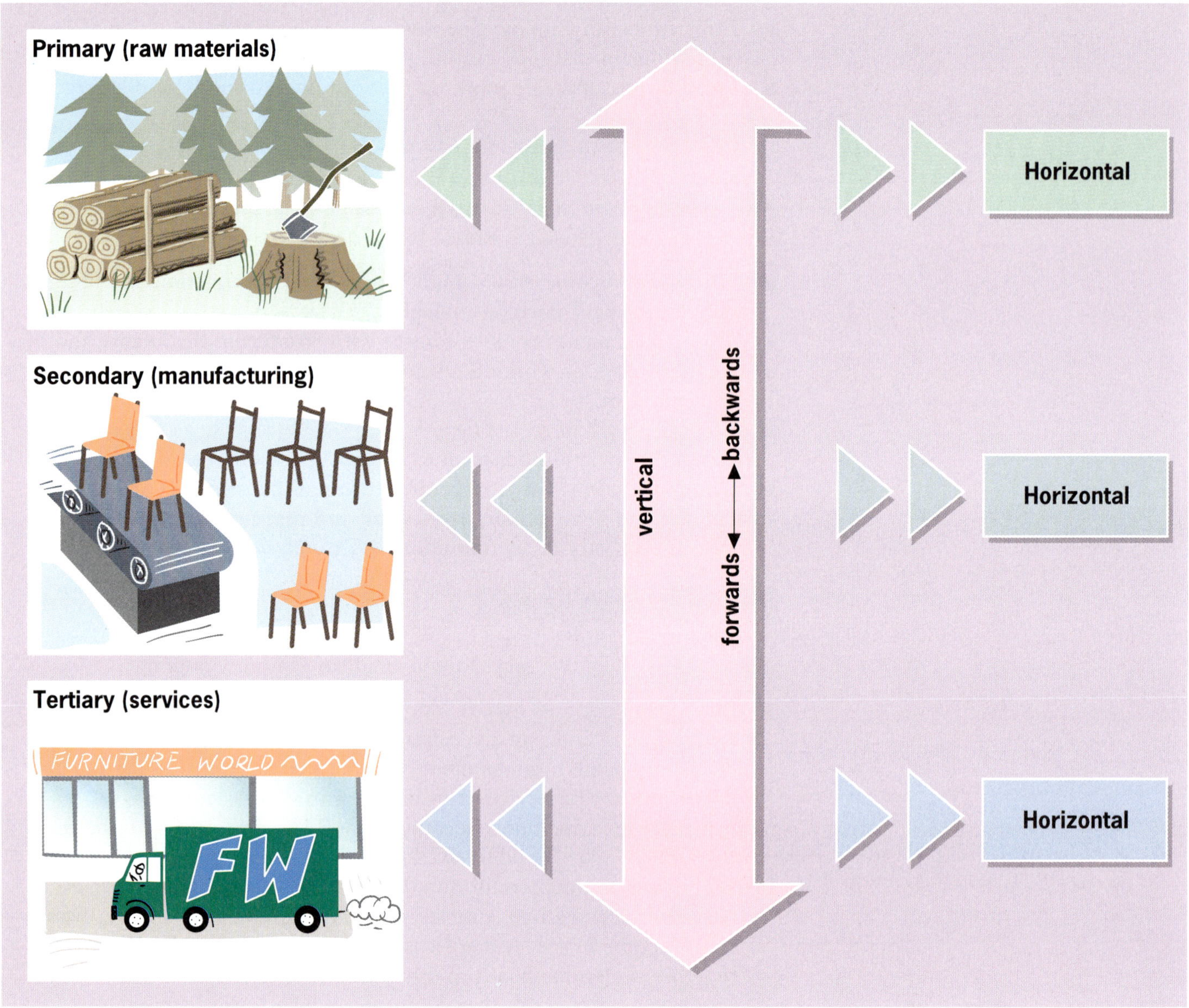

Exercise

Which type of integration?

Say whether each of the following mergers/take-overs is an example of horizontal or vertical integration. If you decide it is vertical, say whether it is backwards or forwards.

1 The merger of National Provincial Bank and Westminster Bank to form Nat West Bank.
2 Brook Bond Tea buying up tea plantations in Sri Lanka.
3 Scottish and Newcastle Brewery buying up public houses.
4 MFI, cash-and-carry discount furniture retailers, buying up Hygena, manufacturers of kitchen units.
5 British Airways' take-over of British Caledonian Airways.

Unilever

Cadbury Schweppes

THE BOOTS COMPANY

Legal & General

The Rank Organisation

ICI

The public limited company

The companies above are examples of public limited companies. Public limited companies have the letters PLC after their names. Any member of the public is entitled to buy shares in a public limited company. The shares of UK public limited companies are bought and sold on the Stock Exchange and their prices are published in most national newspapers. (Some newspapers just show the main shares.)
(See Stock Exchange, page 107.)

Exercise

1 List the above companies and try to name at least one product or service produced by each.

2 Find the share prices in a newspaper and name two public limited companies in each of the primary, secondary and tertiary sectors of the economy.

Why form a public limited company?

Shares in private limited companies cannot be sold publicly. This limits the number of shares which can be easily sold and restricts the amount of finance available to the company. Public limited companies can advertise their shares and sell to the public and financial institutions (such as insurance companies) both in the UK and abroad. Public limited companies may have several million shares owned by a large number of different shareholders, ranging from individuals, with as few as 50 shares, to large financial institutions, which may own 100,000 shares or more.

Ownership of a public company

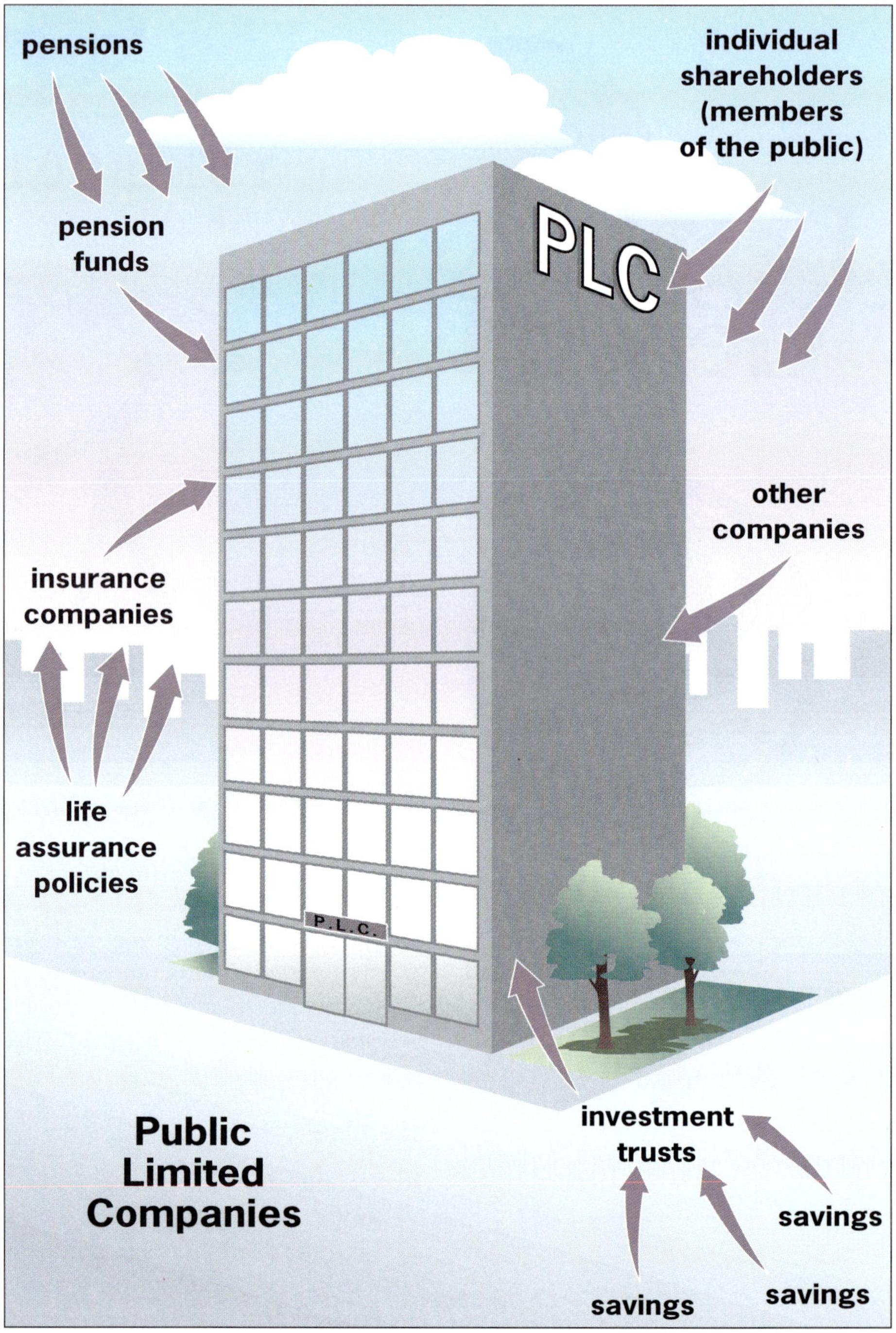

Share-holding percentages

Over the years, the proportion of shares owned by the private individual has fallen while that owned by pension funds and insurance companies has grown.

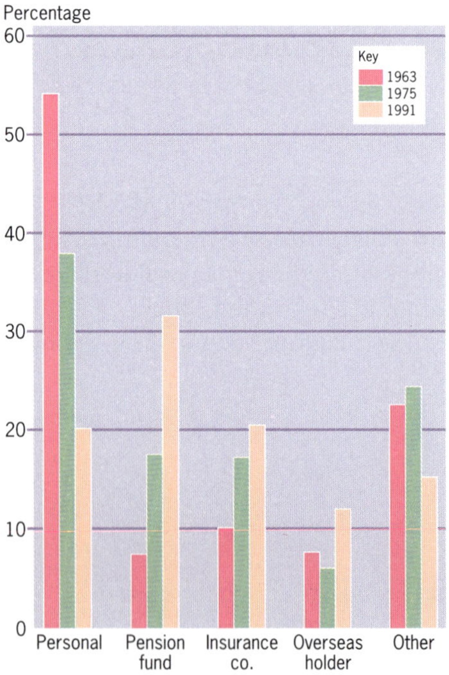

How are public limited companies formed?

Most public limited companies start as private limited companies. Because the shares in public limited companies are sold to the public, there are many more rules and regulations governing their formation and the way in which they operate. It is very expensive to form a public limited company and this type of business organisation is only open to private limited companies with a considerable amount of capital. Public limited companies need a minimum of £50,000 capital and often need to spend at least £250,000 on advertising, legal fees and commission.

Like private limited companies, the PLC must send its Articles and Memorandum of Association to the Registrar of Companies and apply for a trading certificate. It cannot start trading, however, until it has satisfied the Registrar that it has raised sufficient capital and has been approved by the Stock Exchange Council.

How are shares sold in a PLC?

The change from being a private limited company to a PLC is known as a 'Stock Exchange Flotation'.

Virgin Group plc

(Registered in England No. 1568894)

Offer of Ordinary Shares by Tender

by

Morgan Grenfell & Co. Limited

as agent for the Company and the vendors whose names are set out herein

of up to 50,000,000 Ordinary Shares of 10p each to raise £60,000,000

with a minimum tender price of 120p per share

the amount being tendered being payable in full on application

A step-by-step guide to a stock-market flotation

1 A privately-owned company decides that it wants to raise money for expansion of its business, say to build a new factory or start a new brand. It has two main options: either it borrows from the bank or issues shares.

2 If it takes the second route, the company will seek a listing on the London Stock Exchange. It takes advice from a merchant bank in the City of London, which specialises in bringing firms to the stock market.

3 A prospectus listing the details of what the company does, its prospects and the number of shares to be offered will be published.

4 The shares will be offered at a certain price, and buyers invited to apply by a certain date. The three main holders of shares are the public, pension funds and insurance companies.

5 If there are more applications for shares than there are shares available, the issue is said to be over-subscribed and applicants may get fewer shares than they applied for.

6 On the allotted day any shares bought in the offer can be traded. If the issue was over-subscribed, the price is likely to go up.

7 Shares are bought and sold. O this was done on the floor Stock Exchange in Lor but since 1986 bu has been conc on the telepl with stock- using cor termina

Running a public limited company

By law a public limited company must:

- Have a minimum of two shareholders.
- Appoint a Board of Directors to manage the company.
- Hold an annual general meeting of shareholders.
- Give limited liability to its shareholders.
- Publish accounts each year in at least two national newspapers and send very detailed accounts of its affairs to the Registrar of Companies.
- Reveal what any subsidiary companies it owns are doing.
- State any donations to political parties and charities.
- Give details of changes in fixed assets (land and property bought and sold).

Management of the public limited company

The shareholders appoint a Board of Directors to manage the running of the company. The Board of Directors in turn appoint managers to carry out the day-to-day running of the company. The shareholders have the power to sack directors and must be consulted on major decisions, such as merging with other companies. In reality, in many cases, few shareholders bother to attend the annual general meeting. Often the shares are distributed between so many different people that control lies with one or two major institutions who own perhaps as little as 10% of the shares.

Financing large companies

Finance for large companies can either be internal (from within the company) or external (from outside the company).

Internal finance

- **Profits** Shareholders expect to receive a share in the profits of a company, but the company may retain some of its profits to reinvest in the company or use to purchase other firms. A sensible use of profits in this way may result in even greater dividends for shareholders in the future. Over half of all company finance comes from retained profits.
- **Sale of Assets** Companies may raise finance by selling off some of their assets. They may choose to sell whole firms which they have previously purchased or just parts (or 'divisions') of firms. Apart from raising finance, selling off unprofitable parts of a firm may increase the efficiency and profits of the firm. This is called rationalisation.

> is predicted at the end of the financial year.
>
> **£52m for Unipart**
>
> Rover, the vehicle group, yesterday announced the £52 million sale of its Unipart spare parts business to a consortium of City institutions and employees.
>
> It is thought that this is part of a rationalisation exercise by Rover to improve the firm's profitability as well as increase its capital position.
>
> **Share prices rise for**

- **Sale of shares** A company going public will need to sell shares. An existing public limited company may sell more shares to existing shareholders through a rights issue.

Why buy shares?

- To receive a share of the profits. This is paid in the form of a dividend on each share owned.
- Shareholders hope that the price of their shares on the Stock Exchange will rise and that they will be able to sell them at a profit. This is known as making a capital gain. For example, it was possible to purchase shares in Amstrad for as little as 14p in 1984. The same shares in December 1994 were worth £1.34.
- To gain certain 'perks'. Some companies give shareholders benefits in order to encourage people to purchase shares and remain with the company. Examples include European Car Ferries, which give shareholders discounts on ferry crossings to Europe, and British Telecom and British Gas giving vouchers to help pay for telephone and gas bills.
- To have a say in running the company. Each shareholder has one vote for each share owned. Large shareholders can influence company policy.

External finance

Like small firms, large companies can obtain finance from outside of the firm in the form of loans and grants.

Debentures

These are loans to the company by members of the public and financial institutions. They carry a fixed rate of interest. Some carry certain perks, e.g. debenture holders of the All England Club get priority for seats on the centre court at Wimbledon. Debenture holders are not owners of the company and do not have any voting rights or say in the management of the company. They must be paid interest before any shareholders because they are creditors of the company. The company may be declared bankrupt if the debenture holders cannot be paid. If the company is declared bankrupt, the debenture holders are compensated from the sale of assets before any shareholders.

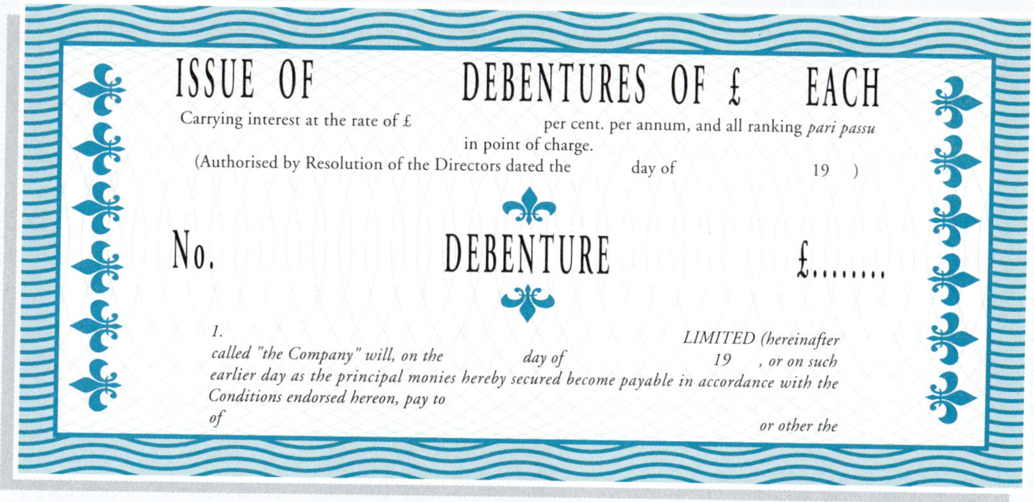
ISSUE OF DEBENTURES OF £ EACH

Carrying interest at the rate of £ per cent. per annum, and all ranking *pari passu* in point of charge.

(Authorised by Resolution of the Directors dated the day of 19)

No. DEBENTURE £........

1. LIMITED (hereinafter called "the Company" will, on the day of 19 , or on such earlier day as the principal monies hereby secured become payable in accordance with the Conditions endorsed hereon, pay to of or other the

Other sources of finance

- **Commercial banks**, such as Barclays, Lloyds, Nat West, etc., give overdrafts and loans (see Unit 5).
- **Merchant banks** These are banks specialising in finance and do not deal with the ordinary public.
- **Insurance companies** Insurance companies currently hold £6 billion worth of funds invested in life assurance policies. Insurance companies buy shares but also loan direct to industry.
- **Pension funds** Huge amounts of money are held in pension funds, some of which is loaned to public limited companies.
- **The Government** We have seen in Unit 5 how the Government makes loans to firms to encourage them to settle and expand in areas of high unemployment. The Government sometimes also makes loans to firms in financial difficulties in order to prevent them from going out of business and increasing unemployment. (This was the case with Rolls Royce and British Leyland.)
- **The European Union (EU)** may give loans to firms, particularly in areas of high unemployment. Large grants have also been given for the improvement of firms, both large and small.

Factoring

Factoring is an increasingly popular alternative to overdrafts for medium and large businesses. The factor (often a bank) agrees to collect debts owed to a firm in return for a fee. For example, TIX Engineering has supplied Bright Bros. with £10,000 worth of components on 30 days credit. TIX Engineering send a copy of the invoice for £10,000 to Lombard Nat West (the factor) and they immediately pay TIX Engineering 80% of the debt (£8,000). After 30 days Lombard Nat West collects the debt of £10,000 from Bright Bros. and pays the remaining 20% (£2,000) to TIX Engineering less the commission charged. Factoring can be expensive but the business receives 80% of the debt immediately. The factor still pays 80% if the customer fails to pay the bill. Factoring also saves the business wasting time in debt collecting.

Exercise

a What advantages are there to a business in using a factoring organisation?

b How might factoring help a business overcome cash flow problems?

c Why is factoring particularly useful to businesses involved in exporting?

Which type of finance?

Large companies generally use a range of different types of finance to suit different purposes. They will need short-term finance, such as overdrafts and trade credit, to meet their immediate needs and long-term finance, such as debentures and bank loans, in order to fund major projects. Like the small firm (see page 51), the large firm will have to consider carefully what types of finance it requires and for what purposes together with its cost.

Extension section

The Stock Exchange

The Stock Exchange is a market place where second-hand shares are bought and sold. The Stock Exchange is located in the City of London but it is linked by computer to other exchanges throughout the UK and abroad. Dealing and information on stocks and shares takes place through the Stock Exchange Automated Quotations System (SEAQ). Some six billion deals take place each year to the value of £350 billion on the Stock Exchange. Shares can only be bought and sold by members of the Stock Exchange.

Stockbrokers can be contacted through banks or by obtaining a list of stockbroking firms from the Stock Exchange. Stockbrokers charge commission for either buying or selling shares. The amount charged can vary between brokers and differs according to the type and number of shares being bought and sold.

Stockbrokers must try to obtain the best possible deal for their clients. When they deal with other brokers they do not reveal whether they are buying or selling shares and will contact a number of broking firms in order to obtain the best price on the shares.

Stockbrokers also offer financial advice to clients, and help to manage various investment trusts and pension funds.

The *Stock Exchange Council* attempts to make sure that any company listed on the Stock Exchange comes up to certain standards and that dealings in shares are carried out correctly.

What makes share prices rise or fall?

BAR WARS!

Now Rowntree shares soar by £50m

Rowntree shares soared by £50m on the stock market yesterday at the prospect of a three-way take-over battle for the company by Swiss confectionery giants Nestlé and Suchard. Nestlé are thought to be preparing to make an offer in the region of £2.1 billion for Rowntree. Suchard, which currently holds 29.9 per cent of Rowntree shares, is also thought to be making a rival bid. Rowntree shares rose by 25p in trading yesterday. The Rowntree Board are strongly opposed to the take-over claiming that it will put jobs at risk and that it will not be in the public interest. They want the bid referred to the Monopolies Commission for consideration…

Guinness shares plummet

Amstrad shares rocket

T.S.B. oversubscribed six times

Shares are like any other product in a free market. If they are in short supply (like fresh strawberries in the winter), their price will rise. This happened when shares in the Trustees Savings Bank were over-subscribed by six times when it went public.

There are various reasons why people start buying up a particular share:

- They expect the company to make large profits.
- The price of the share is low at the current time and it is expected to increase in the future.
- A company is expected to be taken over by another firm. (The firm carrying out the take-over will buy up the shares in the firm being taken over and this will push up the price of this firm's shares.)

Exercise

How good an investor are you? Play the Stock Exchange Game.

You have inherited £1000 from a rich uncle who made a fortune on the Stock Exchange. He was keen that you should try your hand at gambling on shares and a condition of the will is that you invest the money in four companies listed on the Stock Exchange. Pick your four 'winners' from the shares listed in national newspapers. Check their progress over a period of one month. At the end of the month sell your shares and see if you have gained or lost. If you have gained, work the gain out as a percentage of your investment to see how this would have compared to investing £1000 in a bank or building society. (Remember to divide the bank or building society rate by 12 to obtain the rate for one month. You should also deduct 10% commission for buying and selling your shares.)

The game is most fun if it is played by several students either in teams or acting as individuals.

How to read SHARE PRICES

The first two figures denote the highest and lowest the share price has reached in the year.

The two numbers after the name of the company are the price at which they closed in the City the previous evening and their movement on the day.

The last but one figure is the yield and shows that £100 invested in Capital Radio at 224 pence a share would have brought in £3.0 in dividends.

The final column is the price/earnings ratio, comparing the current share price with the amount of money the company is earning in profits. Say a company's profits amounted to £1 a share and its share price was £10, the price earnings ratio would be 10. Generally, the higher the p/e ratio the greater the confidence in the company.

230	171	Capital Radio	224+1	3.0	25.9
818	718	Carlton Com	766–10	2.8	22.6
2080	1615	Central ITV	2003	2.4	21.8

Public limited company accounts and annual report

x

Public limited companies (PLCs) are required to publish annual reports and accounts. We looked at the accounts of a small business in Unit 6. The accounts of PLCs contain similar information to those of small businesses but deal with much larger sums of money and include reference to the capital raised from shareholders and the dividends they receive from the profits. PLCs present their accounts in different ways but they must include certain basic information. Below is a simplified Balance Sheet for Pickwick plc:

Balance sheet as at 31 March 1995	£m	
Fixed assets		
Tangible assets	499	
Investments	2	
	501	
Current assets		
Stocks	2	
Debtors	33	
Investments	46	
Cash and deposits	50	
	131	
Creditors due within one year		
Short term borrowings	(5)	
Other creditors	(70)	
	(75)	
Net current assets	56	
Total assets less current liabilities	557	
Creditors due after more than one year		
Long term borrowings	(70)	
Grants and contributions	(10)	
	(80)	
Provisions for liabilities and charges	(3)	
	474	
Capital and reserves		
Called up share capital	85	
Share premium account	2	
Profit and loss account	387	
	474	

Annual Report

The annual reports of PLCs contain information about the main developments during the past year and comment on the financial position of the company. Below are some of the financial highlights from J Sainsbury plc's report for 1995.

J Sainsbury plc

1995 52 weeks to 11th March £ million

GROUP SALES (including taxes) 12,065.4

GROUP PROFIT BEFORE TAX 809.2
Tax (269.9)

GROUP PROFIT AFTER TAX 539.3

EARNINGS PER SHARE 29.8p

DIVIDEND PER SHARE 11.7p

GROUP SALES

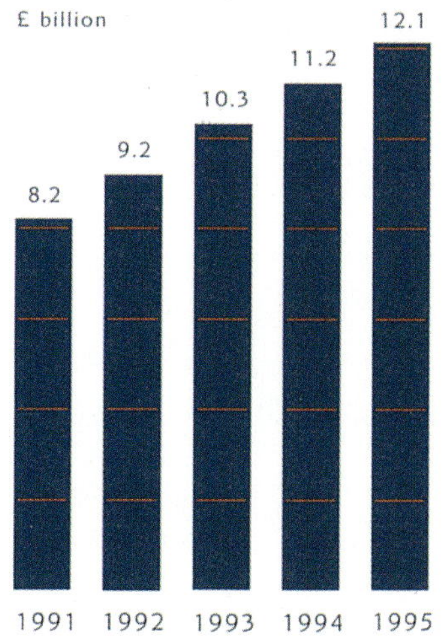

Group sales increased by 7.5% to £12.1 billion.

GROUP PROFIT

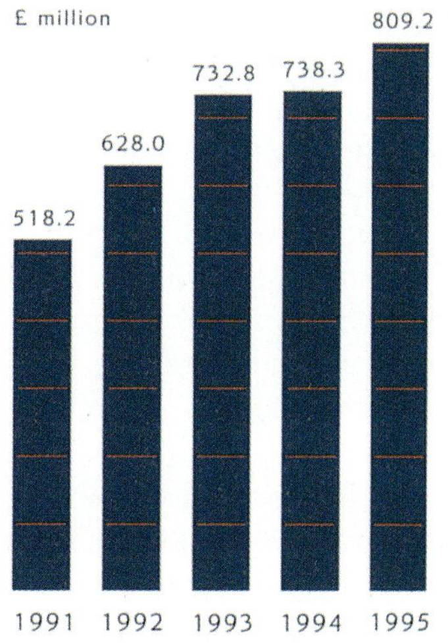

Group profit before exceptional costs and tax increased by 9.6% to £809.2 million.

DIVIDEND PER SHARE

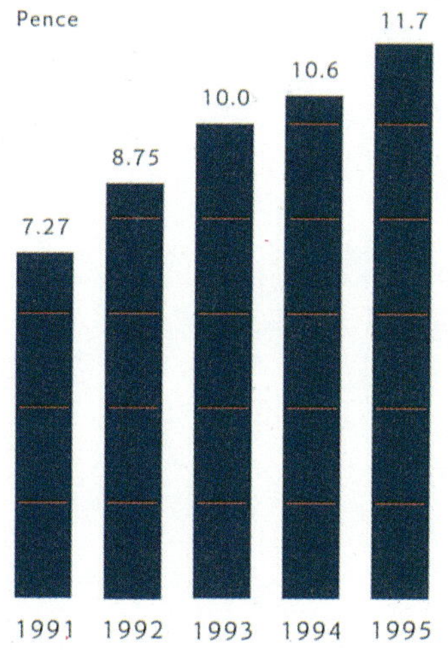

Dividend per share increased by 10.4% to 11.7 pence.

Exercise

1. Between 1994 and 1995 Sainsbury's sales increased by 7.5% but profits before tax and exceptional costs increased by 9.6%. What reasons could there be for profits increasing faster than sales?
2. How have dividends on shares changed since 1991? Why do you think the dividend has changed?
3. Calculate profit as a % of sales for each year between 1991 and 1995. What conclusions do you reach from these calculations?

Summary of key words and ideas

- Large firms are responsible for an increasing share of total output in the UK. This benefits the firms but may result in certain disadvantages for the consumer.
- Firms are keen to expand because it usually brings greater profits.
- **Diversification** is when firms expand into producing a new range of products or services.
- **The economies of scale** are the benefits gained from producing on a large scale. **The diseconomies of scale** are the disadvantages of growing larger.
- Firms can expand either by growing themselves or by taking over, or merging with, other companies.
- **Horizontal integration** is when firms at the same stage of production join together. **Vertical integration** is when firms at different stages of production join together – it can be either **forwards** (a firm buys another at a later stage of production) or **backwards** (a firm buys another at an earlier stage of production).
- A **holding company** is one which buys up other companies but keeps the original names of the companies.
- A **public limited company** is a firm which is allowed to sell its shares to the public and is quoted on the Stock Exchange.
- Large firms can raise finance either internally, through the sale of shares, by using profits, and by selling assets; or externally through various loans.
- **Debentures** are fixed-interest loans which do not carry voting rights but usually have a prior claim on the assets of the company.
- **Dividend** A dividend is the interest paid on a share. In the case of an ordinary share, it will vary according to how much profit the company makes.
- People buy shares,
  - **a** to obtain dividends,
  - **b** to make a capital gain if the price of the share rises,
  - **c** for the 'perks' which some companies give when shares are purchased,
  - **d** to influence company policy.
- Companies will use different methods of finance depending upon their requirements.
- The **Stock Exchange** is a market where second-hand shares are bought and sold.

Test questions

1 Atlantic plc is a holding company with a large number of subsidiaries. It has been particularly successful in the last financial year and has just declared a record dividend on its shares. It is now considering a major expansion of the company which will involve it in several take-over bids. Atlantic hopes that its increasing diversification will result in even higher profits in the future.

a What do the letters PLC stand for?
b How is Atlantic different from a private limited company?

c What are subsidiary companies?
d What is a dividend on a share?
e Give two reasons for being a shareholder in Atlantic.
f What are take-over bids?
g Why do you think Atlantic wishes to expand?
h What is meant by 'increasing diversification'?
i Why might increasing diversification result in higher profits for Atlantic?
j Suggest four different ways in which Atlantic might finance its expansion. (Include at least one internal and one external method of finance.)

2 'Businesses make use of a range of short-term and long-term finance'. Give two examples of short-term and two examples of long-term finance and explain what each type might be used for.
3 'The Stock Exchange is a market for second-hand shares'.
a Explain what this statement means.
b What other functions does the Stock Exchange have?

Extension questions

RP Knight, a manufacturer of potato crisps, has recently won a contract to supply a major supermarket chain. This has resulted in a doubling of output. The firm has found that their average costs of production have fallen by 2p a packet as a result of the increase in output.

1 Explain how the above illustrates the economies of scale.
2 Give two reasons why doubling output may result in lower average costs.
3 What other benefits might increasing output bring to the firm?

Suggestions for coursework

1 A comparison of four public limited companies. Write to the head offices of public limited companies and ask for copies of company prospectuses, annual reports to shareholders and any other information they may have available. Compare the companies in terms of,
a what they produce,
b their assets,
c profits and share dividends,
d how they raise their finance – number of shareholders, debenture holders, etc.,
e how they have performed in the last year.

2 Trace the shares of any five public limited companies over a period of time. Choose shares in very different types of companies to give a good contrast in performances. Draw graphs to represent the price changes. Compare the graphs of your companies with changes in the Financial Times Index (this is an indication of average share price movements). Which share showed the largest percentage change? (Price change ÷ buying price x 100.) Can you offer any explanations as to why the shares have changed over the period you have studied them?
3 Collect newspaper articles on mergers and take-overs. Write a case study of a merger or take-over explaining how it happens, why it happens and the effects on share prices. Discuss who you feel benefits and who loses from the merger or take–over.

unit 10

Organising the business

Aims

At the end of this unit you should understand:

- The need for organisation in firms.
- The organisational structure of a large firm.
- The function of different departments in a large firm.
- The difference between line and staff.
- The idea of a chain of command and a span of control.
- The advantages and disadvantages of centralised and decentralised systems of organisation.

Why do businesses need organisation?

Case study

Business Report – Hot Dough Bakeries – a rising business

Jean Thomas started Hot Dough Bakeries 10 years ago when she set up her first bakery in a London suburb.

Since then the business has mushroomed and she is now the owner of a chain of 20 shops throughout London.

Jean recalls how 10 years ago she and just one assistant ran that first bakery. This meant ordering supplies, carrying out the actual bread making and baking as well as doing all the paperwork involved in running a small business. Jean's job is very different now. She is no longer seen brushing the flour off her apron or serving customers. She is fully occupied now with the management of her 20 shops. She spends her time in discussions with her bank manager and accountant, appointing managers and developing her business further.

Jean has delegated much of her day-to-day responsibilities to her bakery managers and has also appointed a group of specialists to assist her in the running and expansion of the business. She now employs a Buying Manager to deal with supplies, a Finance Manager to assist with the money side of the business and a Marketing and a Sales Manager to take on responsibility for selling the bakery products.

1 How has Jean's job changed as her business has expanded?
2 Why has Jean needed to change the organisation of her business?
3 Explain what is meant by 'Jean has delegated much of her day-to-day responsibilities'.
4 What other specialist managers might Jean consider employing in the future if the business continues to expand?

How are large businesses organised?

Different businesses have different types of organisational structure which vary according to their size, what they do and what the management feels is most appropriate to that particular business. A large manufacturing firm may well have a very different structure from that of a chain of supermarkets.

Talbot Textiles: an example of an organisational structure for a large manufacturing company.

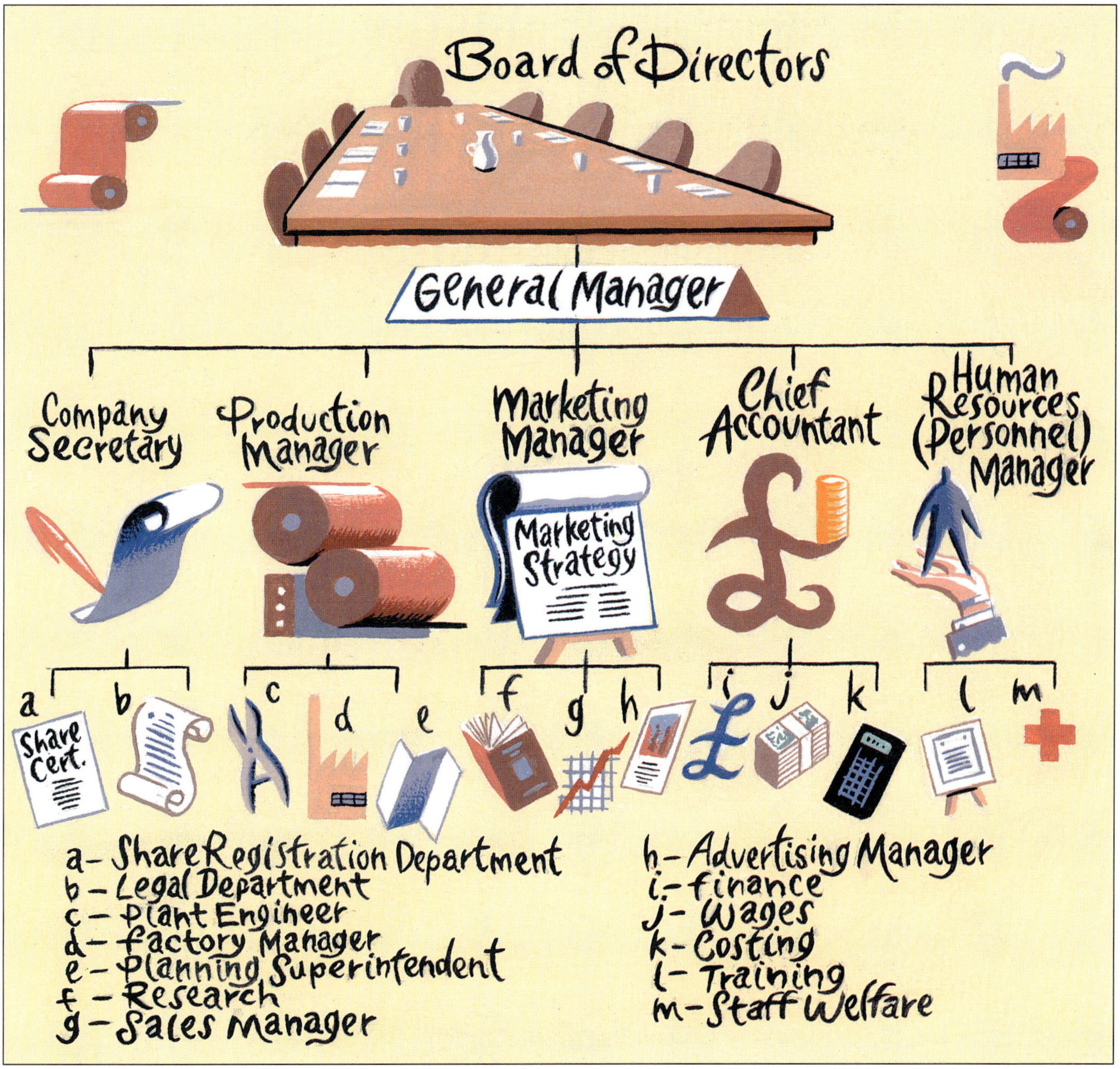

Exercise

1 Draw an organisation chart for the example of Hot Dough Bakeries on page 114.

2 Draw an organisation chart for your school.

The chain of command

The chain of command is the way in which orders and instructions are passed down through the organisation from the General Manager to the workers on the shop floor. The order will pass through a number of levels (or stages) – rather like the rungs of a ladder.

The General Manager of Talbot Textiles decides to stop all overtime work in the weaving shop from next month.

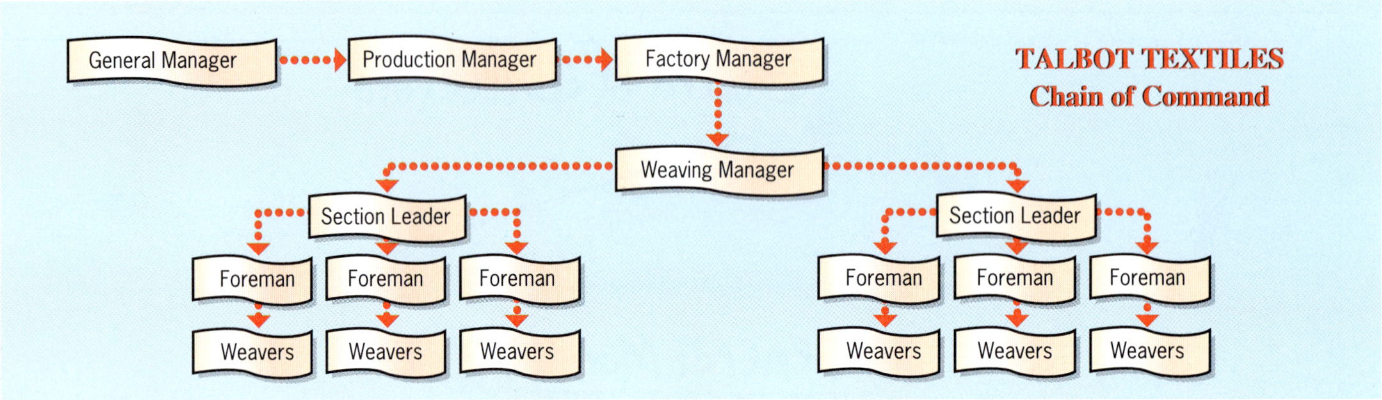

Exercise

List the people involved in the chain of command in the above decision.

The span of control

The span of control (or the span of responsibility) is the number of people or departments which report to a particular manager. In the case of the Marketing Manager at Talbot Textiles, the span of control is 3.

Exercise

1 Draw the chain of command at Talbot Textiles for a decision made by the General Manager to reduce the advertising budget.

2 Draw the chain of command in your school for a decision made by the headteacher to reduce the lunch break by 10 minutes in order to end school earlier.

3 What is the span of control of the Chief Accountant at Talbot Textiles?

4 What is the span of control of the Head of Science at your school?

Extension questions

1 What problems might arise if the chain of command is very long?

2 It is often said that the span of control of any one manager should not exceed six people. What problems might arise if the span of control were to become greater than six people?

Senior personnel at Talbot Textiles

MacDonald J

Profile
John MacDonald
Position:
General Manager

I was appointed to the position of Managing Director by the Board of Talbot Textiles. I have overall responsibility for the running of the company and report to the Directors. I must make sure that the firm conforms to the various rules regarding companies laid down by the Government.

I attend the meetings of the Board of Directors where major decisions are made on company policy. I am responsible for the overall management of Talbot Textiles and it is my job to organise the other managers. I advise the Board on general strategy and make recommendations about the future direction of the firm.

Partridge L

Profile
Lynne Partridge
Position:
Company Secretary

After leaving Exeter University with a degree in law, I spent 10 years working in the legal departments of large firms. I joined Talbot Textiles 5 years ago as assistant company secretary and was promoted to my current position last year. I find my legal background very useful as I spend a great deal of my time dealing with such matters as the Company Acts, contracts, and patents. I have a small team of legal assistants, clerks and secretaries working for me and I report to the Board of Directors and the General Manager. I work closely with several other departments including accounts, finance, and marketing.

Rae K

Profile
Keith Rae
Position:
Chief Accountant

I joined the financial accounting division of a large engineering firm in Leeds after I qualified as a chartered accountant. I was eventually promoted to finance manager in the same firm. I joined Talbot's 10 years ago as assistant chief accountant and took over as chief accountant when my boss retired two years ago.

I am responsible for all finance and accounting which takes place in the firm. My division deals with everything from the accounts for office stationery through to negotiating a £500,000 bank loan. All expenditures and sums of money coming into the firm eventually have to be passed through our books. I need to make sure that any surplus cash we may have is invested wisely. At the same time, I must make sure that the company has sufficient ready cash to meet its current needs.

I report to the finance director and work closely with most other departments in the company. The division is divided into three departments; finance, wages and costing. There is a manager in charge of each of these departments which employ considerable numbers of accountants, clerks and secretaries.

Rees S

Profile
Sue Rees
Position:
Human Resources (Personnel) Manager

I have worked with Talbot's ever since leaving school with A levels. The company has always been keen on training and they gave me day release to do a degree in business and management studies at the local university. I later qualified as a member of the Institute of Personnel Managers.

My job is looking after all matters to do with staff. The human resources department is responsible for recruiting and selecting staff, training programmes, the health, safety and welfare of all workers, the keeping of employee records and negotiations with the trade unions. There are a considerable number of rules and regulations laid down by the Government concerning the employing of staff, their working conditions and their rights and responsibilities and it is my department's job to make sure they are carried out correctly within the factory.

A key aspect of my job is to do everything possible to improve working relationships and avoid the need for industrial action. With this in mind, I set up a Works Council where representatives from all parts of the firm regularly meet together to discuss problems.

I report to the Board of Directors and to the General Manager on staffing policy and my job inevitably involves a great deal of contact with all other departments within the firm.

Hall P

Profile
Peter Hall
Position:
Marketing Manager

I joined Talbot's five years ago after being marketing manager at a much smaller textile factory in Bradford. The success of Talbot's depends upon us being able to sell the finished products to the consumer. That is the work of the marketing department. If we fail, the whole firm fails - no matter how successful and efficient everyone else is.

As head of the marketing department, I am concerned with identifying customer requirements and supplying their needs. This involves market research to find out what our customers require, advising the research department on product design, advertising and sales promotion as well as ensuring a good distribution service.

We employ an agency to run our advertising campaign for us but it is my job to discuss with them the nature of the campaign and to select from several possible alternative approaches.

I report to the General Manager and have particularly close contact with the production and finance departments.

Street G

Profile
Gill Street:
Position:
Production Manager

After getting my degree in production engineering at Salford University, I worked in different size engineering firms to gain practical experience. I went back to university to study for a postgraduate qualification in management and landed this job after being assistant sales manager at a rival firm. Management has taken me away from actual engineering but my knowledge of what goes on helps me to understand the various problems people face on the production side.

The production division is the largest at Talbot's and three departmental managers report to me; the plant engineer, who is responsible for the ordering and maintaining of equipment, the factory manager, and the planning superintendent, who ensures we have adequate stocks of materials to meet production targets. The division is responsible for all aspects of textile production; spinning, weaving, dyeing, and printing. I report directly to the General Manager and have to liaise closely with the marketing, personnel, and finance departments.

Exercise

Who deals with this?

For each of the situations given,

a state which department at Talbot's you think would be mainly responsible for dealing with it,
b name any other departments you feel might be involved and explain how they would help.

1 The company has just won a major export order to supply a chain of retailers in Denmark. This will mean raising output by overtime working and increasing stocks of raw materials. The Danish importers will be paying one month after final delivery.
2 A rival textile firm has just launched a new line which has taken part of your market for duvet covers. The rival firm is using a new synthetic fibre which is proving to be very popular with customers.
3 Talbot's has decided to invest in a new computer-controlled weaving system. The machines for the new system are very expensive and have to be imported from Switzerland.
4 A fall in demand for a particular line has meant the possibility of some redundancies in the spinning shops. The union representing the workers in spinning is resisting any of their members being laid off.

Extension section

Different types of organisational structure

- **Line organisation** This is when there are direct lines of responsibility from senior management to the workers on the shop floor. This method of organisation used to be called 'military' because it is how orders are carried out in the army. Employees in a line organisation work solely in one department.
- **Functional organisation** This is where the firm is organised by function – by what people do. The chief accountant, for example, will deal with all departments. Employees who move between departments are called staff workers.
- **Line and staff organisations** In reality, most firms have a mixture of both line and staff workers.

Centralised and decentralised organisations

How centralised or decentralised an organisation is depends upon who makes the important decisions. In a very centralised organisation the important decisions are made by management at the centre of the organisation and then passed out as instructions to the various departments. Many major chain stores and supermarkets, such as Boots, Sainsbury's and Dixons are highly centralised. Company policy is decided at headquarters, finance is controlled centrally and goods are often bought centrally. Branch managers have relatively little discretion in the running of individual shops.

Centralised organisations

Advantages

- Tight control of decisions
- Decisions made by experts
- Achieve uniformity throughout the organisation
- Avoids repetition of functions – allows bulk buying

Disadvantages

- Lack of motivation for managers – major decisions taken away from them
- Central management may lack knowledge of local conditions
- Central management may lack contact with 'shop floor'
- May be slow to react to changes

Centralised organisations tend to be those where the firm is dealing with the same or very similar products or services throughout, such as chains of shops, banks and fast food restaurants, where the customer expects the same service or provision of goods throughout the UK.

Decentralised organisations

Decentralised organisations delegate many important decisions to managers of divisions and departments. In decentralised organisations managers are given a great deal of freedom to make the decisions they feel are best for their part of the organisation. The central management will only make the really major decisions but will otherwise allow the various divisions and departments to function independently. Examples of very decentralised organisations include Lonhro, Dunlop, and ICI.

Advantages

- Increases motivation of managers
- Encourages initiative and development of ideas for improving the business
- Department managers may have better understanding of what is required in their area
- Decisions may be made quicker because less consultation needed

Disadvantages

- Managers may lack sufficient expertise – wrong decisions may be made
- Local decisions may run counter to policy required by the company
- Firm may fail to benefit from the economies of scale, such as bulk buying

De-layering

During the 1990s the trend has been to reduce the number of tiers in the management structure. This process is known as de-layering. The diagram of the management structure of Talbot Textiles shown on p.115 is known as a hierarchy. It is in the form of a pyramid with the general manager at the top and the production workers at the base. De-layering would result in a flatter pyramid or hierarchy.

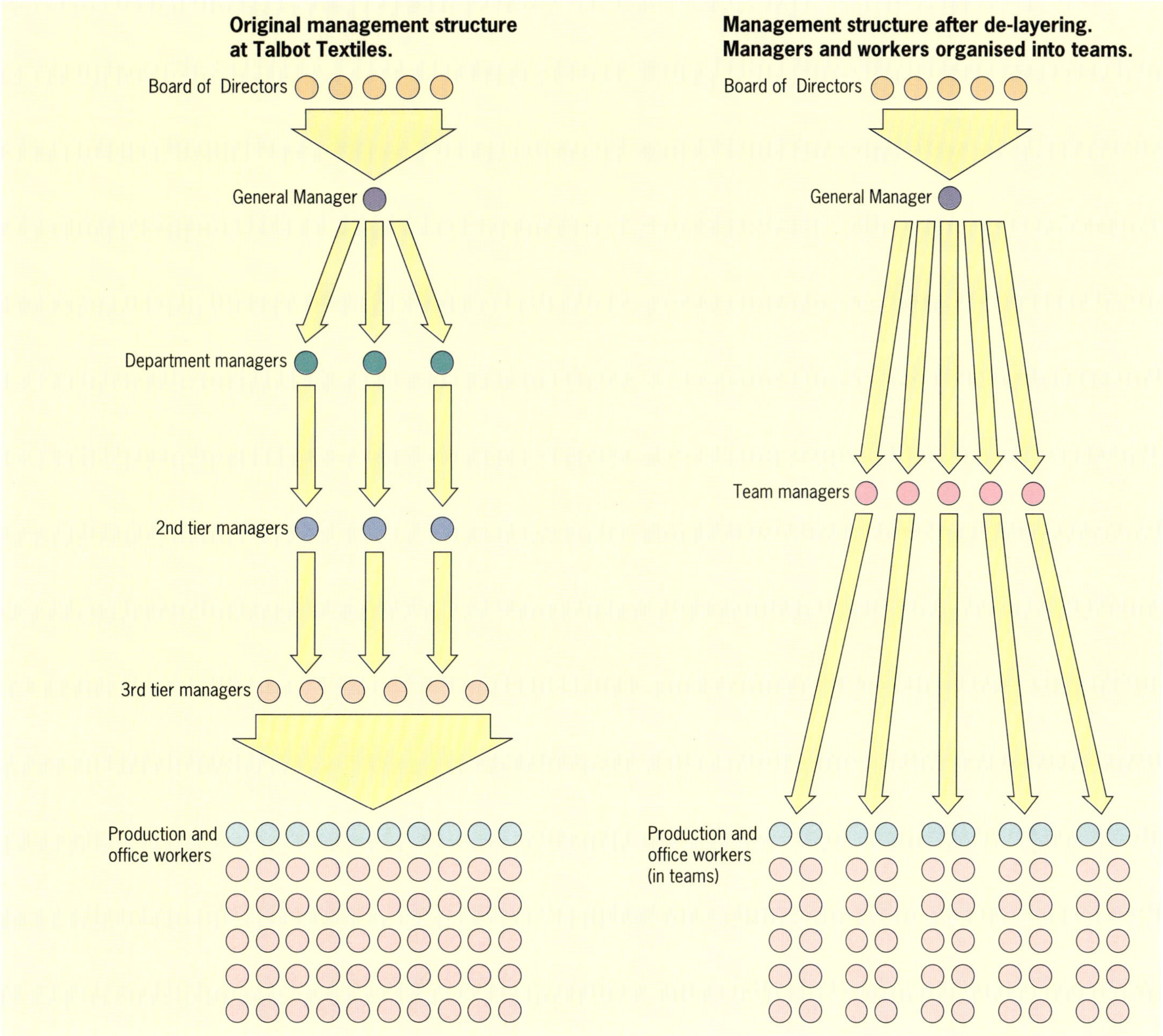

De-layering is closely linked to the idea of de-centralisation. It helps to make the organisation more flexible so that it can respond quickly to changes. The chain of command is reduced and decisions can be made more rapidly.

x (*Note* Unit 12 looks at how quality control operates in flat hierarchies. See Quality Circles, page 152.)

Summary of key words and ideas

- The need for a proper organisational structure increases as the business grows larger.
- **Delegate responsibility** To give authority to others to make decisions on matters previously dealt with by a more senior person in the organisation.
- As an organisation expands, the need for delegation of responsibilities and decision making increases.
- **The chain of command** The way in which decisions are passed down an organisation.
- **Span of control** The number of people or departments reporting to a manager.
- **Line organisation** Employees work in one department and decisions are passed down the organisation in a direct line from senior management to shop floor workers.
- **Functional organisation** Where the firm is organised on the basis of what people do.
- **Staff workers** Employees who move between various departments in their job.
- **Centralised organisation** Where the organisation is tightly controlled from the centre and there is little delegation of responsibility.
- **Decentralised organisation** Where divisions or departments in the firm are given powers to take major decisions.
- **De-layering** The removal of tiers of management.

Test questions

JK Whittaker Ltd is a medium-sized firm making marine engines. The company is organised into five main departments: production, marketing, finance, personnel and distribution. The production department is further divided into three sections: research and development, assembly, and plant maintenance.

The Chairman of the Board of Directors has recently instructed the General Manager to inform all departmental managers of the need to reduce expenditure by 5% in order to meet financial targets in the coming year.

1 Construct an organisational chart for Whittaker's from the information contained in the above passage.

2 Briefly explain the type of work you would expect to be carried out by:
  a The production department,
  b the marketing department and,
  c the human resources (personnel) department.

3 What is the Board of Directors? What types of decisions will it be responsible for?

4 What work is done by a Departmental Manager?

5 What is the span of control at Whittaker's of
  a the General Manager,
  b the Production Manager?

6 What is the chain of command for carrying out the order to reduce spending by 5%?

7 It is decided to subdivide the marketing department into three sections. Suggest an appropriate way of dividing it up.

8 Which department manager would each of the following be mainly responsible to:
   a a delivery driver,
   b a salesman,
   c a toolmaker,
   d the staff training officer,
   e an accounts clerk?

Extension questions

1 Whittaker's, like most organisations, has both line and staff workers. Explain the terms 'line' and 'staff', giving an example of each from Whittaker's.

2 Whittaker's has a centralised system of personnel record keeping but a decentralised system of accounting. Explain the terms 'centralised' and 'decentralised' as used in this context and discuss the advantages and disadvantages of the two methods of organisation as they are used here.

3 What is meant by 'de-layering' the management? Why has the trend in management during the 1990s been towards 'de-layering'?

Suggestions for coursework

1 Draw an organisation chart for any organisation you are familiar with, such as school, a club, sports centre, youth club, etc. Use your chart to illustrate the terms 'chain of command', and 'span of control'. Find out the exact responsibilities of any four people in the organisation and list them. Suggest an alternative management structure giving the advantages and disadvantages of it compared to the existing one.

2 Compare the organisation of any two contrasting firms (large/small, manufacturing/service, etc.) How is responsibility delegated? What are the chains of command in the two firms? Why are the firms differently organised? Compare the responsibilities of two managers in each of the organisations.

3 A 'mini-enterprise' activity taking place in school or college could be used to look at organisational structures. How was the business organised? Was this developed by the group or imposed by someone else? How did it work in practice? Who did what? What problems were there in terms of the organisation? How much work was delegated – how much was centralised?

unit 11 Communicating

Aims

At the end of this unit you should understand:

- The need for good communications in business.
- The range of different types of internal and external communications.
- The suitability of particular forms of communication.
- How communications can be improved and made more efficient.
- How information is stored and retrieved in business.

The need for good communications in business

Communication is the passing of information between people. Good communications are essential for the efficient functioning of a business. These communications may range from informal conversations to the most sophisticated electronic forms of communications available.

Exercise

An urgent order has just come into your firm and you need to pass the details on to the production manager who is in the next building.

1. List all the possible ways of getting the information to the production manager.
2. What might happen if you do not get the information to the production manager quickly and accurately?
3. Which method (or methods) of communication would you choose in this case?

Types of communications

Communications can be divided into two groups: internal (communications used within the firm) and external (communicating with people outside the firm). There is some overlap between the two groups – the telephone, for example, is used both for communicating within the firm and with people outside it. At the same time, some companies may be on many different sites which are spread throughout the country.

Internal communications

Telephone

(+) Fast, avoids the need to move around.

(–) Conversations not normally recorded. No record of information. Verbal message may be misunderstood. (See telephone for external communication, page 133.)

Face-to-face contact

May be informal 'chats' or formal meetings where details are recorded in the 'minutes'.

(+) May sort out problems more rapidly and avoid unnecessary paper work.

(–) People not always available for meetings. Often no record kept and information may be misinterpreted.

Internal memo

MEMO

From: Managing Director
To: J. Smith
c.c. T. Evans
date: 25/11/95

Subject: Kuwait Contract

Following a meeting with the production manager...

Short, hand-written or typed note giving information.

(+) Record kept of information sent out. Less open to misinterpretation than verbal messages.

(–) May come to be disregarded if over-used. Less personal than verbal contact.

Formal report

Long document giving details of, for example, a particular meeting or company policy. May be copied or circulated between staff.

⊕ Provides an accurate and detailed record of the information.
⊖ Can involve a great deal of paper circulating in the firm. Reports may not be read if too long and the staff are short of time. Vital information may be lost in the details of the report if it is not summarised.

Noticeboards

Used to display notices concerning large groups of people.

⊕ Can be eye catching – use of colour, pictures, etc. Saves on copying.
⊖ May not be seen. Needs to be kept up-to-date. No good for confidential documents.

Computer links

Departments linked together by computer. Departments can both input and receive information. The person receiving the message can save it electronically, alter it and send replies.

⊕ Fast means of communicating. Suitable for short and long messages, diagrams and graphs. Departments can select the information required. Messages can be sent instantaneously to all departments.
⊖ Initially expensive to install. Lack of confidentiality. Messages may get overlooked or ignored if used too frequently. (See electronic mail, page 134.)

x

Company magazine/newsletter

Normally a feature of large companies. Used for general information on how the company is performing, social activities, changes of personnel, etc.

- ⊕ Helps to give the company a feeling of unity. Assists employees to see what is going on in the whole organisation.
- ⊖ Costly to produce – needs editing, printing, etc. No guarantee it will be read.

Radio paging

Employees who move around a great deal in the firm may be contacted by 'bleeper'– they then go to the nearest telephone extension.

- ⊕ Paging allows employees to be contacted wherever they are.
- ⊖ Expensive if used for large numbers of employees.

Dictaphone messages

Tape-recorded information. Letters can be recorded whilst awaiting typing. Messages can be left for staff temporarily out of the office.

- ⊕ May mean more efficient use of secretarial staff by having a 'pool' of typists.
- ⊖ Messages easily misunderstood. Training needed in accurate and clear dictation of letters. Need for audio-typists.

Exercises

Choosing the best way of communicating

1 For each of the following situations, suggest three possible ways of communicating the information. Choose the way you feel is best and say why you have selected this particular method.

   a The Managing Director wishes to call a meeting of all departmental managers in two weeks' time.

   b The Marketing Manager wishes to have a letter typed but her secretary is out at lunch and she has to go to an important meeting before the secretary is likely to return.

   c The Production Manager urgently requires details of an order from the Despatch Department which is located some distance from his office.

   d The Personnel Manager wishes to inform all staff of the arrangements for the Christmas Party.

   e One of the secretaries in the Marketing Department wishes to arrange special leave to look after a sick relative.

2 Prepare a notice on A4 paper for the staff noticeboard announcing the formation of a social club in the firm. Make your notice as eye-catching as possible and include all relevant information, such as when it meets, what activities are on offer, the names of the organisers, etc.

3 Write a memo from the Distribution Manager to Ms J Roberts in the Packing Department, asking her to ensure that all orders for PR Supplies Ltd are completed by the end of the month.

The Rules For Good Communication

- Keep it as simple as possible. Think about what you really want to say and avoid information which is unnecessary or irrelevant.
- Be accurate. The message must be understood in the way you intend it. People respond differently to spoken and written words.
- Choose the most appropriate form of communication – an informal chat may be more effective than a formal letter.
- Think of your audience. Who is the message intended for? Different styles of communication are required for friends, customers and managing directors.
- Be clear about what you expect to happen as a result of the communication. Do you expect an immediate response? Is it something to discuss further? Is the message for information or is it trying to influence someone in their thinking?
- Timing of the communication. There may be some times which are more appropriate than others. A busy executive may not wish to engage in a lengthy discussion five minutes before an important meeting.

The post

- Despite many advances in communications, the postal system is still very heavily used by nearly all firms. Examples of common use include: the sending of documents such as orders and invoices; sending advertising information to possible customers; sending letters to suppliers, customers, and other firms.
- The postal system is a relatively cheap and safe way of sending written information.
- The main disadvantage of the postal system is that it is relatively slow.
- There are also some special postal services which are quicker than the normal letter delivery but which cost considerably more than ordinary letters.

Special delivery

Guarantees delivery of letters and parcels the next day.

Datapost Sameday

Provides delivery during the sameday within and in between most UK business centres.

International Datapost

Provides guaranteed express delivery to most countries throughout the world.

Other postal services

Registered post

A safer way of sending valuable items or documents through the post. A signature is obtained upon delivery of the item. The sender is compensated if the item is lost or stolen.

Recorded delivery

The service is cheaper than registered post and provides proof of posting, and confirmation that it has been delivered. There is limited compensation if the item is lost or stolen, so it is not suitable for very valuable items. It is useful in sending such items as bills, and final demands for payment, as evidence that they were posted and received.

Certificate of posting

This is a free service which shows the date of posting. This may provide useful evidence in business in the event of a dispute.

Freepost

This allows customers to write back to a business free of charge. This encourages people to respond to advertisements and enquire for further details. A similar system is the Business Reply service where customers are provided with special pre-printed envelopes to reply free of charge. In both cases the business offering Freepost or Business Reply services pays the cost of the postage.

A motorcycle courier delivering an urgent parcel to a company

Private courier

Businesses are making increasing use of private courier services for both short and long distance delivery of letters and parcels. The courier will collect the letter or parcel from the business in person and deliver it to its destination. It is fast but relatively expensive.

The telephone

The telephone remains one of the most important forms of external communication. It is a rapid and relatively cheap form of verbal communication. The cost of using it depends upon the time of day (it is most expensive in the mornings during working days), the length of the call, and the distance. Most places throughout the world can be reached by direct dialling without using an operator. Mobile phones make it possible for business people to stay in touch almost anywhere.

Fax

This is a popular method of sending black-and-white printed material or drawings very rapidly between two firms. The information on A4 paper is copied and sent electronically between two Fax machines using the telephone lines. The cost of sending the message depends upon the distance between the two firms and the length of time it takes to transmit the information.

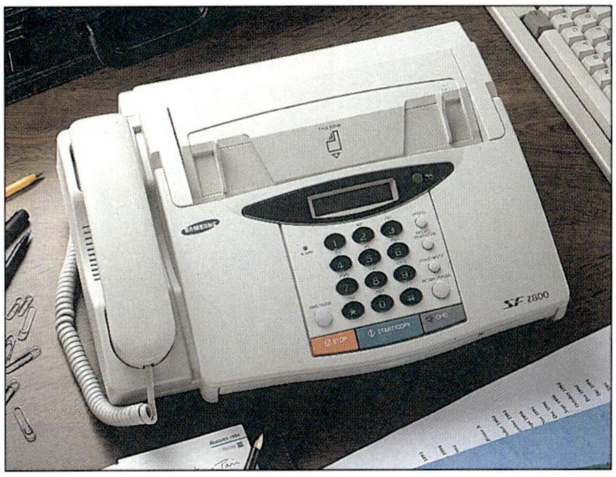

Video conferencing

To save managers travelling long distances for meetings, they can be linked by sound and vision to managers elsewhere in the country using video conferencing links.

Computerised information systems

In the past few years there has been a very rapid growth in a variety of computerised information systems.

Prestel

Prestel is the British Telecom information system. Firms connected to Prestel can receive information on a wide range of topics such as Stock Exchange prices, financial reports, and travel information. The system also allows users to request particular pieces of information and to make bookings for items such as airline tickets.

Electronic mailing

Electronic mailing systems allow firms both to receive and input information. The information is received through a computer terminal linked to the telephone system by a modem. Each firm involved in the system has a post box number to which information can be sent.

Electronic mailing systems are very useful to firms spread over a number of different sites and requiring frequent contacts to be made between the various offices. It also allows a head office to maintain centralised control over its branches. (See page 121). Business people with a portable computer and a modem can receive and send messages in hotels and business centres by simply plugging into the telephone lines.

The information superhighway (INTERNET)

The information superhighway is the next step up from electronic mail. This enables people with access to the superhighway to tap into a vast network of databases, receive video and send messages to all other users throughout the world through the telephone system. The replacement of copper telephone lines with fibre optic cable will allow even more information to be transmitted.

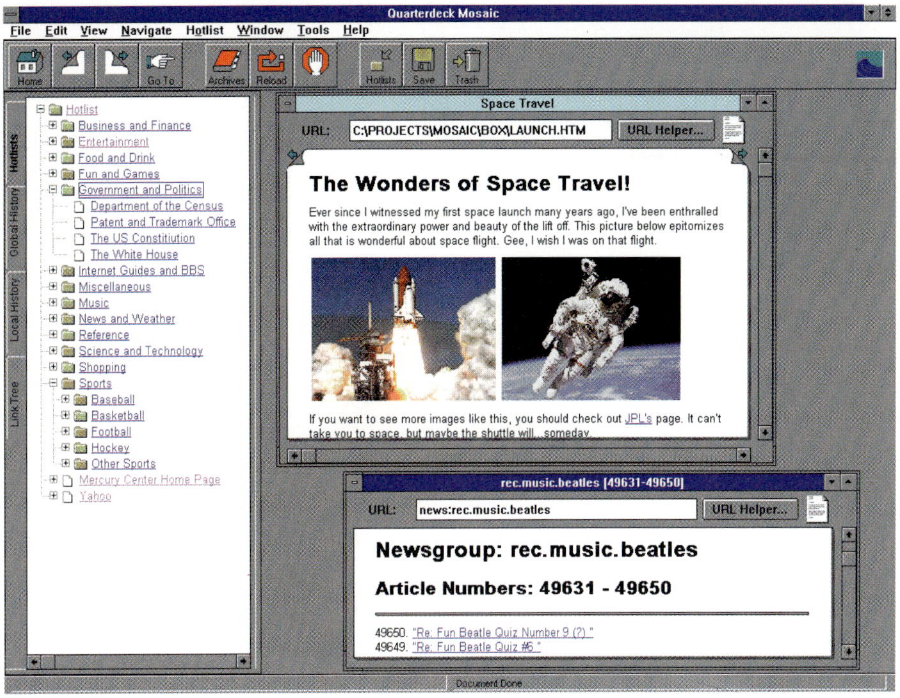

Exercise

1 For each of the following situations choose the most appropriate form of communication and say why you feel that this would be the best in the circumstances:

- a The head office of a supermarket chain wishes to communicate regular price changes to its branch stores.
- b A firm in London needs to send an important contract to a firm in Birmingham to arrive the following day.
- c A firm in Newcastle wishes to contact its agent who is currently in a small town in Kenya.
- d A marketing manager in York wishes to discuss a proposal with an advertising agency in London.
- e An investment trust in Norwich wishes to obtain regular information on share prices and interest rates.
- f A firm in Manchester wishes to send a written estimate to a firm in Cardiff the same day.

2 Use the Post Office and British Telecom guides to calculate the cost of:

- a A ten minute telephone conversation between London and Manchester at peak rate.
- b Sending computer data weighing 100gms from Birmingham to London to arrive the same day.
- c Sending a package weighing 500gms from Newcastle upon Tyne to Hong Kong by the fastest means possible.

Storing and retrieving information

So far in this unit we have been concerned with the ways in which information is passed between people. Businesses also have to store information and be able to refer to parts of it when it is required in the future. For example, firms need to store information on their clients, keep copies of invoices and customer records, and to retain copies of contracts and other legal documents. The sending, storing, classification, and retrieving of information is called information technology. Firms may have systems ranging from simple filing cabinets through to the most up-to-date computerised data storage.

Electronic data storage is becoming increasingly important as the amount of information to be stored grows. Computerised systems have the advantage of being able to store huge quantities of information on disk and this can be 'found' very rapidly. Information recorded in a database can be rearranged and extracted in a variety of ways to suit the user. This is illustrated in the case study on Direct Fashions Ltd on page 137.

Where large quantities of information change frequently, such as stock prices, a firm's records can be updated by receiving a computer disk with the alterations on. This information is then very rapidly fed into the firm's computer.

Whatever system of storage is used, the firm needs to decide upon a method of organising the information. A filing system can be organised in a variety of ways – by name of subject, by date, by account number, etc. The method chosen will depend upon the type of information being stored and the way in which it needs to be most frequently retrieved.

Case study

Direct Fashions Ltd

Direct Fashions is a mail-order clothing firm. It has a large number of customers throughout the UK and uses a computer system for storing information about them. Apart from keeping details of the customer's account, Direct Fashions records a great deal of information about each of the customers. The computer is able to give information on what each customer has bought, their age, social class, their tastes in clothes and what their *spending power* is likely to be. This information is of great value to the Marketing Manager who can construct *profiles* of the company's customers. When a new range of fashions comes in she can quickly extract information from the computer as to which customers are likely to be most interested in it. This saves time and money sending advertising to customers whose profiles indicate that they are very unlikely to buy the new fashion range. From the company's database the Marketing Manager could, for example, obtain a list of all customers in the age range 35-45 who have previously bought knitted items from Direct Fashions.

1 What advantages are there for Direct Fashions of using a computerised system of storing customer information?

2 What is meant by a customer profile?

3 Imagine that you are a customer of Direct Fashions. Draw up a computer print-out of the information Direct Fashions might have on you.

Example

```
NAME  Philip Spencer
ACCOUNT NO. PS/3456/82
ADDRESS  21, The Rise, East Bainbridge, Notts.
AGE  27
DATE OF FIRST PURCHASE  2-4-82
DATE OF LAST PURCHASE  5-9-95
```

Communication problems

Case study

How poor communications cost Spender Bros. £20,000.

Spender Bros., a firm making electrical components, were contacted by telephone for an urgent quotation to supply Trend Electronics with a large quantity of specialised switches. The telephonist transferred the call to the Sales Manager. The Sales Manager was at a meeting and her secretary was out at lunch. The caller from Trend Electronics was left hanging on for five minutes before being told that there was nobody available to take the call. The caller left a message with the telephonist asking the Sales Manager to telephone him as soon as possible. The telephonist forgot to inform the Sales Manager of the call from Trend Electronics until the next day.

The following day the Sales Manager telephoned Trend Electronics and jotted the details of the request for a quotation down. She passed these on to the Production Manager later the same day. Unfortunately, the Production Manager was not told that the matter was urgent and did nothing about it for three days. Trend Electronics again contacted the Sales Manager at Spender Bros. to remind her about the quotation. The Sales Manager had not made a copy of the order but thought she could remember the details. Unfortunately, the Sales Manager got the type of switch wrong.

The quotation finally arrived at Trend Electronics late and incorrect. Not surprisingly, Spender Bros. did not get the contract and lost £20,000 worth of business.

List all the mistakes which were made in communications by Spender Bros. and suggest how the matter should have been properly dealt with, starting from the initial telephone call from Trend Electronics.

Communication nets

One problem often faced by large firms is a lack of understanding by any one section of the company as to what the other sections are doing. This was one of the diseconomies of scale mentioned on page 97.

It is very important that information within the organisation is received by all those that it may have an effect upon. A very common complaint in large organisations is that workers on the factory floor are not informed of decisions made by management until it actually starts to influence working conditions. This has frequently been a cause of industrial action. This is dealt with in detail in Unit 14.

Exercise

How information is passed around in an organisation is very important for the efficient running of the firm. Here are several different types of communication nets which show who communicates with who in an organisation. For each one,

a describe how it operates and,
b say what you think the advantages and disadvantages of the particular method are, e.g., Who receives the information? How rapid is the system? Who does it involve in decision making?

Summary of key words and ideas

- As firms expand the need for a system of communications increases.
- **Good communications** are vital for the efficient running of a firm. Poor communications can lead to loss of business and poor relationships between various parts of the workforce.
- **Internal communications** are those taking place within the firm and include: face-to-face contacts, telephones, memos, reports, noticeboards, computers, newsletters, and dictaphones.
- **External communications** are when a firm communicates with those outside the organisation and include: letters, telephone, electronic mailing, and information systems.
- Different types of information are suited to particular methods of communication depending upon their nature, the speed with which they need to be received, and whether they are best presented in written or verbal form.
- **Information technology** is the exchange, classification, storage, and retrieval of information.
- Electronic systems of storing information are becoming increasingly important in organisations. They can store large quantities of information in a small area and can reorganise information to best suit the purpose of the user.
- **Communications nets** are the patterns of how communications are organised in a firm.

Test questions

1 JM Martyn Ltd are a large firm producing office equipment. They sell their products mainly in the UK but import some materials from Germany.

a Name four forms of internal communication the firm would use. Give a specific example of how the firm would use each method of communication.

b Name four types of external communication the firm would use. Include two methods of communication that the firm would use for its dealings with Germany. Give an example of the use of each method chosen.

2 You have recently taken up a post with the Easiway Travel Agency. They have purchased a computer which is linked by modem to the major travel companies and is also used for storing information on their customers.

a Explain how their computer link with the travel companies would be used.

b List the types of information Easiway might hold on each customer.

c Suggest two other uses that Easiway might make of the computer.

3 Explain the use a large manufacturing company might make of the following forms of communication:
a Electronic mail,
b Datapost,
c Confravision,
d Fax.

4 A large estate agents has several different ways of filing information. One method it uses is to file alphabetically according to the name of the customer. Suggest two other methods of filing which the estate agent might make use of. In each case explain how the system would work and what use it would be to the estate agent.

Extension questions

1 The marketing department in a large manufacturing firm feels that the finance department too frequently fails to communicate important information. Suggest two ways in which communications could be improved between the marketing and finance departments.

2 Draw two different types of communication nets. For each net chosen suggest,
a the type of information it would be used for,
b its advantages and disadvantages for communicating information.

Suggestions for coursework

1 Invent a firm and describe what methods of internal and external communications are used. Give precise examples of how the various methods of communications would be used. Draw diagrams to show how different departments communicate with each other.

2 Carry out the above task with a real firm. The task could be further improved by making a comparison of two different organisations.

3 Using data from the Post Office Guide, British Telecom, and Mercury carry out a comparison of the cost and speed of sending a variety of types of information by different methods of communication.

4 Develop either a paper (manual) or electronic database for an estate agent.
Store information,
a by customer requirements,
b by types of property for sale.

Explain how you have organised your information and how it could be used by the estate agent.

unit 12 Production

Aims

At the end of this unit you should understand:

- The factors influencing the location of a firm.
- The different methods of producing a product.
- How businesses seek to assure quality.
- The division of labour.
- The impact of changing technology on production.

Locating the enterprise

Where shall we put our firm? There are a large number of factors which may influence where a firm is located. A great deal depends upon what the firm is producing. A firm involved in writing computer programs may well be able to locate almost anywhere in the country, while a heavy engineering firm will be much more limited in its location.

Materials versus markets

Some firms tend to locate close to where their materials are available. This may be close to the source of the materials, such as mines, quarries, forests, etc., or where the firm can obtain easy access to materials by being close to ports, major roads and rail links.

Firms locating close to raw materials, or where there is easy access to them, are often bulk reducing industries. This means that the product being produced is lighter, or less bulky, than the raw materials needed to make it. It is therefore cheaper to make the product as close as possible to the raw materials rather than pay high transport costs to move the materials to a factory some distance away. A good example of this is the steel industry.

Bulk reducing

It takes 5 tonnes of materials to produce 1 tonne of steel. Early steel works tended to be located on those coalfields which also had iron ore and limestone. More recent steel works, using imported iron ore, tend to be located near to ports which also have easy access to coal.

Other firms which tend to be located close to the source of raw materials include those dealing in perishable items, such as fish canning and vegetable freezing.

The pull of the market

Firms which are bulk increasing tend to be located close to the market for their products. Bulk increasing means that the good being produced is larger or heavier than the materials being used to make it. Examples of such industries include firms making boxes for packing, soft drinks manufacturers and baking. It is clearly cheaper to transport the raw materials to the market than to move the more bulky finished good.

Bulk increasing

Other industries which normally locate close to their market include services, such as banking and finance, where close contact with customers is important. Perishable foods which cannot be processed, such as lettuces, are also often produced close to their market – although improvements in transport and growing methods have meant that they can now be grown further from their market.

Other factors influencing location

Planning permission

Firms normally require planning permission from the local authority in order to set up a new factory. Certain areas will often be designated for industrial development while restrictions may be placed on developments close to housing or in rural areas.

Site facilities

Some manufacturing firms require large, flat sites and may have particular needs, such as a gas supply, special waste disposal facilities, and a good water supply.

Above left: The ICI Wilton works, with the village of Lazenby and main road connections. ICI also own the houses in the village

Above right: The ICI chemical works at Runcorn, situated on the Mersey estuary

The cost of the land

The price of land for rent or purchase varies between different regions and within areas. Rents in the centre of large cities will be a lot higher than 'greenfield' sites in more remote areas.

Transport facilities

Many manufacturing firms need good transport facilities in order to obtain materials and components and to move the finished products to the customer. Because of congestion, many firms have moved out of towns and cities and have located close to motorways outside of urban areas. Major airports have also attracted firms which have close connections with other countries.

Skilled labour

Some industries rely on particular types of skilled workers. Certain areas develop a reputation for possessing specialist skills. A recent example of this has been the growth of high-tech industries around Cambridge, partly based on the skills and research facilities available at the university there.

Historical factors

Sometimes the reasons for an industry developing in a particular location in the past have disappeared and yet the industry remains there because it is well established in the area and because the costs of moving are high. This is known as industrial inertia. An example of this is the Cumbria pencil industry, which was originally based upon local supplies of graphite, but which now uses synthetic materials.

Government influence

We have seen in Unit 5 how government and local authorities have attempted to attract industry to areas of high unemployment by offering them grants and other incentives. This has certainly influenced the location of at least some firms. A recent example has been the locating of the Nissan car factory near Sunderland in the north-east of England. (See Unit 17.)

Linkages

Some firms are very dependent upon others. They may supply components to a large firm or deal in the by-products of other firms. (A by-product is something produced in the making of another product.) Other firms, particularly those providing services, often need to be in close personal contact with similar types of organisations. This can be seen in the City of London where there is a tremendous concentration of financial businesses close to the Bank of England and the Stock Exchange.

Below left: Incentives offered by Strathclyde Regional Council to encourage businesses to set up in Strathclyde

Below right: The Bank of England

Case study

Location

Notes

Lodwick is the main town in the area with a population of 500,000 residents. It is a centre for trade and commerce and has excellent shopping facilities which service the town and the surrounding area.

New Berkley – a new town developing with a population of 50,000. There is local authority assistance for firms locating there. It has several industrial estates and there is a range of modern factory accommodation.

Port File has a population of 120,000. It has a harbour which will accommodate large ocean-going ships. There is a small fishing fleet based in the west of the town and a number of industries connected with the town's function as a port.

Seaton – a popular holiday resort as well as a retirement town. It has a population of 30,000. There is a range of holiday accommodation and a small shopping centre.

1 For each of the following firms choose the best location in the area shown on the map opposite, giving your reasons for each decision:
   a A steelworks.
   b A firm concerned with freezing and processing fresh fish.
   c A light engineering firm requiring a large, flat site and good road communications to obtain its components and to transport its finished products.
   d A firm offering a range of personal financial services.
   e A DIY hypermarket.
   f A craft shop.

2 A firm producing chemicals wishes to locate in the area shown on the map. They are informed by the local authority that there are three areas where they will not be allowed to locate.
   a Which three locations do you think they are referring to and why?
   b Where do you think the best location would be for the chemical works?

3 Suggest types of firms, apart from those already mentioned, which might be found in:
   a Port File,
   b Seaton,
   c New Berkley,
   d Lodwick,
   and say why you feel that they would be located there.

4 a Why do you think the firm pictured below is located where it is?
   b Say how the factors influencing its location may have changed in the past 30 years.

Below: The British Steel works at Port Talbot in South Wales

Organising production

There are three types of production organisation: Job, Batch, and Flow.

Job production

This is when a firm gets one-off orders so that each product is built to the customer's specifications. This type of work is often done by relatively small, specialist firms. It is difficult in this type of production to have a flow line (see below).

JC Buchanan Ltd are specialists in luxury motor boats. Each boat is built to the customer's requirements, which means that no two boats are ever identical. The workers at Buchanan's tend to work as a team and there is little specialisation in the production of each boat.

Right: Job production

Above: Flow production at a Nissan car factory

Batch production

Batch production lies between job and flow production. A clothing manufacturer, for example, may receive batch orders for 1000 particular skirts. The firm can set up a production line for this type of work because it involves some repetition of particular tasks. After the batch is produced, it will switch to something else.

Flow production

Flow production is where assembly is on a production line. The product is moved along a conveyor belt to the workers who add components and carry out tasks. Unlike batch production, the work is continuous. Each stage of production does not have to wait until a batch is passed on and production lines often run 24 hours a day. Flow production often results in workers specialising in specific tasks, this is known as the division of labour. (See The division of labour, page 153.)

Flow production is best suited to products that can be mass produced such as cars, washing machines, and computers. Mass production requires products to be similar but not necessarily identical. Modern production methods mean that a particular model of car can be produced with a range of engine sizes, in different colours and with different levels of trims on the same assembly line. However, a completely new design of car will require substantial changes to be made to the production lines and this will be very costly.

Above: Using CAD to design a new model of car

Recent developments in production

CAD/CAM

Computer aided design and manufacture helps to reduce the time it takes from a new design for a product to full mass production. Clarks Shoes pioneered the use of CAD/CAM in the footwear industry. Clarks aims to bring out a new range of shoes twice a year which means frequent changes to the pattern cutting machines. Under CAD/CAM the designers produce their designs on computers and this is translated to the computers controlling the cutting machines on the production line.

CIM

Computer integrated manufacture is where computers control large parts of production. CIM involves the use of industrial robots to replace humans. The modern car industry makes extensive use of CIM with robots doing such tasks as spot welding, tightening bolts and carrying out quality control.

Right: CIM – robot welders in a car factory

Just-in-time systems

The efficient operation of production requires a business to keep stocks of materials and components. On a production line there needs to be supplies of components ready to add to the product being assembled on the conveyor belt. The whole production process might be disrupted if components were not ready to be fitted on any part of the assembly line. On the other hand, over-stocking is inefficient because money is tied up in components and materials and they also take up valuable space.

Just-in-time systems attempt to keep stock to a minimum by having replacement stock arrive at the point where it is required just before it is needed. The use of computers to keep a check on stock levels and send messages to the supply centre has helped in the development of just-in-time systems. Large supermarkets also adopt just-in-time methods by keeping a limited stock and relying on an efficient transport and delivery system.

Case study

Just-in-time

In Example A the business decides it wants to keep a minimum of 5000 components in stock (this is known as the 'buffer stock' and is there to meet emergencies, sudden changes in demand or delays in deliveries). It takes 5 days between re-ordering and delivery. On average, the business uses 2000 components in 5 days of production so it re-orders when stock falls to 7000.

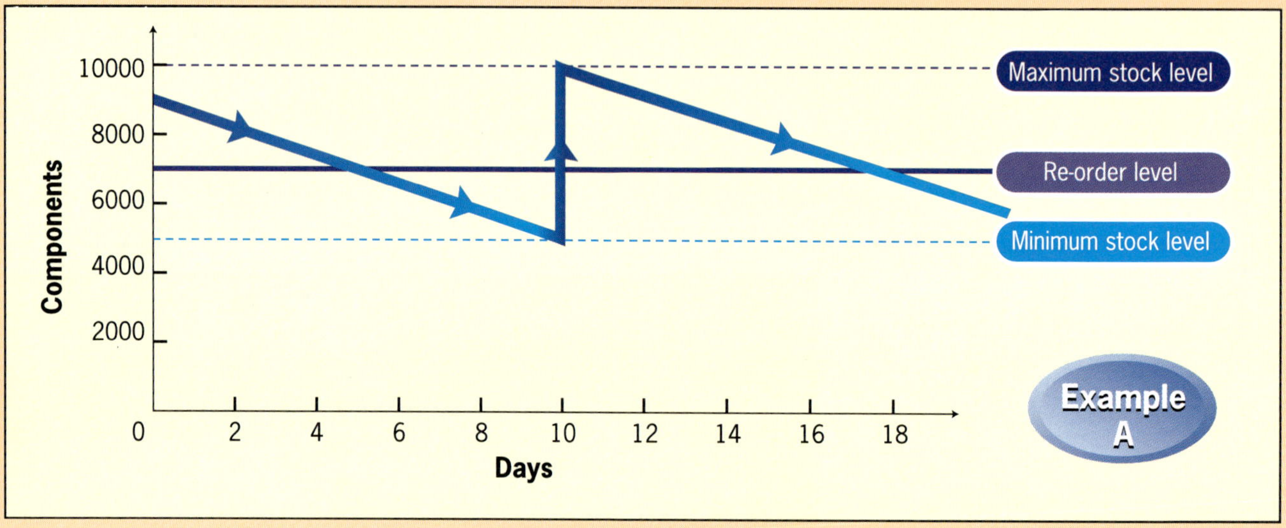

In Example B the business adopts a just-in-time system. It has reduced the time between re-ordering and delivery to two days and does not keep a buffer stock.

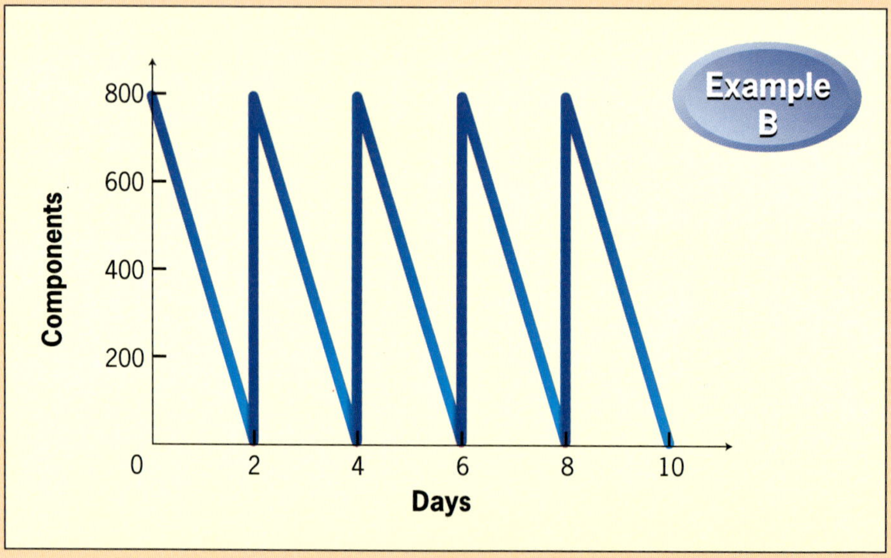

1 Why do businesses hold a 'buffer' stock?
2 What benefits does the business gain by adopting a just-in-time system?
3 How is the business in Example B able to hold less stock?
4 What dangers might there be for the business adopting the just-in-time system shown in Example B?

The flow of production

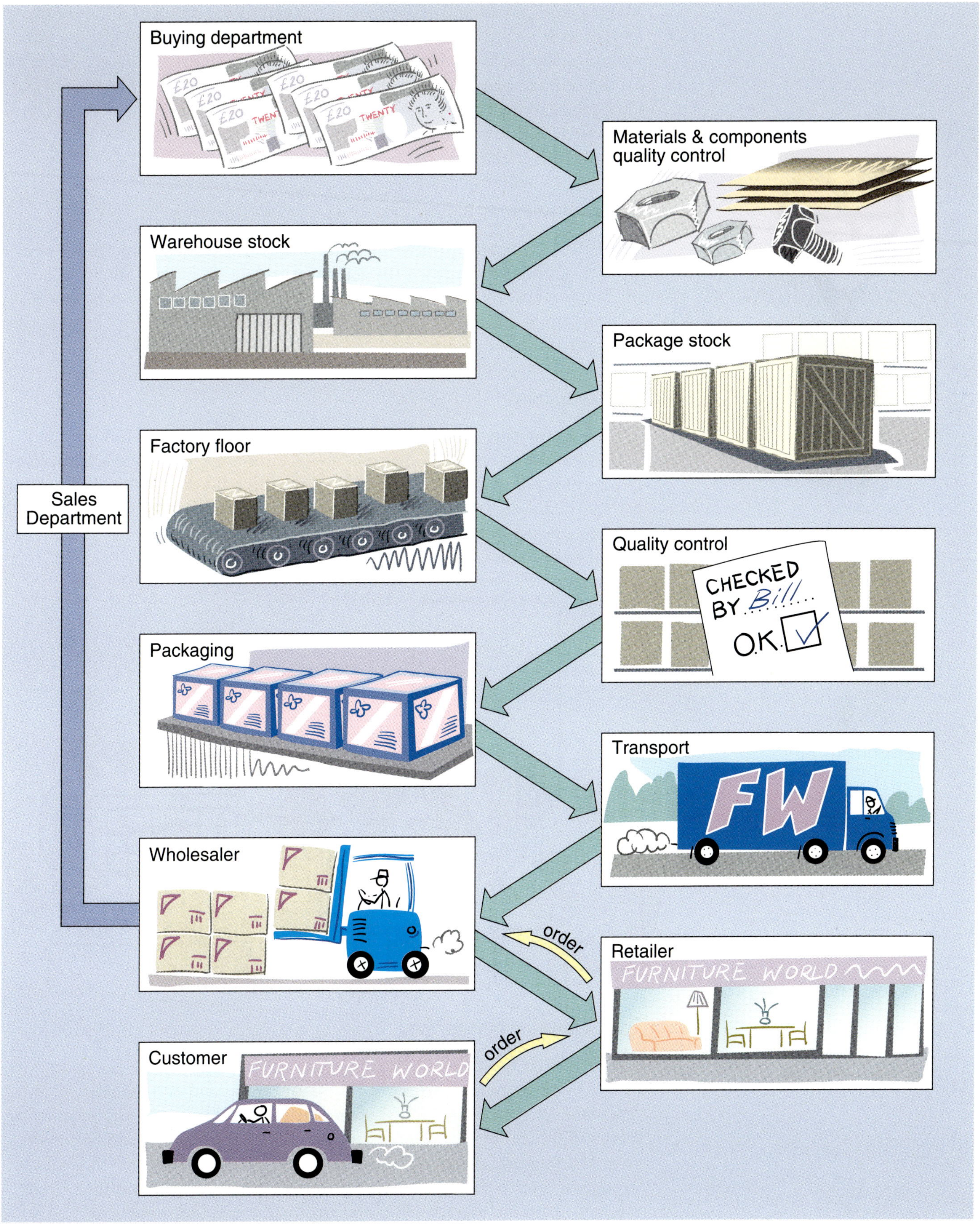

Assuring quality

Making sure goods and services are produced to the standard required by customers is vital to the success of a business. Firms using flow production will normally build in checks at each stage in the process and carry out tests on the finished product. It is obviously better to detect errors as they occur rather than trying to discover where the fault is after the product has been assembled. The inspection of goods and services to make sure they are up to standard is known as *quality control*.

Below: The Kitemark

British Standards Institution

The British Standards Institution (BSI) sets quality standards for goods and services. Goods which reach the standards laid down by BSI are awarded the Kitemark. Regular checks are carried out by BSI to make sure goods awarded the Kitemark continue to reach the standards required. Having the Kitemark is a good selling point for businesses. (See page 215.)

Quality Circles

The idea of quality circles was developed in the Japanese car industry and has now been taken on by many Western businesses. Quality circles involve groups of workers and managers taking responsibility for quality in their part of the production process. The circles meet regularly to review quality and the level of output achieved and to suggest ways of improving their part of the production.

Total Quality Management

Closely linked to quality circles is the idea of total quality management (TQM) which attempts to get everyone in the organisation to take responsibility for quality. TQM aims as far as possible to 'get the product or service right and to get it right first time'. This cuts down waste, lowers costs and increases customer satisfaction. TQM also encourages all workers to suggest improvements in the production process. This is summed up by the Japanese word *Kaizan* which means 'continuous improvement'.

Specialisation and the division of labour

Modern mass production methods normally require a considerable degree of specialisation by the workforce. Each worker carries out a small part of the total assembly, often alongside a conveyer belt which brings the components to each worker. It is argued that the division of labour results in higher productivity (the amount each worker produces in an hour) and that this leads to lower average costs of production.

This is because:

- Each task is very simple, so workers get very quick at carrying it out.
- Little training is required to learn each task.
- Workers can be allocated to the tasks they are best at.
- Workers may find better ways of carrying out a particular task.
- Machines are in constant use.
- Use of assembly-line methods with less time wasted moving around the factory.

The division of labour may however have disadvantages, and some of these are illustrated by the following case study.

Case study

A day in the life of Brett Graham, car worker

'I am on the day shift today which means clocking in at 8.30am. I'm working in the engine assembly plant fitting pistons. I've been doing this for the past ten shifts. You get moved around every three weeks but it still gets pretty boring. You can learn how to do most of the jobs in ten minutes and you start getting bored after the first hour. I can fit pistons now without even thinking about it. As soon as the belt starts up I let my mind wander – its the only way to stay sane, and it helps to pass the time. I think about where I'm going on my holidays next month, what's on TV tonight or about the girl I met at the Club last Saturday – my mind's on anything except the job I'm doing. Sometimes I make a mistake because I'm not thinking about what I'm doing and back the block comes from Quality Control.

Every two hours we get a twenty-minute break. It's so far to go to the canteen that they bring food and drink round on a trolley now. I can't say I get much satisfaction from this job – apart from the money at the end of the week. There's not much to talk about when I go home after the shift.

This afternoon we got an unofficial break. Something went wrong down the line which brought all of us to a standstill. I've thought about changing jobs a few times – I couldn't stick this for the rest of my life. The problem is, jobs are not easy to come by these days and this one doesn't exactly give you much of a training for anything else.'

1. What disadvantages of the division of labour are illustrated by the case study above?
2. What satisfaction did Brett get from his job? How would this compare to the satisfaction a cabinet maker would get from his job?
3. What improvements could be made at the car factory to help to overcome some of the disadvantages of the division of labour?

Improving assembly line work

- One of the main disadvantages of the division of labour is that the workers fail to gain satisfaction from the job and this leads to boredom and consequently to poor standards of output. It is also claimed that this is one cause of strike action and loss of production. Workers are made to feel that they are 'a very small cog in a large wheel' and this results in them not having an interest in the product as a whole: they feel *alienated*.

- Some firms have tried to overcome these problems by:
  - a Moving workers between jobs more frequently.
  - b Giving workers more involved and interesting tasks to do.
  - c Having groups of workers make a particular section of the product.
  - d Offering bonuses and other incentives. (See page 176.)
  - e Making the working conditions more interesting – playing music, having a factory radio station, etc.
- The Volvo car company of Sweden used some of these methods and found that the quality of their cars increased and fewer were rejected because of faults. Productivity increased compared with when they had a very intensive division of labour.

Case study

People in production

Johnston Domestic Appliances (JDA) Ltd

The following people all have jobs in production at JDA Ltd, a factory making and assembling washing machines. Here they briefly describe their jobs and how modern technology has changed the nature of production.

Render J

Jean Render
Factory Manager

I was the only woman on the mechanical engineering degree course at my university and it is still unusual for a woman to be a factory manager. I am responsible for everything that happens - or fails to happen - in my factory. I am also responsible for the factory itself. I lead a team of specialists. I did several of their jobs before becoming manager and my knowledge has proved very useful.

Modern technology has had a big impact on our company in the last few years. Machines have replaced many workers and we are now producing more washing machines with a much smaller workforce than ten years ago. I can see more jobs disappearing from the factory floor in the next few years too. It's a great pity to see the decline in jobs but we have to remain competitive.

Bux J

Joseph Bux
Production Controller

Everything produced in the factory is done according to a plan and it is my job to see that everything runs smoothly. I need to make sure that we have enough of the correct materials in stock in order to meet production targets, that there are no unnecessary hold-ups in the production flow and that things get done on time. Hiccups in production may mean a loss of revenue if we are unable to meet our orders.

I said that everything is produced according to a plan and this is being increasingly done by computer technology. Computers assist greatly in stock control and help to achieve a smooth flow of materials through the factory. The computers can also pinpoint very quickly where any problem is occurring in production. This has meant a lot of retraining for me but it has made my job more interesting.

Lemont J

June Lemont
Quality Control Inspector

I have been working here since I left school. I started on the shop floor as a machine operator and worked my way up to this position. Gaining promotion meant getting some training and qualifications and the firm was very good in allowing me day-release to go to the local technical college and then to polytechnic. My job is to make sure that what is being produced comes up to the correct standards - what's laid down in the specifications. This means checking quality at every stage in production - from the materials through to the finished machine.

Every year we use more sophisticated methods of quality control in order to improve the reliability of our products. We used to check everything by hand using gauges and scales or by just looking at it. These days a lot of that is done by machines linked to computers. They can tell straight away if a part is the minutest amount out from the specifications. We used to check the quality of the paintwork by eye, that's now done by lasers which can tell the thickness and level of the paint. All this has changed my job and those of the people who work in my department. There are fewer people working in my department than 10 years ago, but I feel that the standards of quality control are much higher now.

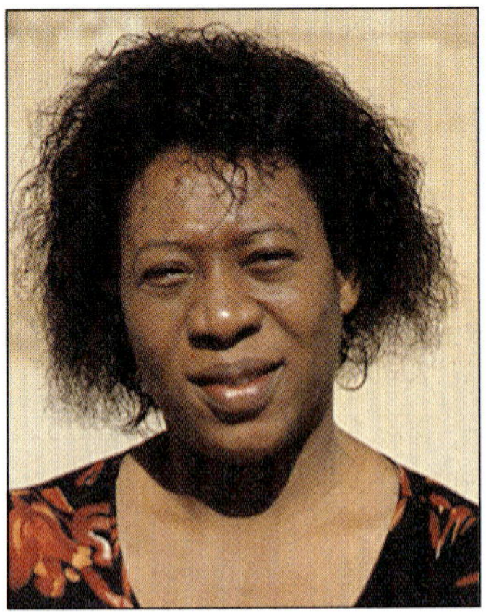

Ryman M

Mark Ryman
Machine Operator

I've been here for fifteen years and I have seen a few changes in my time. The job used to involve hard physical work and it was dirty too. Now most of the machines are controlled by computers. They work more quickly and accurately than I was ever able to do. I just push the buttons and away it goes. There's not much for me to do now unless something goes wrong. The job is physically less demanding and not so noisy and dirty but in some ways it is less satisfying. Still, I mustn't complain: there are plenty who have lost their jobs through machines taking over.

1. List all the ways that new technology has affected production at JDA Ltd washing machine factory.
2. How has the company benefited from new technology?
3. Who has lost out through new technology?
4. What is meant by the 'specifications' of a particular machine?
5. What is the purpose of quality control?
6. What is meant by 'everything is produced according to a plan'?

Summary of key words and ideas

- **Bulk reducing industries** tend to be concentrated close to their source of raw materials.
- **Bulk increasing industries** tend to be located close to the market for their product.
- **Industrial inertia** is when the original reasons for a firm's location have disappeared but the firm remains where it is.
- The three main methods of organising production are **job**, **batch**, and **flow**.
- **CAD/CAM** – computer aided design/computer aided manufacture speeds up the time between the new design of a product and full mass production.
- **CIM** – computer integrated manufacture. Computers control robots and other machines on the assembly line reducing the need for human labour.
- **Just-in-time systems** keep the level of stock to a minimum and rely on the delivery of materials and components to the point where they are needed just before they are needed.
- **New technology** can help raise productivity and reduce costs. It may lead to the loss of some workers' jobs and reduce the level of job satisfaction for others. It may also create jobs for other workers and make some tasks less physically demanding and unpleasant.
- **Quality control** is checking that the product is being produced according to the standards laid down for it.
- **Quality circles** are groups of workers who take responsibility for quality assurance on a particular part of the assembly line.
- **Total Quality Management** (TQM) encourages workers at all levels to take responsibility for quality.
- The **division of labour** means dividing work up into small units with workers specialising in particular parts of the production.
- **Productivity** is how much on average each worker produces in a given period of time.
- The division of labour normally increases productivity but may result in less job satisfaction.

Test questions

1 Oasis is a manufacturer of a range of soft drinks. It is considering setting up a new bottling plant somewhere in the UK. Suggest three things it will need to take into account when deciding where to locate its new factory.

2 Explain one way in which *central government* and one way in which *local government* can influence the location of a firm.

3 Name any manufacturing industry which is normally located close to its market and explain why this is the case.

4 Three methods of organising production are job, batch, and flow. Explain what is meant by each of these terms and suggest a product which might be suited to each method.

5 Cars are normally made on an assembly line. Explain what is meant by an assembly line, and why this method of production is suited to the car industry.

6 RK Greens Ltd are a manufacturer of wooden garden furniture. At present each worker on the shop floor makes each individual piece of garden furniture. You are appointed as the new production manager and you propose to reorganise production by introducing a greater division of labour. This will mean an assembly line with workers each carrying out small tasks.
   a What arguments would you put forward for the scheme?
   b Why might some workers resist the introduction of such a scheme?

7 a Describe a piece of new technology introduced at a firm.
   b State how the new technology has benefited the firm.
   c In what ways has the introduction of new technology been, **i** an advantage to workers, **ii** a disadvantage to workers.

Extension questions

1 A new major airport is to be built in the UK. Which industries is the airport likely to attract which are directly involved with the work of the airport? Which industries not directly connected to the airport are likely to be located in the vicinity? Give reasons for your choice of industries.

2 The division of labour is often said to cause 'worker alienation'.
   a What is meant by the term 'worker alienation'?
   b How can a firm attempt to overcome this problem?

3 'Quality control is about making sure products are of an acceptable standard – this does not mean that they are all perfect.' Explain what is meant by this statement.

4 a Explain why some firms are introducing just-in-time methods of stock control.
   b What does the success of these methods depend upon?
   c What are the dangers of adopting these methods?

5 What methods do businesses use to try to assure quality?

Suggestions for coursework

1 Location studies: **either**
   a Do a survey of industrial location in your local area trying to find out why firms have decided to locate there, **or**,
   b Compare two different types of area, e.g. a city centre and a suburb or market town, showing what types of firms are located in each area and indicating why they are there.

2 Division of labour: **either**
   a Show how the division of labour operates in any one firm. Try to interview workers on a production line to see how they feel about the type of work they are doing. Show any ways in which the management is attempting to overcome some of the problems associated with the division of labour, **or**,
   b Set up a classroom experiment where two teams of students have to produce a simple object (e.g. a paper aeroplane) with a limited

amount of capital equipment (scissors, rulers, pencils, etc.). One team uses a division of labour and the other works individually. See if the division of labour does result in greater productivity. Write up the results of your experiment as you would in science.

3 The impact of new technology. Study the impact of any one piece of new technology in a firm, e.g. the introduction of computers into an office. Try to find out if it has improved productivity, what employees feel about it, whether it has caused any job losses, and whether it has involved retraining.

4 Quality assurance. Compare the methods used to try to achieve quality in a manufacturing business and a business in the service sector.

unit 13 Managing people

Aims

At the end of this unit you should understand:

- The methods firms use to recruit and select workers.
- The need for different types of training.
- The different methods of paying workers.
- How firms use incentives other than wages to motivate their workforce.
- The laws governing the employment of labour.

The recruitment, training, development, and welfare of the workforce is a vital part of any large organisation. Managing people in the organisation is known as personnel management or management of human resources.

We met Sue Rees, Personnel Manager at Talbot Textiles, in Unit 10. Here is an example of a typically busy day for her.

A day in the life of Sue Rees, Personnel Manager, Talbot Textiles

- *8.15 am* Arrive early to prepare myself for interviews to find a new Sales Manager. Check over applications from the short-listed candidates. Check interview arrangements with my secretary.
- *9.00 am* Meeting with Peter Hall, Marketing Manager, to discuss the candidates for the Sales Manager appointment.
- *9.30 am* Start interviews – these go on for the remainder of the morning.
- *12.45 pm* A working lunch with the rest of the interview team to decide upon the appointment.
- *1.45 pm* Back in the office. Meeting with Gill Street, Production Manager, to draft an advertisement to fill a vacancy for a foreman in the weaving shop.
- *2.15 pm* Meeting with union shop stewards to draw up agenda for next Works Council meeting.
- *3.00 pm* Meeting with John West, Training Manager, to discuss YTS training programme.
- *4.00 pm* Read through notes supplied by the Health and Safety Officer on an accident yesterday in the spinning shop. Write memo to Health and Safety Officer suggesting we start disciplinary proceedings.
- *5.00 pm* Meeting with Managing Director to discuss the latest pay claim.

Exercise

1 List all the different types of work that the Personnel Manager is involved in

2 List the other departments she needs to involve herself with.

COMPUTER NETWORK PRODUCTS

MAJOR ACCOUNTS SALES EXECUTIVE
£30,000
on Target Earnings plus car

YOUNG SALES EXECUTIVES
£25,000
on Target Earnings plus car

A knowledge of Plastics &/or Packaging? ... Share in our Success

Part of a major international group, our clients are recognised as a leading force in the plastics/packaging industry and have a reputation for the application of advanced technology to the production process. They are now looking for two experienced people – with exemplary negotiating skills – to join a division which is engaged in the manufacture of injection moulded packaging products. Growing rapidly, this particular division has a variety of prestigious UK and overseas customers who in turn supply diverse consumer markets.

Export Marketing Manager
£18,000 North London

This successful, small company, purchase and re-sell pistachio nuts in the domestic and world market. A recently secured agreement with a German company for the development of sales in the world's export markets, has resulted in them selling this commodity both in the UK and abroad.

VACANCIES

CURTAIN MAKER. Skilled curtain maker (or skilled factory machinist) to work either in workshop or at home. To sew by hand and machine, previously cut pieces of fabric

GENERAL ASSISTANT To help in a local hotel. Silver Service Waiting and general house-keeping duties. Full training given. Some shift work. £80 per week – live in. £100 per week – live out

STOCK CONTROL/VDU OPERATOR. Local cosmetics company to feed stock control details into digital computer and to liaise with sales/purchasing, and production departments. Experience in VDU operating essential. £7,750 to start, rising to £8,000 per annum after 3 months trial.

It is the job of the Personnel Department to recruit and select workers to fill particular vacancies, from the most junior office assistant up to senior executives. The first step is to advertise the vacancy. Depending upon the job to be filled, this may take the form of local, national or even international advertising.

Exercise

All of the above advertisements were taken from either local or national newspapers.

1 Which jobs do you think were advertised locally and which were advertised nationally?
2 How do you think the Personnel Manager in a firm decides whether to advertise locally, nationally or internationally?

Methods of recruitment

Advertising in newspapers is only one way of recruiting staff. Firms may also:

- Advertise internally within the firm.
- Advertise on radio and television.
- Notify Job Centres.
- Use private recruiting agencies, such as Reed Employment.
- Headhunt – some top staff are in such short supply that one firm will recruit directly from another by offering the employee more money and perks, such as cars, to join their firm.
- Recruit people they know already.

Job description and job specification

Before the Personnel Manager advertises a vacancy s/he must decide exactly what the job entails. This is done by writing a job description – a definition of the job. This will include details of the responsibilities of the person appointed, together with information about hours, holidays, pay and conditions.

The Personnel Manager, in consultation with various departmental managers, also needs to decide in advance what type of person they are looking for. This is known as the job specification. This will contain details of the type of qualifications and skills required, together with the likely age and experience of the candidate.

Some aspects of the job specification and job description normally appear in the advertisement for the vacancy. Candidates are normally sent more details when they apply for application forms.

Exercise

For the job advertisements on page 161:

a List the information contained in each under the headings of Job Description and Job Specification.

b For any two advertisements, say what additional information you would require if you were considering applying for the job.

Applying for a job

The next stage in recruitment is to look at job applications. The following case study looks at it from the applicant's point of view.

Case study

Job Vacancy

■JOB VACANCY■

Job: Office Junior
Employer: Swanson Bookings, High Street, Middleton

Job Description: Swanson Bookings are a travel and theatre booking agency. They require an office junior to assist with basic record keeping, filing and reception duties. 40-hour week.

Start at £100 per week.

Requirements: Good GCSE grades in English and Mathematics desirable. Keyboard skills and knowledge of record keeping systems useful.

Applications: By March 10th. Application forms and further details available from the above address.

21 The Grove
Sunbury
Kent

20th February 1995.

Dear Sir

Would you please send me application forms and further details for the post of Office Junior at your firm. I enclose a stamped addressed envelope for your reply.

yours faithfully A Khan

Ahmed Khan has seen the above job advertisement at his local Careers Office and has decided to apply.

Ahmed's application

The Application Form

Swanson Bookings
High Street
Middleton
Tel: 01468 382612

APPLICATION FORM

NAME: Ahmed Khan

ADDRESS: 21, The Grove
Sunbury
Kent

TEL NO: 01468 312398

DATE OF BIRTH: 3rd November 1977

EDUCATION: Sunbury High School
1989–present

QUALIFICATIONS: GCSE Maths (D)
Eng (C), Geog (E),
Bus Studies (C),
Int Science (E)
Technology (D)

CURRENT COURSE:
GNVQ (Intermediate) Business

INTERESTS: Sport, reading, photography

ADDITIONAL INFORMATION IN SUPPORT OF APPLICATION:
I have had work experience at a Solicitors, Estate Agency, and Travel Agent, and worked part-time at British Home Stores

Letter of Application

Swanson Bookings
High Street
Middleton
Kent
26th February 1995

Dear Sir
With reference to the post of Office Junior. I enclose a completed form and include the following additional information to support my application.

I am at present a 6th form Student at Sunbury High School taking the GNVQ intermediate level in Business.

The GNVQ course has allowed me to develop my general education as well as gaining some practical experience of the Business world.

The course has included three work experience placements and I spent one of these at a local travel agent. I very much enjoyed my time at the travel agency and feel I would like to make this my career.

My GNVQ course has also included some keyboarding and wordprocessing and two of my work experience placements offered me the opportunity to try out my skills.

I feel that I would be well suited to the post of Office Junior and ask you to give my application serious consideration.

yours faithfully A Khan

Although Swanson Bookings did not ask for it, Ahmed included with his application a copy of his curriculum vitae. A curriculum vitae formally sets out the applicant's personal details and experience.

CURRICULUM VITAE

Name:	Ahmed Khan
Address:	21 The Grove, Sunbury, Kent
Telephone No:	(01468) 312398
Marital Status:	Single
Date of Birth:	3/11/77
Education:	Sunbury High School, 1989–present.
Qualifications:	GCSE Maths (D), English (C), Geography (E), Business Studies (C), Integrated Science (E), Technology (D).
Current Course:	GNVQ Intermediate Business.
Employment Experience:	Part-time sales assistant British Home Stores. Work experience in Solicitors, Estate Agent, and Travel Agent.
Interests:	Hockey, tennis, photography
Positions of responsibility:	Captain of 1st XI Hockey team. School Prefect.

Exercise

You are the Personnel Manager at Hollards and Barnett Department Store. You have a vacancy for a part-time sales assistant in the toy department. Wages are £3.00 an hour plus subsidised meals. The hours are Friday 5–8pm and Saturday 8.30am–5.30pm. Minimum age 17.

a Design an advertisement for the job to go in a local newspaper.
b Prepare an application form for candidates applying for the job.
c Complete an application form and include a letter of application for the job (assume you are 17).

Selection

After the Personnel Manager has received all the applications for a job a shortlist of the most appropriate candidates is drawn up. This may be done in consultation with the manager of the department in which the person is going to work. They may well draw up a list of qualities they feel are required for the job.

Exercise

1 Draw up a list of qualities you would expect candidates to have for the job at Hollards and Barnett Department Store.
2 Put these in two columns under the headings *Essential Qualities* and *Desirable Qualities*. For example 'Age 17+' would be an essential quality while 'previous shop experience' might be a desirable quality.
3 How does Ahmed match up to these qualities?

The interview

The next stage in the selection procedure is to invite the shortlisted candidates for interview. Exactly who does the interviewing will depend upon the size of the company and the importance of the job. In a large company the Personnel Manager may only be involved with appointments at a senior level. Department managers may well be responsible for appointments at a lower level.

Interviews can take many different forms:

- The candidate may be interviewed by one person or by a group of people (known as a panel interview).
- The candidate may be interviewed separately by a number of individuals.
- At higher levels of recruitment candidates are sometimes interviewed as a group in order to discover qualities such as how they get on working with other people, whether they are a group leader and how they react to other viewpoints.
- Candidates may also be subjected to intelligence tests, aptitude tests or be asked to write an essay on a particular topic.

Appointment to the job

References

Some firms will ask for references before deciding upon their choice of candidate. They may use references to help them to decide upon their shortlist of candidates. Other firms may only ask for references after they have decided to offer the job to a particular candidate. In this case, the offer of the job will be made 'subject to suitable references being obtained'.

Firms may also ask for a *testimonial*. This is an open statement from someone who knows the candidate well and normally refers to such qualities as honesty, reliability, etc. The candidate brings this to the interview. This is different from the reference, which is confidential and sent direct to the employer.

The job contract

As soon as a person accepts the offer of a job there is a contract between the employer and the employee even if there is no written contract. Most firms have a written contract which sets out the rights and obligations on both sides, but there is no legal requirement for a firm to have such a contract. The employer is legally obliged, however, to send the employee a written statement of the terms and conditions of employment after the worker has been at the firm for 2 months. This must include such details as:

- The title of the job.
- The rate of pay.
- Hours of work.
- Holidays.
- Payments during sickness or injury.
- Pension rights.
- Length of notice to be given by the employer or employee to terminate (end) the contract.
- Procedures regarding dismissals.

x Some of the employee's rights depend upon the length of time they have been with the firm. (See Unit 14, page 192 for further details)

Contract of Employment

JOB TITLE: Filing Clerk

JOB HOLDER: C. Kovaakis

SALARY: £8000 per annum

HOLIDAY ENTITLEMENT: 21 days per annum in addition to statutory days

HOURS OF WORK: 37 hours per week

Training

Training is a very important part of the Personnel Department's work. In some large firms there is very often a separate training department. Ideally, training should involve the worker before they actually start the job, during the first few weeks of employment and throughout their careers.

The purpose of training

- To train new workers for particular jobs.
- Help to improve the efficiency of existing workers.
- Avoid accidents at work.
- Retrain workers so they can cope with new technology.
- Help workers gain promotion to better jobs within the firm.

Case study

Induction training: 'My induction course at Talbot Textiles'

This was my first day at the factory. I can tell you I was pretty nervous when I walked through those factory gates. I wondered what I would be asked to do – I was scared I'd make a fool of myself. I felt better when I was shown to a room with several other new recruits – they all looked as worried as me.

I think we all felt more at ease when the Personnel Manager spoke to us and explained that we wouldn't be thrown onto the production line straight away without any training. She also explained that the purpose of the day was to introduce us to Talbot Textiles. She then told us what her job was in the firm and one or two of us asked some questions about pay and conditions.

We had a very interesting talk by the Production Manager who showed us a short film about what the firm did and how it was organised. This was followed by a talk from the Health and Safety Officer who frightened us by telling us about the sort of accidents that could occur if we didn't stick to the safety code.

After coffee we had a tour round the whole factory. This was useful because it gave us an idea of where we would fit into the organisation. We were also introduced to the people we would be working with.

After lunch we were given talks by a representative from the trade union and by a nurse from the firm's medical room. We finished up with a talk from the secretary of the firm's social club and a final discussion with the Personnel Manager.

Sue, newly appointed machinist

1 What was the purpose of the induction course?
2 How do you think Sue would benefit from the course?
3 If you were joining a new firm, what would you consider to be the most important things to be included in an induction course?

Simulation training

After her induction course, Sue spent two days in the department where she was going to work, learning about her job. She was given training on a machine very similar to the one she would be working at but it was not on the production line. The advantage of this was that it could be stopped at any stage if Sue got into difficulty. It also allowed Sue to learn each stage in the process before tackling the whole task.

Job training

After two days, Sue felt confident enough to work on the proper production line. Her supervisor kept a close watch on her and helped her whenever she made an error or was uncertain about what to do.

After a week on the production line, Sue was capable of working unsupervised, but her training did not end there. It was the policy of Talbot Textiles, to move workers around in a department so that they understood how to do a range of jobs. Each move meant more training for Sue, first on a simulator and then under supervision on the actual job. Sue enjoyed learning how to do different jobs; it made the work more interesting as well as increasing her skills.

Appraisal

Each year Sue has a meeting with her line manager to discuss how well she is doing and what her training needs are. This discussion is known as an appraisal interview (see motivation, pages 176–177).

1 What is meant by 'simulation training'?
2 Why do you think firms use simulation training before allowing new recruits to do the actual job?
3 Name another job which would involve simulation training.
4 What is meant by 'on-the-job training'?
5 What are the advantages
  a for Sue,
  b for Talbot Textiles,
  of giving Sue training in a number of different jobs?
6 How might appraisal benefit
  a Sue
  b Talbot Textiles?

Apprenticeship training

An apprenticeship scheme combines practical training at the firm with more theoretical training at a College of Further Education or a University. At Talbot Textiles there are a number of different apprenticeship schemes.

Craft and technical apprentices

They mainly joined Talbot Textiles straight from school. They spend a day a week at a local College of Further Education taking National Vocational Qualifications (NVQ s). They are paid by Talbot Textiles whilst they are doing their apprenticeships.

Youth Trainees

In the last few years, Talbot Textiles has taken on a number of youth trainees. They are on a two-year course and spend up to three days a week in the factory. The rest of the time they are at the local College of Further Education. They are different from other apprentices in that they are not employees of Talbot Textiles and are paid an allowance by the government. Their training is supervised by the College, which acts as Managing Agent for the scheme.

Undergraduate apprentices

These apprentices have joined Talbot Textiles after gaining A levels or GNVQ qualifications. They spend some of their time at the factory and the remainder at the University where they are studying for Degree qualifications. Most of these apprentices are on what are known as *thick sandwich courses*. This involves blocks of one year at either the university or the firm. *Thin sandwich courses* involve shorter blocks at the university and at the firm.

Examples of sandwich courses

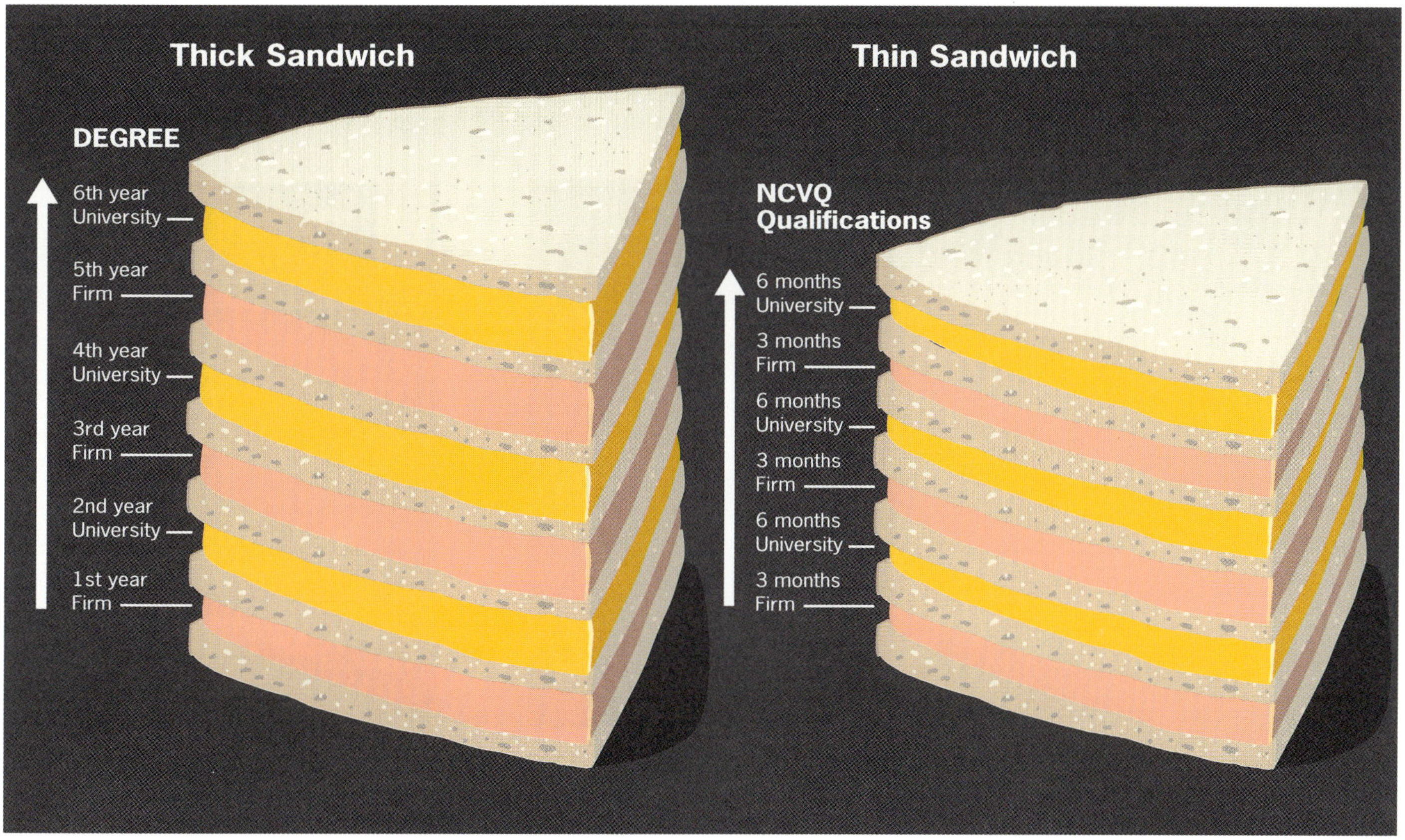

Off-the-job training and retraining

Talbot Textiles continues to train and retrain their employees throughout their working lives. They recently sent some of their top managers to learn about a new weaving machine in Germany with a view to installing it at Talbot Textiles. If they decide to buy the new machine, it will involve sending some of the workforce on training courses in Germany so that they are able to use the equipment as soon as it is installed.

The Government and training

Training is seen as important by all political parties. Businesses will only remain competitive and successful if they invest in training. The Government supports training and re-training to try to make sure that the nation has the right skills to meet future challenges.

Training and Enterprise Councils

There are over 80 local Training and Enterprise Councils (TECs) which are managed by employers and Government agencies. Their purpose is to support the needs of local businesses and to help to generate more enterprise. They receive money from the Government to operate a range of training and re-training courses for young people and adults. They also administer the Enterprise Allowance Scheme and give advice to small businesses on training, sources of finance, and expansion.

Training credits

Unemployed school leavers are guaranteed a place on this two year government scheme which provides training at Colleges of Further Education and in firms. Trainees receive a small weekly allowance during the time they are on the course. (See page 170.)

Paying the workers

Contract Hire Manager
£22-25,000 + Car

Exceptional Role in Training
£25,000 + Car + Benefits

CASUAL FARM LABOURER
required £3 per hour. Must be reliable

VACANCIES

DISPLAY ASSISTANT. To work in a town centre department store arranging window displays, internal banners, ticketing, etc. You should preferably have had some experience or have an artistic flair. Wage: £3.50 per hour + staff discount. Hours: 8.50am-5.35pm Mon-Fri. **Ref 7217.**

COOK SUPERVISOR

26 1/4 hours per week, term time only. Wage £68.83 inclusive of plus rate. Application forms available from and returnable to the

Wages and salaries

Staff workers are paid an annual salary. This is divided into twelve equal parts and normally paid directly into the employee's bank account each month by a credit transfer. The amount paid each month does not usually vary a great deal because staff workers do not tend to receive overtime or piece-rate payments (see below).

Wages are paid each week. Manual workers are sometimes paid wages in cash. The amount paid each week may vary considerably, depending upon overtime and bonus payments.

Methods of payment

There are two basic methods of paying workers:

- **Time Rate** – workers are paid according to how many hours they work.
- **Piece Rate** – workers are paid according to how much they produce.

  Some firms combine both these methods. They pay so much for a 40-hour week and a bonus if the worker produces more than a certain target level of production. This is known as a productivity agreement.
- **Commission** is a special form of piece rate payment. This is often applied to salesmen who get paid according to what they sell in the form of a percentage of the value of the sales.
- **Overtime** payment is for hours worked over and above the basic week. This is normally paid at a higher rate than the basic wage, e.g. a worker gets paid £6 per hour and 'time and a half' for overtime. This means that each hour of overtime is paid at £9 an hour.
- **Flexitime** – Staff workers are not normally paid overtime but some firms have a system of flexitime. An example of such a system would be to require staff to work a minimum 40-hour week and allow them to start and finish work at any time provided that they were at the firm between the 'core' hours of 10am-4pm. If staff work more than 40 hours in a week they are allowed time off: if they have 8 hours credit they are allowed a flexiday holiday.
- **Performance related pay** (PRP) is similar to bonus schemes but normally applies to employees on salaries. The employee and the line manager agree on the targets to be met during the year. These are reviewed at the annual appraisal interview and the employee is awarded extra pay according to how well they have performed. (See page 170.)

Exercise

1 For each of the following employees say which methods of payment you feel would be most appropriate giving reasons for your choice. Set out your answer as shown.

Methods: wage/salary, time rate/piece rate, commission, overtime, bonus, performance related pay.
Employees: Supermarket checkout operator, double-glazing salesperson, advertising executive, knitwear outworker (this is someone working for a firm from home), company accountant, delivery driver, assembly-line worker in an electronics factory

> **Example:**
>
> ***Supermarket checkout operator.***
> ***Wage - Time Rate - Overtime.***
>
> ***Reasons: Fixed hours / need longer hours for late night opening and Christmas period/difficult to apply piece rate methods.***

2 Try to find examples of jobs from advertisements in local and national newspapers which illustrate the following methods of payment: salary, wage, time rate, piece rate, commission, bonus.

3 Put the following statements under the headings of *time rate* and *piece rate* depending upon which one you feel they refer to:

- Difficult to apply to jobs where each person's output is difficult to measure.
- Can be applied to almost any job.
- More suited to production of a good than a service.
- Gives an incentive to workers to produce as much as they can.
- Workers may waste time because they get paid whether they produce or not.
- May lead to poor workmanship and the need for a great deal of quality control because workers are tempted to work too quickly.

4 Josh gets paid £5 an hour as a machine operator. His basic week is 40 hours and he gets time and a half for any work done on top of this.

a How much does he get paid in a normal week?
b How much would he get paid if he worked 45 hours in a week?
c How many hours overtime did he work if he got paid £230 last week?

5 You are a salesperson for a firm making birthday and Christmas cards. You currently get paid a regular salary but the firm wants to alter this and pay you mainly on commission. Explain whether you would be for or against this change.

The pay slip

Pay Slip: J.C. SWEETMAN LTD

NAME F R JONES	**GROSS PAY** 772.00
PAY NO. 8031670	**OVERTIME ETC**
MONTH SEPT 1995	**GROSS PAY AFTER ADJUSTMENT** 772.00
DEPT 038	**SUPN.** 50.00
N.I. NUMBER YP31-498-670	**INCOME TAX** 180.00
TAX CODE 156L	**N.I.** 25.00
PAY TO DATE 4660.11	**NET PAY**
TAX TO DATE 905.80	
SUPPN. TO DATE 335.71	
N.I. TO DATE 224.31	

Notes

- **N.I.** = National Insurance Contributions This is money paid to the Government which is used to finance such things as sickness and injury benefits.
- **SUPN** = Superannuation This is money used by the government to help pay for pensions.
- **Tax Code** This shows how much a person is allowed before they are taxed. A married man, for example, gets a higher allowance than a single person. Every worker is notified of their tax code each year by the Inland Revenue.
- **Gross Pay** is pay before deductions for National Insurance, Superannuation and Tax are made.
- **Net Pay** is what the worker actually receives after deductions are made.
- **PAYE** (Pay As You Earn) Most employees pay tax each month to the Inland Revenue. It is deducted automatically from their wages and is shown on the pay slip.

Exercise

1 Calculate F.R. Jones' net pay for September 1995.
2 What other information might be included on the pay slip?
3 What percentage of income does F.R. Jones lose in deductions?
4 What is the purpose of the deductions? How does the Government make use of the money it takes from the pay packet?

Motivating the worker

It is part of the work of the Personnel Department and all managers to try to make sure that the workforce is well motivated and that each employee is keen to do their best. A well motivated workforce helps to raise productivity and reduce the number of days' work lost through absenteeism and strikes.

How do we increase motivation?

In order to find ways of increasing motivation we need to look at the reasons why people work – what satisfaction do they get from their work?

- **Pay** Probably the most important reason for people working is the pay they receive at the end of the week or month, which can then be used for buying goods and services. The chance to earn higher pay clearly helps to motivate employees. This may be achieved through promoting members of the workforce to higher paid positions or by offering various bonus and performance related pay schemes. For example, a firm may give a bonus to workers in a particular department for increasing productivity (output per worker) by a certain amount. (See page 153.)

  Firms may also give non-monetary rewards, such as cars, houses, holidays, expenses accounts, first-class travel, and discounts on the firm's products. These are sometimes called the perks of the job.

Pay and perks are not the only satisfaction people get from work

- Workers may get satisfaction from making something well or achieving an objective, e.g. a potter may get it from making a beautiful vase, or a manager from increasing the sales in his department.
- Workers may gain status by being in positions of authority and leadership.
- Workers may enjoy the social side of work - meeting other people in 'formal' groups (departments, sections etc), or in 'informal' groups (e.g. groups of friends meeting in the canteen).

Other ways of improving motivation

- **Training schemes** which help workers to gain promotion or do more skilled work.
- Making the work more interesting by giving workers larger tasks to do, perhaps working in a group.
- Giving workers more **responsibility**.
- Involving workers in making decisions which affect their lives.
- **Profit sharing** If workers know that they are going to get a share of the profits, it will be an incentive for them to try to help the firm gain larger profits. Some firms do this by making their workers shareholders in the company and paying them partially in extra shares (a worker co-operative would be an extreme form of this).
- **Staff appraisal** Many firms have a system of annual reporting which identifies each employee's strengths and weaknesses. The report is then discussed and ways of helping the employee to be more effective are identified. (See page 170.)
- **Social facilities** Many firms have found that offering good social facilities, such as sports clubs and subsidised canteens, helps to motivate the workforce.

x

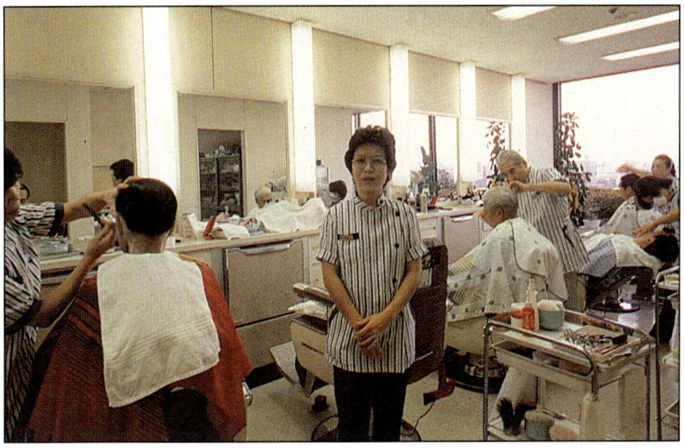

Above left: A staff canteen at an industrial plant

Above right: Japanese newspaper employees having a haircut at the on-site hairdressers

- Giving workers a feeling of 'belonging'. Large Japanese firms and some American companies place a great deal of emphasis upon loyalty to the organisation. They help to gain loyalty by looking after both the financial and non-financial needs of both their workforce and their families.
- **Employee suggestions** Employees are encouraged to suggest ways of improving production and are awarded bonuses if their ideas are successful. The Japanese idea of Kaizan (continous improvement) encourages employees to suggest better ways of doing things through regular meetings. (See Quality Circles, page 152.)

x

Exercise

You are Personnel Manager at a large manufacturing firm. Suggest ways of increasing the motivation of the following workers:

a Production-line workers with little possibility of promotion.
b A middle manager who has been doing the same job for 10 years.
c A new recruit in the Finance Department.
d A salesperson.

Summary of key words and ideas

- The **Human Resources (Personnel)** Department is concerned with the recruiting, training, promotion, and welfare of the workforce.
- **Job description** is a definition of what the job involves.
- **Job specification** is a statement of the qualities a firm is looking for to fill a vacancy.
- **Applications** for jobs may involve the completion of forms, a letter of application and a curriculum vitae (details of a person's experience, under headings).
- Taking up a post involves a **contract** which places certain legal obligations on both the firm and the person being employed.
- **Training** may involve: **induction** (an introduction to the firm), **simulation training** (learning on a simplified version of the real job), **on-the-job training** (learning whilst actually doing the job), **off-the-job training** (training courses away from the firm), **apprenticeships** (a combination of work and study at an educational institution).
- **Sandwich courses** involve blocks of work alternating with blocks of time in education.
- **Training and Enterprise Councils** (TECs) are local organisations responsible for administrating the Government's training programmes and promoting business within an area.
- **Time rate** is being paid according to the number of hours, weeks or months worked.
- **Piece rate** is being paid according to how much is produced.
- **Commission** is earnings in the form of a percentage of the sales a person makes.
- **Bonuses** are payments above the normal wage or salary when employees have exceeded their targets. They may also be special payments such as at Christmas.
- **Performance Related Pay** is an addition to the basic salary paid when the employee meets their agreed targets.
- **Motivation** is encouraging workers to perform better. This might be done through different systems of payment, by offering 'perks' such as cars, or by encouraging employees to be more interested and involved in their work.

Test questions

JOB CENTRE

POST	Trainee Accounts Clerk
FIRM	S W Brindley Engineering Ltd
DISTRICT	South Moulton
SALARY	Starting at £8500 (rising to £10500 on completion of training). Plus fringe benefits, profit sharing, and training package.
HOURS	40 hour week. Monday-Friday. Flexitime working.
TRAINING	Day and block release available, plus on the job training.
REQUIREMENTS	Minimum age 18, good general education including high grade GCSE Maths and English. A level or GNVQ Advanced preferred.
APPLICATIONS	By letter of application to Personnel Manager (S W Brindley is an Equal Opportunities Employer)

1. What is a job centre?
2. Describe two other ways in which SW Brindley could try to recruit labour.
3. Name two 'fringe benefits' the firm might offer.
4. What is meant by 'profit sharing'? What is its purpose?
5. How would 'flexitime' operate if the 'core hours' were 10 am–4 pm?
6. What is meant by,
   a. day release,
   b. block release,
   c. on-the-job training?
7. Describe two other types of training the firm might use.
8. List all the information contained in the advertisement under the headings of Job Description and Job Specification.
9. What does 'equal opportunities employer' mean?
10. Imagine you are 18 with the qualifications required for the post. Write a letter of application to SW Brindley.

Extension questions

1. Compare the likely job satisfaction of a nurse with that of a production line worker in an electronics factory.
2. Describe two ways, apart from pay, of increasing worker motivation.
3. What are the advantages and disadvantages of using,
   a. time rate,
   b. piece rate,

   as methods of paying workers?

Suggestions for coursework

1. Imagine that you are the Personnel Manager in a firm.
   a. Decide on a job vacancy.
   b. Write a job description and a job specification.
   c. Prepare an advertisement to go in a local newspaper.
   d. Make a list, in order of importance, of the qualities you will be looking for in a candidate for the job.
   e. Draw up an application form for the job.
2. For any one firm, investigate the types of training that the firm uses. Try to obtain interviews with workers who have undergone different forms of training to find out its nature and how they felt they had benefited from it.
3. **Either**, do a survey of local training schemes provided by the TEC, finding out:
   a. how they operate,
   b. what trainees like and dislike about them,
   c. the number of trainees who get taken on in full time employment, etc.

   Or,

   Do a survey of job vacancies in the local area, using newspapers, Job Centres, and the Careers Advisory Service. Find out:
   a. the type of employment being offered,
   b. the wages and salaries being paid,
   c. what type of person is required.

   Try to draw some general conclusions about job vacancies in your local area.

unit 14 Employee relations

Aims

At the end of this unit you should understand:

- The reasons for the existence of trade unions
- The different types of trade unions and professional associations.
- How trade unions are organised.
- How collective bargaining is carried out.
- The causes of conflict between workers and employers.
- The legal rights of workers and employers.

Above left: Voting in a union meeting

Above right: A union protest march outside Parliament

Right: The annual conference of the Trades Union Congress

Functions of Trade Unions

- Trade unions exist to represent the interests of employees in their negotiations with employers on *wages*, *hours of work*, *holidays*, and *conditions of work*. Workers are more powerful by combining together rather than trying to negotiate individually. The process of workers combining together to negotiate with employers is known as *collective bargaining*.

Trade unions also:

- Provide legal representation for their members over unfair dismissal, injuries at work, and issues to do with equal opportunities and employee rights.
- Support workers on strike by providing pay.
- Negotiate benefits for their members such as lower rates of insurance, discounts at particular shops and special rates of travel. Some unions have their own social and leisure facilities.
- Support training and education.
- Act as a pressure group by trying to influence the Government through sponsoring Members of Parliament and through the TUC. (See page 183.)

x

Benefits to Businesses

Most businesses find it easier to negotiate with unions rather than with many individuals. Some companies such as Nissan operate a single union agreement where all workers are represented by one union. This makes negotiations simpler than dealing separately with several different unions.

Case study

Why join a union?

Scene: Josie has recently joined the Printing Department of Talbot Textiles. She is having a coffee in the canteen with Marie. Marie has worked at Talbot Textiles for ten years.

Marie: Are you coming to the union meeting at lunchtime then?

Josie: No, I'm not a member. I can't be bothered with all that sort of thing.

Marie: You ought to join.

Josie: What for? They never do anything, do they? Besides, I'm quite happy, I don't want to go around stirring up trouble!

Marie: The union has done a lot here to improve things. And there's been just the one strike since I've been here - and that only lasted for a week.

Josie: What are all these things the union's supposed to do then?

Marie: Well, they negotiate our pay each year. I know the wages are nothing to write home about, but they would be a lot worse if we didn't join together to present our case. We'd just have to accept what the firm offered us if there was no union. They know we'd take action if we didn't get something like a reasonable deal. But pay isn't the only thing the union's concerned about. Last year they helped us get two days' extra holiday. They've improved conditions too. They helped persuade the management to get that new extractor fan installed in our area. And this new canteen was a result of a meeting between the union and the management – we do work together, you know. We're not always at each others' throats.

Josie: Well, I'm still not sure. I don't know whether I can afford it.

Marie: That's ridiculous. Look at the benefits you get. How would you pay legal fees if you were injured and had to take them to court to get compensation? Who would fight your case if they tried to dismiss you or make you redundant? I suppose you'd just accept it!

1 Make a list of all the reasons mentioned in the case study for being a union member.

2 'I know the wages are nothing to write home about, but they would be a lot worse if we didn't join together to present our case.' Marie is referring here to what is known as *collective bargaining*. Explain in your own words what collective bargaining involves and how it benefits the worker.

How trade unions are organised

In 1994 there were 9.5 million trade union members in the UK. Approximately one third of workers are members of trade unions; this proportion has declined over the past 20 years. There are 275 different unions ranging from very small unions with less than 100 members to large unions like the Transport and General Workers Union (TGWU) with over a million members. Some unions, such as the TGWU, have members from different occupations and types of work. Other unions, such as the National Union of Mineworkers (NUM), are only open to workers in a particular industry. *'white collar'* unions, such as Civil Service unions, are for non-manual workers, as opposed to *'blue-collar'* unions, such as the NUM, for manual workers. Professions such as solicitors, doctors and accountants have *Professional Associations* rather than unions; the Law Society, the British Medical Association and the Institute of Chartered Accountants are examples.

The Trades Union Congress (TUC)

Most, but not all, unions are members of the TUC. The TUC does not have the power to tell individual unions how to run their affairs, although it can advise them to take a particular course of action. The TUC, through its General Council, represents the views of its members to the Government and attempts to influence policy. The TUC also carries out research into various aspects of the trade union movement and publishes a wide range of policy documents. The TUC will, on occasions, help to settle industrial disputes - particularly disputes between unions. The TUC meets once a year for its conference to debate various motions and elect members to the General Council. The Council attempts to put the decisions made at the conference into action during the rest of the year.

People in the union

Not all unions are organised in the way shown in the diagram. Different types of unions also have different names for their officials. White collar unions have representatives rather than shop stewards. In the print unions, the local branch is called a chapel and the shop stewards are called fathers of the chapel.

Shop stewards are the elected representatives of the members in the workplace. Large firms will have several shop stewards who meet together with the convenor of the shop stewards - a type of chairman. Shop stewards are full-time employees of the firm and are not paid for their work by the union.

Depending upon the size of the union, there will be full-time, paid employees of the union who carry out the union's work at local, branch and national level. These officials may be elected by the members or appointed by the union.

The Shop Steward

Collins S

Profile: Sam Collins, Shop Steward, Talbot Textiles

I've been at Talbot Textiles for 6 years now. I joined straight from school and spent four years in the weaving shop before moving to finishing. The people I worked with in weaving persuaded me to join the union and I've got more and more involved. I've always been prepared to put my views forward and I guess that's how I got elected as a shop steward last year.

My job is to represent the views of the 30 members in my part of the factory. I also attend meetings with the convener of the shop stewards. He discusses what's been happening at branch and national level in the union. The convener also meets with the Personnel Manager at the Works Council meetings. I take all this information back to our members on the shop floor at our regular meetings.

The union has given me some training in industrial relations and this has already been useful. Just last week I helped sort out a problem to do with sick pay for one of our members with the Personnel Manager. Last month there was a problem with a change of shift working hours. This could have led to a real dispute if I hadn't got the matter settled through our Works Council.

I'm the first person the members in our section turn to if there's a problem. I try to get the matter settled before it becomes a big issue. We want to avoid industrial action if possible - that doesn't do anyone any good.

The Paid Union Official

Williams J

Profile: June Williams, full-time union official

I spent the first 10 years of my working life on the production line at a biscuit factory. There was no union when I started and conditions were terrible. Some of us joined the Transport and General Workers Union to see if we could do anything to improve matters. I suppose they elected me as their shop steward because I was prepared to say what I thought to the management.

I got really involved in the union when we had a strike for higher pay. Sometime after this I was asked if I was interested in working for the union full-time. I jumped at the opportunity and the union paid for me to go to college and attend their training course.

I find the work very interesting. My job is to get to know all I can about the local firms our members are employed in. This helps me to assist the shop stewards in obtaining the best deal for their members. I also have to know about union policy so that I can inform branch members about what's going on. I meet regularly with the conveners of the shop stewards and attend as many meetings of our members as possible. It's my job to recommend to the union that a strike becomes 'official'. I am also responsible for organising elections and ballots in our area and making sure that they are carried out according to the requirements laid down by the union.

Exercise

1 Describe a day in the life of either a shop steward or a full-time union official to show as many of their functions as possible.

2 List the functions of the person you did not choose in (**1**).

Industrial disputes

Some facts

- The UK does not have a bad strike record compared with other countries.
- 90% of industrial disputes are settled without the need for strike action.
- Many more days of work are lost through accidents, sickness, and absenteeism (unexplained absences) than through strikes.
- In 1993 the number of days lost through industrial disputes was the lowest since records began 100 years ago.

Left: An official union picket line during the 1989 dock workers' strike

Case study

Bakery Workers Threaten Strike Action

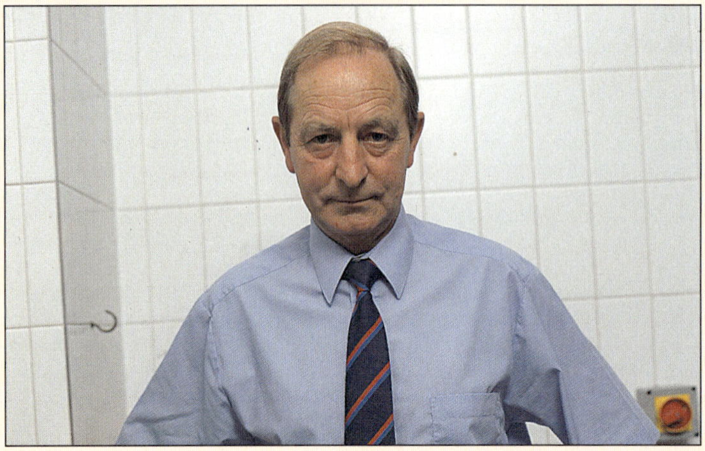

Workers at the Freshbake factory were last night threatening strike action if the management did not substantially improve their latest pay offer. Negotiations between the employers' side and the union finally broke down after four hours of discussions. Convener of shop stewards, Bob Morris, said after the meeting, 'The management just can't see sense. Their offer is totally unreasonable. The bakery made very substantial profits last year and the workers want a share of them. We're not asking for a fortune – just comparability with other workers in the industry. The pay at Freshbake has fallen well behind what other bakery workers are getting throughout the country.'

Managing Director, Pam Brown, commented, 'The offer is a very reasonable one. It gives all workers at least an 8% rise – that's a real increase of 5% when you take account of the rate of inflation. Freshbake can't afford to pay any more than this – we have our shareholders to think of too.'

1. What is the cause of the dispute?
2. What does comparability mean?
3. What is the management's case?
4. What does a real increase of 5% mean?
5. What was the rate of inflation?
6. Explain what is meant by 'we have our shareholders to think of too.'

Strike to go on

The strike at Freshbake, now in its second week, looks like continuing after workers rejected an improved pay offer from the management. A round-the-clock picket line has been maintained outside the factory and delivery drivers have refused to cross it. 'Most workers, union and non-union, have not crossed the picket line and production is at a standstill' said Bob Morris, convener. Management agreed that the strike was proving to be very costly in terms of lost output. 'We are losing something like £10,000 a day at the moment,' said Managing Director, Pam Brown. 'We needed to reduce the workforce this year and we were hoping to do it by voluntary redundancies and natural wastage, but this strike will mean some compulsory redundancies now.'

Terms Connected with Industrial Disputes

Picketing

This is when union members stand outside the workplace and try to persuade fellow workers not to go to work by handing out leaflets and explaining the reasons for the dispute. 'Crossing the picket line' means entering the factory when it is being picketed.

The law and picketing

Picketing has been a sensitive area in industrial relations during the past few years. Only peaceful picketing is allowed and fellow workers must not be intimidated by the picket line. Secondary picketing is when pickets come from workplaces not directly involved in the dispute; this is now illegal.

Redundancy

This is when workers lose their jobs because the firm needs less labour. This is different from being sacked or dismissed because of poor time keeping, failure to do the job, etc. Workers who are made redundant are entitled to compensation – the amount depends upon their current earnings and how long they have been with the firm. Voluntary redundancies are when workers accept redundancy without it being made compulsory – early retirement is an example of this.

Natural wastage

There will normally be a turnover of staff during the year with workers retiring, leaving for other jobs or taking maternity leave. A firm can reduce its labour force if these workers are not replaced by others. This is referred to as natural wastage.

Exercise

Before reading on in the case study, try to think of a solution to the dispute at Freshbake. The management have now offered 9% and cannot afford any more without something in return. The unions have reduced their claim from 12% to 11% and are determined to continue with the strike.

How the Freshbake dispute was settled

The strike went on for a further two weeks before both sides agreed to refer the matter to ACAS. This is the Government's Advisory, Conciliation and Arbitration Service. A conciliator was appointed to help settle the dispute. A conciliator is an impartial person whose job is to bring the two sides in a dispute together to try to find grounds for a settlement.

(Note In some disputes the matter is referred to arbitration. The arbitrator, or panel of arbitrators, looks into the dispute and makes a recommendation as to how it can be settled. Both sides may agree to accept the decision before the report is made.)

After more discussions, the management at Freshbake agreed to increase their offer to 10.5%. In return, the union agreed to some voluntary redundancies, a more flexible shift system and a productivity deal. The deal was accepted by the members of the union and there was a rapid return to work.

1 Suggest how the strike at Freshbake could have been avoided.
2 How was Freshbake eventually able to pay more than a 9% increase?
3 What is a productivity deal?
4 Describe how a shift system operates over 24 hours.
5 How might a flexible shift system work?

A role play

The situation Aero-Devices Ltd is a medium-sized 'high-tech' electronics firm making components for the aircraft industry. The firm has recently won a large order which it needs to meet urgently. In order to do this it wants to introduce a new system of flexible working.

The workers You are used to working a regular 40-hour week and are opposed to the plan for a new system of working. This will involve working early and late shifts as well as some weekend work.

The managers You must fulfil the order on time otherwise a large financial penalty will be imposed on you. The new shift system will help increase productivity which is vital if the deadline is to be met. You are prepared to offer normal overtime rates for weekend working but are keen to keep other wage costs as low as possible.

The independent arbitrator Your presence has been agreed to by both parties involved in the dispute. You must listen to both sides of the argument and then put forward a solution to the dispute.

The role play starts with the management announcing that the firm has won the new order and its plans for flexible working. Management explains what this involves and the reasons for it. The unions then present their reactions and suggest alternatives to the flexible working plans proposed by management.

Management reject the union proposals. Both sides agree to appoint an individual arbitrator who listens to the arguments and presents a solution.

Case study

A demarcation dispute

There are two main unions at Smith Brothers, a firm making wooden garden furniture. The Craft Union represents the skilled carpenters and joiners. The General Union represents less skilled manual workers. The skilled workers are paid more highly than the other workers.

Smith Brothers have recently been taken over by another firm. The new management have decided to revolutionise production methods by introducing new machinery which will enable the furniture to be mass produced on a flow line. The new methods involve less skill and the management proposes to abolish the distinction between craft and general workers. It is intended to pay all workers at the craft rate as they will all be doing similar jobs.

The proposal has provoked a hostile reaction from the craft workers. They have already banned all overtime working and are considering taking further action in the form of a go slow or a work to rule.

The Craft Union objects to the loss of pay differentials and fears that their members may lose jobs in the future to the general workers. They consider that custom and practice means that certain jobs are only done by their members.

The General Union is equally determined that their members will receive the same pay as the craft workers for doing identical work.

More terms connected with industrial disputes

Demarcation dispute

A dispute between two unions as to who does what work. One function of a union is to protect members' jobs and this includes the taking over of jobs by members from another union.

Go slow

Deliberately working at a slower pace. It is difficult for the management to do anything about this if workers are not being paid piece rate.

Work to rule

Working completely according to the rule book. This might involve carrying out long winded safety checks, not working in certain conditions, etc. This has the effect of slowing down production and there is again very little the management can do about it.

Differential

The difference in pay between one group of workers and another. Skilled workers may object to an 'erosion of differentials' because they expect to be paid more than less skilled workers.

Single union agreement

It is because of demarcation disputes and the difficulties involved in negotiating with several unions that some companies have introduced single union agreements. Under these agreements all workers are members of the same union.

Custom and practice

This is when something has been done in a particular way for a long period of time. Even though this is not written down anywhere it may be accepted as law in certain cases.

Lock out

This is action taken by an employer to prevent workers from entering the workplace. Employers may do this in a dispute if they feel that workers will severely disrupt production in some way.

Closed shop

Where workers have to be a member of a particular union to work at a firm. At present it looks likely that the closed shop will not be legally enforceable as it is regarded as a 'restrictive practice.'

Works council

A committee made up of representatives from the workforce, and from management, which meets regularly to discuss problems and to make suggestions as to how they might be best dealt with. This is a form of industrial democracy – allowing workers to have a say in the running of the firm.

A works council

Grievance procedure

An agreement made between the unions and the employer as to the steps to be taken in the case of industrial problems and disputes. This normally involves an agreement not to take industrial action before the matter is referred to a particular body.

No strike agreement

Sometimes in return for higher wages, a union might agree not to take strike action for a specified period of time.

Exercise

1 As a representative of the Craft Union (p 189), make a case out to an arbitrator as to why you oppose the management scheme.

2 Make a case out to an arbitrator as a representative of the General Union.

3 What decision would you make as the arbitrator in the dispute?

The legal rights of individuals at work

- As soon as a person accepts the offer of a job, there is a contract between the employer and the employee even though there may be nothing in writing.
- Employees working 8 or more hours a week are entitled to a written statement of terms and conditions within 2 months of starting a job.
- After one month's employment, the employee, if s/he wants to leave, must give at least one week's notice that they intend leaving. This may be longer if it is stated in the job contract.
- The length of notice an employer must give to an employee depends upon the length of time a person has been working at a firm. After one month, they are entitled to a minimum of one week's notice; after two years, they must be given two weeks' notice; after three years, three weeks, and so on, up to twelve weeks for twelve or more years service. The contract may specify longer periods of notice which an employee is legally entitled to.
- Employees are entitled to a written explanation if they are dismissed, if they have worked for the same employer for 2 years or more.
- Employees who have been working for a firm for a minimum of two years can appeal to an *industrial tribunal* if they feel that they have been unfairly dismissed. (The two-year rule does not apply in the case of dismissals on grounds of gender, ethnic group, trade union membership, or because the worker is pregnant.) Tribunals are set up under the guidance of ACAS and consist of a legal expert and one representative from the employer's side and one from the employee's side. The employee will be reinstated (given their job back) or offered compensation if it is found that they have been unfairly dismissed.

■ Employees who are made redundant by a firm and who have worked for them for two years or more, are entitled to a lump sum redundancy payment. The amount of this depends upon the length of time a person has been with a firm and their earnings at the time of being made redundant.

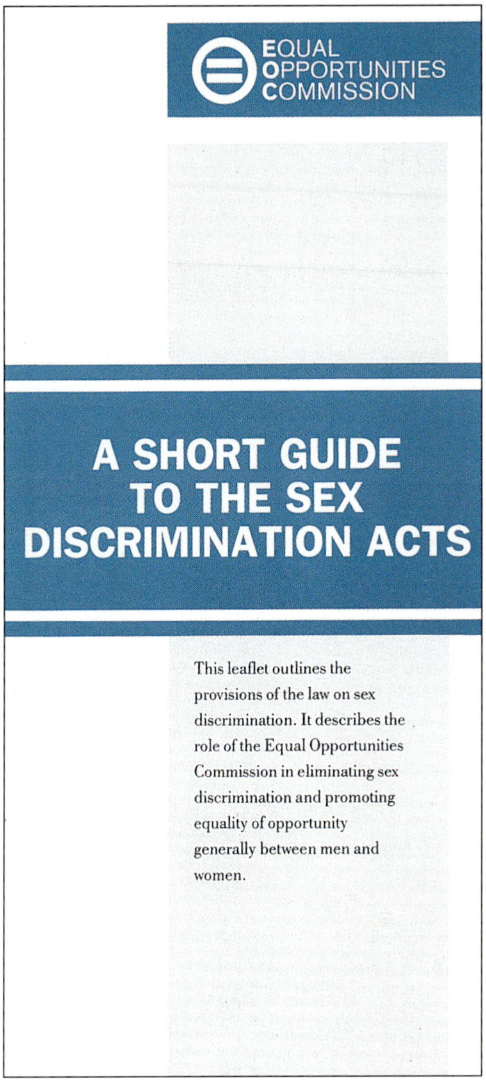

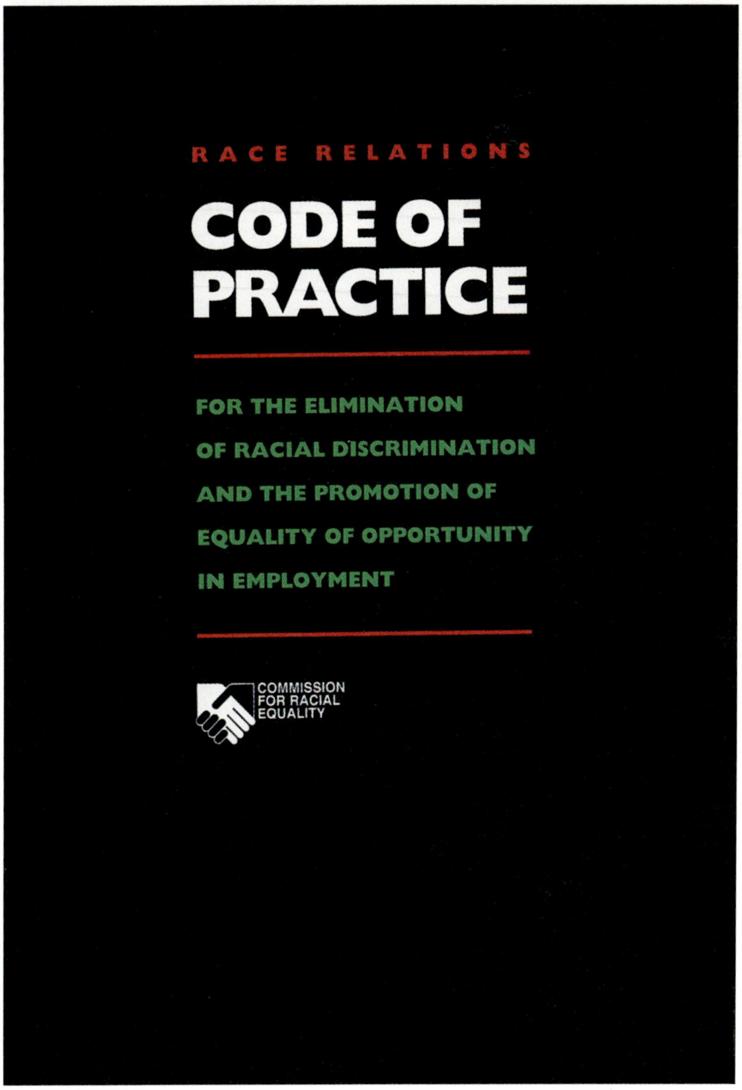

■ *Equal Opportunities* Workers are not allowed to be discriminated against on the grounds of ethnic group, gender or marital status. This applies to recruitment, pay, promotion and other conditions of service. A person who feels that they have been discriminated against can appeal to an Industrial Tribunal. They can also ask the Equal Opportunities Commission or the Commission for Racial Equality for advice. (There are currently no rules about discrimination on the grounds of age or disability.)

■ All women are entitled to maternity leave regardless of their length of service or hours of work.

(*Note* The UK is affected by some European legislation on employee rights. Consideration is currently being given to providing completely equal rights for part-time and full-time workers.)

Equal pay success for canteen girls

Women canteen workers at R.K. Factors have been awarded substantial pay increases following an Equal Opportunities Commission ruling. The women claimed parity of pay with male workers on the factory floor. The E.O.C. agreed that the work of the canteen staff was equal to production line workers. R.K. Factors had claimed that the work of the canteen workers was less skilled than the assembly workers...

1 Is working in a canteen as skilled as assembly-line work?
2 Should equal work always be rewarded by equal pay?

Summary of key words and ideas

- **Collective bargaining** When a union negotiates with an employer on behalf of a group of workers rather than each worker negotiating individually.
- **Unions** look after their members' interest in terms of pay, conditions, and job protection. They also assist in training and education and attempt to influence Government policy.
- **Shop stewards** represent the members at factory level. They are employees of the firm and are not paid by the union for their work.
- **Full-time union officials** are paid by the union for their work in organising union matters at branch and national level.
- **Unofficial strikes** are those strikes which have not received official backing from the union.
- **Pay comparability** is receiving similar pay for similar jobs.
- **Real wage** is the amount a person receives after inflation is taken into account. It is what the wage is worth in terms of the goods and services it will buy.
- Workers and shareholders both make demands on the profits of a company. The proportion each group obtains depends upon the outcome of pay bargaining each year.
- The **Advisory, Conciliation and Arbitration Service** is a Government agency set up to help settle industrial disputes. It does not have the power to enforce a settlement in a dispute but offers advice and appoints neutral conciliators and arbitrators.
- A **demarcation dispute** is a dispute between unions over who does what job.

Test questions

1 As a shop steward, make out a list of reasons why a new recruit to your firm should join the union.

2 What benefits are there to a firm of having trade unions? Why do some firms operate a 'single union agreement'?

3 What is the purpose of the TUC?

4 Briefly explain the function of each of the following:
a shop steward,
b convener of shop stewards,
c full-time union official,
d General Secretary of a union.

5 Name four causes of industrial disputes.

6 What is meant by an unofficial strike?

7 Describe how ACAS might help to settle a dispute.

8 Describe three types of industrial action a union may take, apart from strikes.

Extension questions

1 A decline in orders for the car components firm of CT Lewis means that 50 fewer workers are needed. The union accepts the need for some redundancies but has put forward four suggestions as to how the firm could avoid making all of them compulsory.
a Explain the difference between redundancy and sacking.
b What four suggestions do you think the union might put forward?

2 Explain why unions will take account of the rate of inflation when they submit their wage claims.

3 'Unions increase wages and make it more difficult for workers to get jobs'.
'Without unions, wages would be lower and more workers would lose their jobs'.
Explain both these statements.

4 'Most of the work of unions is not concerned with pay disputes'.
Explain what areas unions are engaged in apart from wage negotiations.

Suggestions for coursework

1 Follow an industrial dispute through from start to finish using newspapers, television and radio. Show how the dispute came about, how it developed and how it was settled.

2 Find out how industrial relations operate in one large firm. Try to obtain interviews with a shop steward and a personnel manager to find out their roles and how they operate during disputes. How do the firm and the unions attempt to settle disputes? What are the main causes of industrial disputes in the firm?

3 Act out the role play on page 188. Write a detailed account of the background to the dispute, the events which take place, and how it is settled.

unit 15 Marketing and selling in a large firm

Aims

At the end of this unit you should understand:

- The stages in the life cycle of a product.
- How large firms carry out market research.
- Pricing strategies.
- Advertising and sales promotion methods used by large firms.
- How the consumer is protected.

Reminder The marketing mix involves the 4 P's of Pricing, Promotion, Product, and Place. In this unit we look in more detail at some aspects of the marketing mix. (See Unit 8.)

The life cycle of a product

New products pass through a series of stages, and this is called their life cycle. This is particularly true of branded products. A brand is the trade name for a particular good, e.g. (baked beans) Heinz, Crosse and Blackwell, HP, Tesco.

Case study

Life cycle of the Scout chocolate bar

Stage 1 Research and development

Features Market research, product design and development.
Advertising and sales tests in selected areas.

Profits No sales, high fixed costs of research and development. Loss making.

Stage 2 Introduction

Features The launch of the product on the national market.
Heavy advertising and sales promotion.
Introductory special offers to tempt public into trying the product.

Profits High initial sales revenue because of novelty of new product and head start on competitors. But high fixed costs and special offers mean that an overall loss is being made.

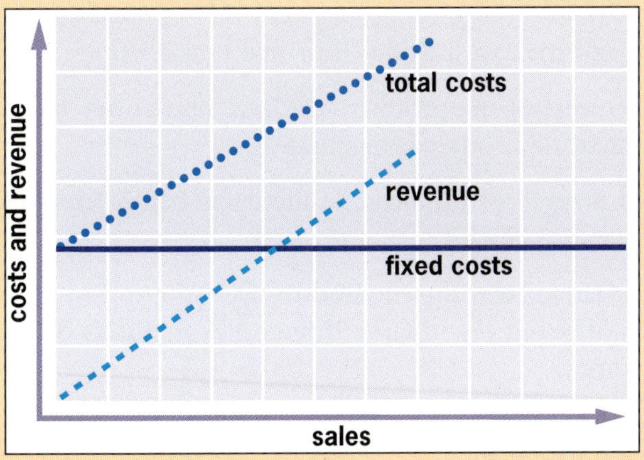

Stage 3 Growth

Features Product now being established in the market. Advertising and promotion less intense than in introductory stage, but remains important.

Profit More profit being made on each unit but total costs still not covered.

Stage 4 Maturity (saturation)

Features Product well established in market. Competitive advertising to keep product in the mind of the public.
Sales promotions to maintain market position for as long as possible.

Profits Period of maximum sales. Total costs now being covered. Overall profit being made.

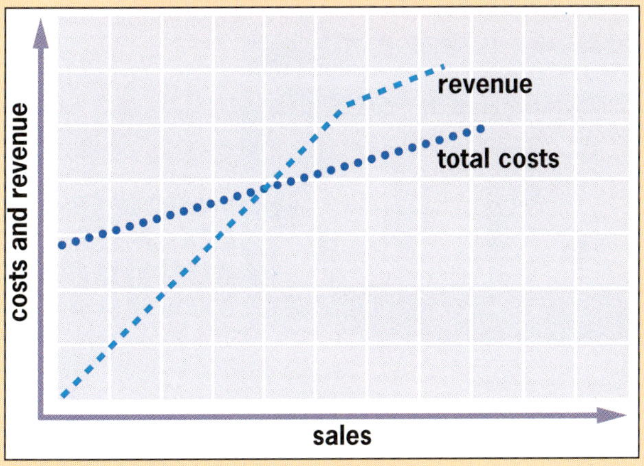

Stage 5 Decline

Features Introduction of rival brands and competitive advertising. Patent may expire allowing more competition. Changes in style and taste. Loss of market share. Advertising and sales promotion fail to regain share.

Profits Declining profits but still adding to total profits on the brand.

Stage 6 Obsolescence

Features Decision made to stop production of brand. Stocks sold off at reduced rate. Little or no advertising expenditure.

Profits Products sold at reduced profit or cost to avoid unsold stock and losses. Overall substantial profit made. Some profits invested in developing new line.

Exercise

1 Choose any product and make a list of at least five brand names.

2 How do the manufacturers of the product you have chosen try to make their brand seem different from another firm's brand?

3 Why did it take until Stage 4 of the product life cycle before an overall profit on the Scout Bar was made?

4 'Win a holiday of a lifetime' was the method of sales promotion chosen by the manufacturers of Scout Bar. Name three other methods of sales promotion that firms use.

5 Name two brands of different products which are now obsolete.

More about market research

Large firms spend a great deal of time and money on market research in order to get their product design correct. Firms may either carry out the research themselves or employ a market research agency to do the work for them. A new product line will involve a firm in considerable expenditure on new machinery, marketing, and advertising – so it must make sure that its product will sell enough to recover its costs and make a profit.

Case study

The launch of Yorkie

Background

The market for chocolate in the UK is a very competitive one and is dominated by Cadbury-Schweppes and Nestlé Rowntree. During the 1970s, sales of bars of chocolate were declining. This was partly due to a rapid rise in the price of cocoa, which made the bars more expensive, and partly due to a change in tastes. The manufacturer's response to rising cocoa prices was to make the bars thinner and this was also proving to be unpopular with consumers. It was against this background that Nestlé Rowntree decided to develop a new product line.

How Nestlé Rowntree researched the market

Nestlé Rowntree spent several years researching the market for bars of chocolate. They did this in a number of ways.

- They looked at existing data available on sales of chocolate products, market shares and consumer trends. This is known as desk research.
- They used survey information already collected by various market research agencies. These agencies maintain information on people's spending patterns, who buys what and when, what television programmes they are likely to watch, which newspapers they are likely to read, etc. This type of information enabled Nestlé Rowntree to target the groups of consumers who were most likely to buy a new line in chocolate.
- Further research was carried out on existing brands to find out why people bought them, what made them switch brands and their attitude towards advertising claims.
- Nestlé Rowntree, together with their advertising agency, J Walter Thompson, came up with five new product concepts. These were tested on four different groups of consumers. Consumers tasted each new product and looked at mock ups of the type of advertising that would go with the product image. Four out of five ideas were very rapidly rejected but there was considerable interest in the remaining product.This product was called Rations and was a thick, sustaining bar which was associated with open-air activities. The advertising image showed pictures of mountaineers and used slogans such as, 'When you've got to keep going'.

- Although market research showed that consumers liked Rations it also showed that they did not like the name. Several alternative names were thought up, together with different wrapper designs. These were again tested by market research and eventually the name of Yorkie was chosen.
- Finally, a range of advertisements was tested on consumers in order to select the right image for the product. The idea of the long-distance truck driver proved to be the most popular and this formed the basis of the advertising campaign.
- Yorkie was test marketed in certain areas of the country.

The outcome

Yorkie was launched nationwide in 1976 and proved very popular, taking 20% of the market for bars of chocolate. It still remains popular 20 years later.

Exercise

1. Explain what is meant by the following terms:
   a. target market,
   b. product concept,
   c. product image,
   d. test marketing.
2. List the methods of market research used by Nestlé Rowntree and their advertising agency and describe the type of information that each method discovered.
3. Why do you think the name 'Rations' was less popular than 'Yorkie'?
4. What product image do you think Nestlé Rowntree were trying to create by using the truck driver advertisements?
5. Using the advertising examples below to help you, make a list of the methods and images large firms use in advertising their products, e.g. sex appeal, etc.
6. Choose any three examples of advertisements and say who you feel they are targeted at, e.g. age range, male/female, rich/average income earner, etc.

Pricing strategies

x

How do businesses price their products? We looked briefly at how small businesses might set their prices in Unit 8. This section considers pricing in more detail. (See page 81.)

Market pricing

Prices in a free market economy are decided by the interaction of demand (the amount of a good or service people are prepared to buy) and supply (the quantity of goods and services firms are prepared to supply). We can show this on a diagram:

The market for petrol

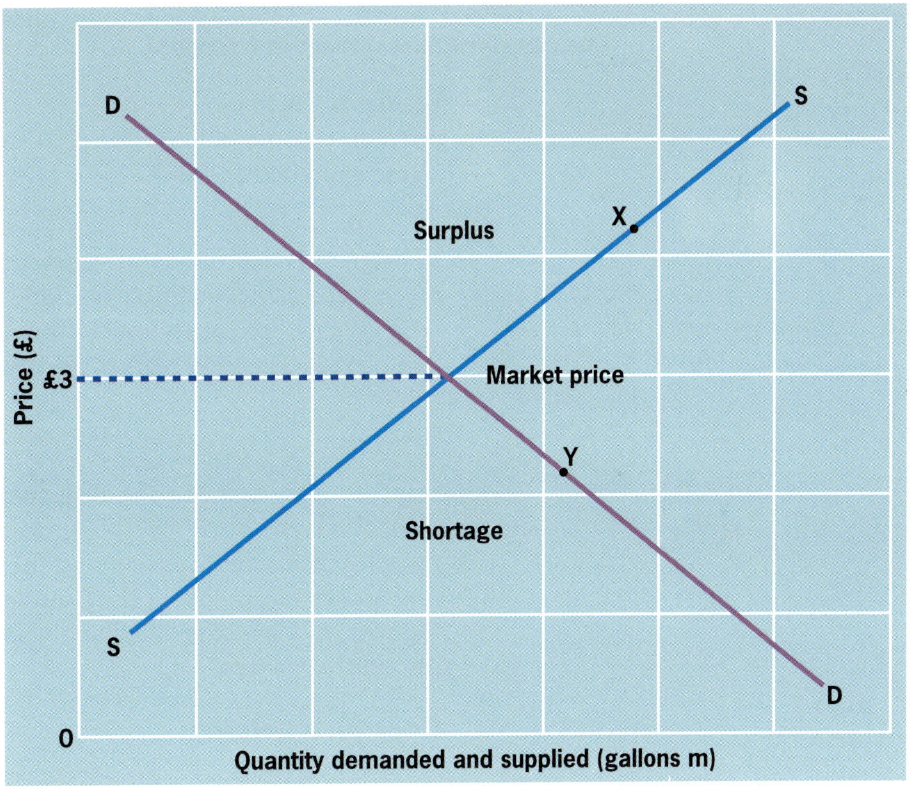

Line DD shows the demand for petrol. The higher the price, the less consumers are prepared to buy. Line SS shows the supply of petrol. The higher the price, the more producers are prepared to supply. If producers supply X million gallons of petrol, supply will exceed demand, there will be a surplus and the price will fall. If consumers want to buy Y million gallons there will be a shortage and the price will rise. Where demand and supply intersect demand will equal supply – there will not be a shortage or a surplus. This is known as the equilibrium or market price. In the diagram the market price is £3.

Generally, the greater the number of producers, the more the competition and the lower the price will be. Thus firms have to take account of market conditions when they are deciding on their prices.

Shifts in demand and supply

The market for Gamex computer game consoles

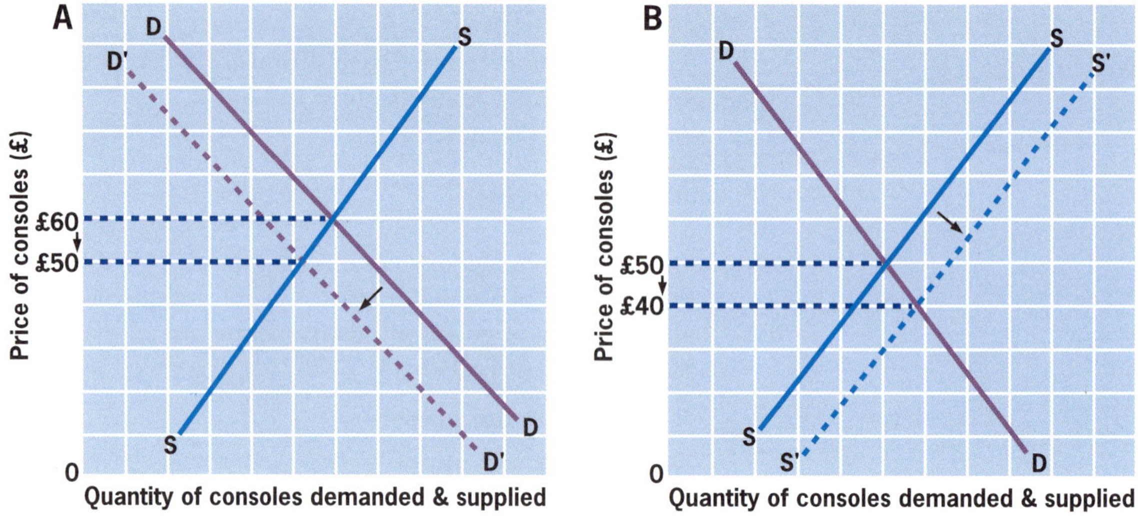

In diagram A the market price for the Gamex is £60. A rival firm cuts the price of its games console by £10. Less people are prepared to buy the Gamex and demand shifts from DD to D1D1. The market price falls to £50.

In diagram B the market price for the Gamex is £50. Gamex negotiates a lower price for its components and this reduces production costs. Gamex is now prepared to supply more consoles at each price and supply shifts from SS to S1S1. The new market price is now £40.

Exercise

Draw a supply and demand diagram for Gamex showing a market price of £60. Show the likely effects of: (**a**) a rival firm increasing the price of its console; (**b**) more firms entering the games console market; (**c**) an increase in the costs of producing the Gamex; (**d**) greater economies of scale for Gamex; (**e**) Gamex producing a very popular new game which will only run on the Gamex.

Cost-plus pricing

Cost-plus pricing takes the average cost of producing a good or service and adds on a certain percentage (called the mark-up) to arrive at a selling price.

Example: The cost of producing 1000 mountain bikes is calculated at £200,000. the average cost is £200. The producer decides on a mark up of 50%. This gives a selling price of £300.

The amount of mark-up will be determined by market conditions – what consumers are prepared to pay and what competitors are charging.

Businesses will monitor sales of their good or service, check on the prices of similar goods or services, and continue to carry out market research to find out how much consumers are prepared to pay for the product. In the light of this information businesses may well change the amount of mark-up and the selling price.

Market skimming v market penetration

Businesses have a choice of setting a high price and selling fewer goods or services but making a high profit on each item sold, or setting a low price and selling more but at a lower profit on each item.

Market skimming involves setting a high initial price. Businesses introducing new and unique products into the market might adopt this pricing strategy. Computer games are a good example of this. When a new game is produced it is often sold at a high price. Consumers who are very keen to buy the latest game will be prepared to pay this high price. Later, as this part of the market is 'skimmed' the price will be reduced to attract other consumers.

Market penetration is the opposite strategy. Here, producers deliberately charge a low price in order to get the product established in the market. Later, as the product gains a foothold in the market and gains consumer loyalty, the producer might increase the price. Eventually, the revenue from the sales must more than cover costs if the business is to make a profit. This strategy has sometimes been adopted by Japanese car companies breaking into the European market.

Loss leader is where a business prices a product below what it costs to make it. It might do this as a form of market penetration, hoping to increase the price when the product is established. The business might also hope to make the profit through the accessories sold with the product. Gamex might sell its computer game consoles at below cost but the games which are designed to run only on the Gamex will be sold at substantially above cost. Supermarkets will sometimes offer a number of products as loss leaders in order to attract customers to the store in the hope that they will do the rest of their shopping there to.

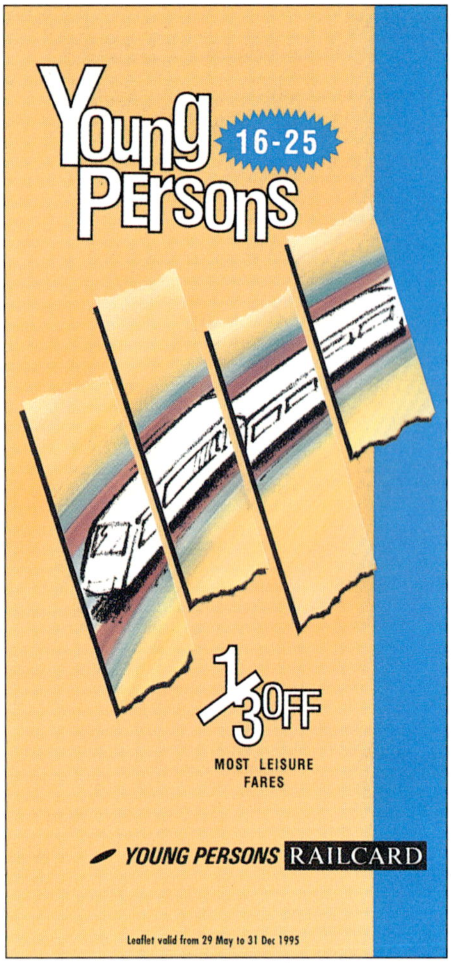

Price discrimination

A business might charge different prices to different groups of consumers for the same product or service. The railways charge different fares for the same standard class journey. Car manufacturers have charged up to 30% more for the same car bought in the UK rather than in Germany. Businesses operate price discrimination because it results in greater profits. They can only do this if they can control sales and there are groups of consumers who are prepared to pay different prices for the same product or service. Business people need to travel at certain times of the day and at short notice. They are prepared to pay higher prices for rail travel than the family who can book well in advance and can travel 'off peak'. It pays the railways to fill all their seats even if some travellers are only paying £10 for a journey for which the peak rate is £80.

Promoting the product in a large firm

In Unit 8 we looked at sales promotion in the small firm. Many of the same ideas apply to the large firm but more expensive methods of sales promotion are open to the large organisation.

Advertising Large firms will make use of national advertising in newspapers, on billboards, and on television. Firms are prepared to spend very large sums of money promoting their products. Pepsi Cola and Coca Cola annually spend several million pounds on advertising – paying well known stars large sums of money to appear in adverts, and producing elaborate and costly television and cinema advertising campaigns.

Direct mail This is a form of advertising growing in importance. Firms or their advertising agencies send 'mail shots' through the post to consumers, or pay newspapers and magazines to include them as inserts. The advertising will often include a pre-paid or freepost reply for those consumers interested in receiving more details of the product. Direct mail is commonly used by insurance companies selling their financial services and charities asking for donations.

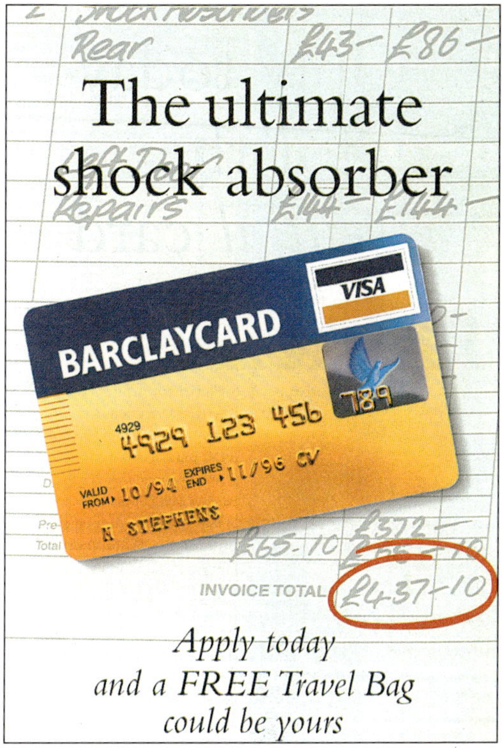

Branding Branding is a form of product discrimination, trying to make the product appear different from its competitors. (See page 82.) Brand names for washing powders include Daz, Ariel and Persil. Producers try to encourage brand loyalty to a product so that consumers will continue to purchase it in preference to the brands of rival firms. Some brands have become household names, so that people refer to a 'Biro' for a ball point pen or a 'Hoover' for a vacuum cleaner.

Different brands of crisps

Sponsorship We saw in Unit 8 how small businesses might sponsor local events and sports teams. Many large firms sponsor national events and top teams. Benetton have sponsored a motor racing team, Carling the premier football league, and Mars the London Marathon. The sponsorship is a form of advertising which helps get the company more well known.

Left: David Coulthard driving for the Williams Renault Formula One team in 1995

Case study

Coca-Cola launches £4m UK campaign

COCA-COLA has embarked on a £4 million television advertising campaign – one of the biggest ever seen in Britain – in what will be seen as a direct attack on supermarket copycat brands.

The six-week campaign, which opened last night, is part of an attempt to boost the size of the £6 billion-a-year UK soft drinks market. Fierce competition from brands such as Sainsbury's Classic Cola and Virgin Cola backed by Richard Branson, has dented sales at certain outlets.

The drinks giant denies the new advertisements are a response to the 'cola wars' that have raged in supermarkets this year, but admits to localised damage. George Bradt, consumer marketing director for Coca-Cola in the UK and Ireland, said: "We have a 108-year-old brand that is doing very nicely thank you but needs to do better. My mission, our mission, is to grow our business."

Mr Bradt is one of 30 executives recruited to key posts around the world as part of a drive by Coca-Cola to focus on regions. The "one sight, one sound, one sell" theme seen in ads during the 1970s and 1980s has given way to a tailored approach.

The company claims third-quarter sales are up 21 per cent year on year. Sales fell sharply when Sainsbury's Classic Cola was launched in April.

Coca-Cola is not the only drinks giant to embark on an expensive marketing drive. Moet et Chandon, the world's best-selling champagne label, this week launches its first advertising campaign, at a cost rumoured to be in the region of £1 million.

1. Why is Coca-Cola launching a £4 million advertising campaign?
2. What is meant by the 'cola wars'?
3. How is the new advertising campaign different from previous campaigns?
4. What strategies might Coca-Cola use in promoting its product against the competition?
5. Moet et Chandon 'the world's best-selling champagne label' launched its first ever national advertising campaign in the UK in 1994. Why have they not gone in for advertising before 1994? What reasons might there be for them launching this campaign?

Image Some companies have attempted to promote themselves through their image with the consumer. This is often associated with a concern for the environment. Producers might use re-cycled materials to make their packaging. Firms selling cosmetics and toiletries might claim that their products are not tested on animals and they do not use CFCs in their sprays.

Free gifts and special offers Consumers might be attracted to products because they contain a free gift or a special offer. Breakfast cereals are often promoted to children by containing a free gift in the package. Consumers are persuaded to purchase several of the same product in order to collect vouchers for a 'free' gift or a discount on something. Sometimes such promotions go disastrously wrong. In 1992 Hoover offered two free flights to anyone purchasing products worth over £100. Large numbers of people took up the offer and sales increased dramatically for a short while. Unfortunately for Hoover, the cost of the flights greatly outweighed the extra profits on the sales and the promotion ended up costing them £48 million!

Hoover comes clean over £48m cost of free flights fiasco

HOOVER'S free flights fiasco cost its American parent company £48 million, it was disclosed last night.

The full scale of the disastrous promotion, which Hoover initially claimed had cost £20 million, emerged with publication of the 1993 financial figures of the Iowa-based Maytag Corporation.

Hoover says that 220,000 people have flown or are booked to do so. But about 400,000 are still waiting for their flights, most of which were supposed to have been arranged by the end of this month. Members of the pressure group are flying to America today for talks with senior officials at Maytag.

Hoover said last night that it had taken on 250 extra staff to handle the promotion which offered two free flights to customers who purchased any Hoover appliance costing more than £100.

Market segmentation Large firms can often divide their consumers into a number of different groups with different life styles, levels of income, and buying habits. They are then able to 'target' the promotion of the product in different ways to each 'segment' of the market. International companies will often have different brand names and run different advertising campaigns depending upon the country where they are promoting the product.

Protecting the consumer

Advertising and techniques of sales promotion are very powerful methods of persuading people to buy goods and services. In the past, there was no legislation or body to stop firms making all types of misleading claims about their products.

Why might the adverts below not be allowed today?

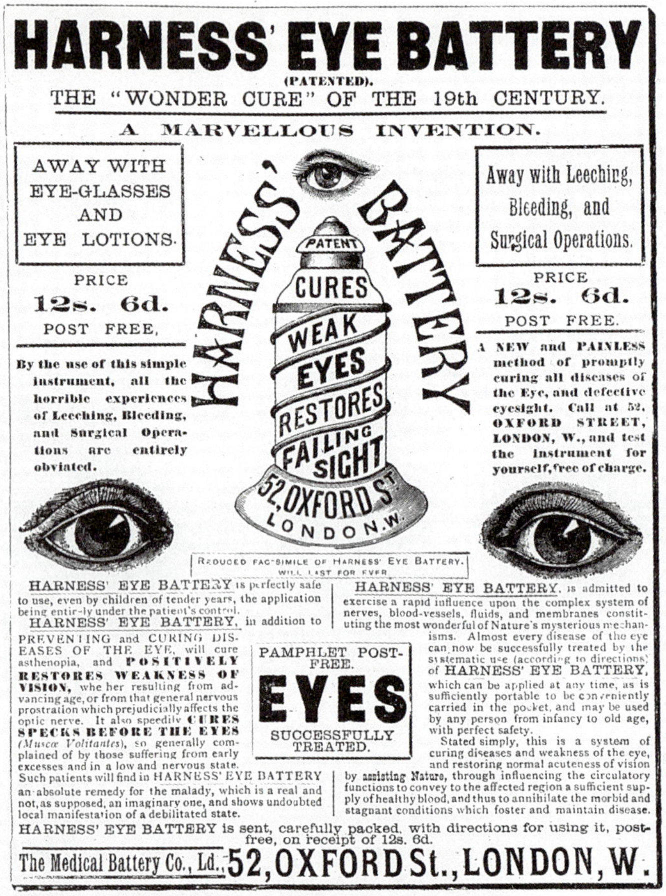

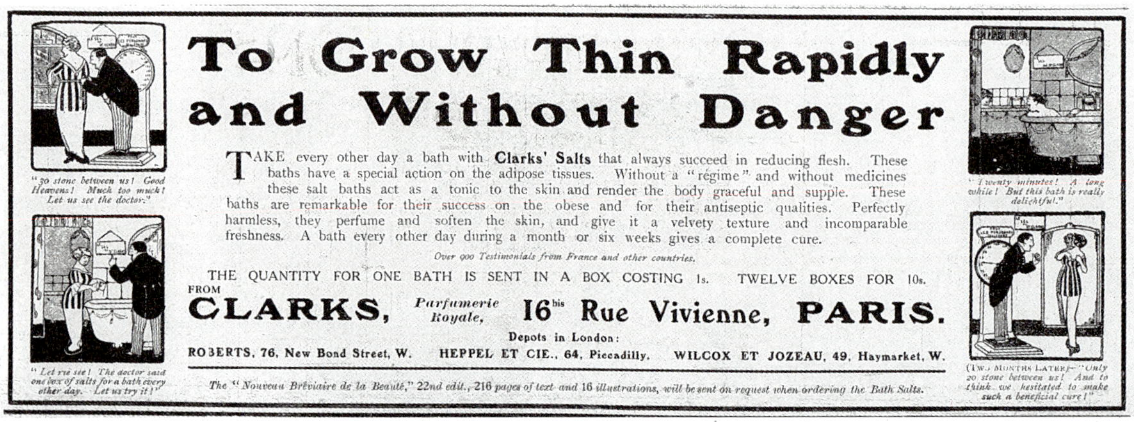

Controls on advertising

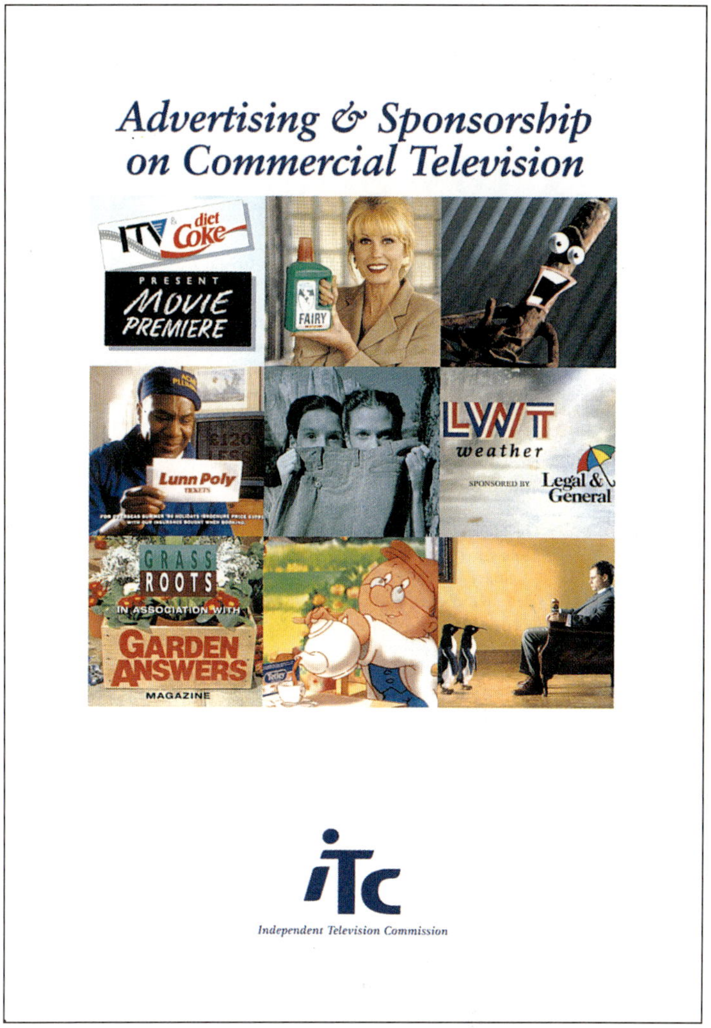

All advertising, apart from broadcast advertising, is monitored and controlled by the Advertising Standards Authority. The ASA makes sure that the British Codes of Advertising and Sales Promotion, drawn up by the advertising industry, are carried out. Advertisements are supposed to be *legal*, *decent*, *honest*, and *truthful*.

People who feel that an advertisement breaks these codes can complain to the ASA and the offending advertisement will be investigated. The ASA can recommend that an advertisement be withdrawn if it considers that it is breaking the codes.

In addition to investigating specific complaints, the ASA also monitors areas of public concern such as slimming advertisements; and provides an advice service for advertisers to check their advertisements against the codes before publication.

The Independent Television Commission (ITC) does the same for television advertising.

There is much debate as to what is regarded as being offensive. Are advertisements which show women or men in particular roles offensive? Should advertisements which are directly aimed at children be banned?

Case study

A toy shop in your living-room

THE Child Poverty Action Group last week called for television advertising of toys to be investigated and possibly more tightly regulated.

Their demands are timely, for in the lead up to Christmas, parents have been pressurised even more than usual to buy toys for their children. The largest influence is television - not just the advertisements, but also the programmes themselves, which are often based on a toy product.

Although the broadcasting authorities have taken some steps to meet these worries, current children's programmes and advertising suggest that the broadcasters' own rules are being broken in spirit, if not in the letter:

– Bought-in American cartoon series, where effective editorial control lies with the toy manufacturers, questions the basic principle of British public service broadcasting – that advertising and editorial are separate.

– The level of advertising on both TV-am and Children's ITV seems close to exceeding the ITC's guidelines.

– Despite strict regulations on children's advertising, there is still misunderstanding.

Toy advertising has been particularly important to TV-am, helping to save it from financial crisis in its first year. Earlier this year the company decided, after discussions with the ITC, to cut toy advertising as a proportion of total advertising volume from 20 per cent to 17.5 per cent next year and to 15 per cent in 1988.

However, a recent edition of the Saturday morning 'The Wide-Awake Club', the main vehicle for toy advertising, showed 14 minutes of advertising between 7.40 and 9.25 am, and, if the proceeding commercial break was included, 15 minutes in two hours. Of the 45 advertisements in that two hours, 35 were for toys. Again, on children's ITV on 4 th December between 4 pm and 5 pm, there were 7 1/2 minutes of advertisements, and of 16 advertisements, 12 were for toys or games. The ITC says there should be a maximum of seven minutes of advertising in any clock hour.

The advertisements themselves, disturbing to many parents, are, in fact, to be reviewed by the ITC's Advertising Advisory Committee when it discusses children's advertising next month.

While sex role stereotyping is not dealt with in the ITC's code on advertising standards, virtually without exception, boys are shown with action or construction toys and girls with kitchen or cuddly toys. Next month's ITC meeting will look at 'over-emotional' appeals and 'fantasy' situations in a number of American-made advertisements.

The 'toy-linked' programmes – such as 'He-Man', 'Transformers', 'My Little Pony', 'Care Bears'. and 'Mask' - stem directly from the de-regulation of broadcasting in America.

In 1969, when toy maker Mattel, together with the ABC network developed a series based on Mattel's Hot Wheels toys, the Federal Communication Commission banned it. In 1983, when toy manufacturers tried again, the FCC accepted their arguments. As a result, most other kinds of children's programming have now been driven off the screens of the American networks.

Peggy Charren, president of Action for Children's Television, calls the FCC policy 'tainted speech, not free speech'. 'There are now more than 60 shows where editorial control lies with the toy companies', she claims.

While Britain does not yet suffer such problems, the influence of the toy manufacturers, particularly the American ones, is important. Hasbro, market leader in the British toys market, had its 'Transformers' running earlier this year on TV-am. Mattel is second in the market, and currently has 'Mask' on TV-am and 'Inspector Gadget' on children's ITV.

Earlier this year the ITC warned ITV companies not to run too many toy-linked series at any one time. It also ruled that advertisements for toys related to programmes should not be shown on the same channel on the same day.

Traditionally, British TV has kept the separation between advertisement and programmes as wide apart as possible. Last year for example the ITC banned a 'My Little Pony' series because it was set to run too close to an advertising campaign. Yet many British parents, especially with an eye on American TV de-regulation, are already very concerned. That concern will grow if British TV goes down a de-regulated path.

1 Why is the Child Poverty Action Group concerned about toy advertising?
2 Why might the ITC be reluctant to reduce toy advertising?
3 How might the 'Wide Awake Club' have broken the ITC's guidelines on advertising?
4 What are toy-linked programmes? Why is there concern about these types of programmes?
5 What is meant by 'sex role stereotyping'? (2nd column, para 3). Why do many parents find this type of advertising disturbing?
6 Discuss whether or not toy-linked programmes should be banned.

Complaints considered by ASA

AUSTIN ROVER GROUP
Canley Road
Canley
Coventry, CV5 6QX

Agency: DFS Dorland Ltd
(Previous complaints upheld during last 12 months: 2)

Complaints from: Kingston; Ayr

Basis of Complaint: Two members of the public objected to a national press advertisement for the Rover 800 Series, and which included the following claim: "It's first and foremost a car to be driven. The 2.5 litre, V6 fuel-injected engine and its twenty four valves see to that. Generating full-blooded power that will take you to over 130 mph before you know it. But the real excitement comes in the way the Sterling handles that power". The complainants objected that the advertisement encouraged and condoned driving at speeds which are both dangerous and illegal. (B2.2; B.19)

Conclusion: Complaints upheld. The advertisers were advised that the copy approach went beyond what is permitted under the Codes in that the description of the speed capability of the vehicle and the presentation of the information was unduly emotive; furthermore it suggested that the driver could experience the direct effect of such speed. The advertisers were asked to ensure that future advertisements suggested neither that it was permissible nor acceptable to drive at speeds in excess of the legal limit.

BRISTOL HIPPODROME
The Centre
Bristol
BS1 4UZ

Agency: EAP

Complaint from: Portishead, Avon

Basis of Complaint: A member of the public objected to a local press advertisement for the show "Allo, Allo" which gave details of ticket bookings and which claimed "Monday night 2 for the price of 1". The complainant, who made enquiries about the offer, was advised that tickets were no longer available for Monday night. The complainant therefore questioned the continued appearance of the claim. (B.14.2).

Conclusion: The advertisers stated that when they were aware that all tickets had been sold they had been unable to stop the appearance of a further advertisement and at their request an editorial article had appeared to that effect. They added that a large number of initial reservations had limited the availability of tickets but when reservations were not later confirmed and paid for, over 20 tickets were released on the opening night and were sold at the two for one concession. The Authority considered the advertisers to have acted responsibly in the circumstances.

Exercise

Explain the background to each case and say why the complaint was either upheld or rejected by the ASA.

The Government and consumer protection

The consumer was given very little protection against unscrupulous traders in the early part of this century. There was some protection given against being sold short measures and dangerous goods but most legislation came in the 1960s and 1970s. There is now a whole range of legislation designed to protect the consumer and only the more important ones are listed below.

Acts

Sale of Goods Act, 1979

The sale of a good from one person to another is a contract between those two people. The Sales of Goods Act gives the buyer extra rights by stating that the good must be fit for the purpose it is sold for and any defects in the good must be pointed out at the time the good is sold. (This also applies to goods bought in sales at reduced prices.) Goods should stand up to normal wear; shoes, for example, should not fall to pieces the first time they are worn.

Goods must match the description of them given. A shirt, described as 100% pure cotton, must not contain any nylon (see also Trade Descriptions Act below).

The Act only covers sales from a business – private sales are not covered.

The trader cannot remove the buyer's statutory rights by displaying notices such as 'no refunds'.

Trade Descriptions Act, 1963

Traders must give an accurate description of their goods or services. Beefburgers described as '100% beef' must not contain anything else. Services should be completed to a reasonable quality in a reasonable period of time.

Unsolicited Goods and Services Act, 1971

Under this Act, a person does not have to pay for goods and services which have not been asked for. If you receive through the post a good which has not been requested, you do not need to return it or pay for it. If the good is not collected after a period of six months the good becomes yours. This period of time is reduced to 30 days if you write to the firm asking them to come and collect it.

Weights and Measures Act, 1963

It is illegal to sell goods which weigh less than the amount stated on the packaging or in an advertisement. Pre-packed goods must show both the weight of the product and the unit weight (weight per pound).

Consumer Protection Act, 1987

Prices must not be displayed in a misleading way. Sale prices which show a reduction must have been offered for sale at the higher price for 28 days in the past six months. This is to prevent a shop from artificially raising the price of a product for a day and then reducing it to make it look a real bargain in the sale. Prices must show extra charges such as VAT and delivery. (Restaurants, for example, must clearly display a menu with prices and this must include VAT and any service charges).

Consumer Credit Act, 1974

This Act covers all goods and services bought on credit up to £15,000. The main points are:

- Customers must be given full information on the credit sale, including the Annual Percentage Rate of interest (APR) being charged, the cash price of the item and the total credit price. (See Unit 7, page 66.)
- A customer who signs a credit agreement at home has 15 days to change their mind and cancel the agreement. (This is to avoid people being 'pressurised' by door-to-door salesmen into taking on agreements.) This does not apply to agreements signed on trade premises.

Fair Trading Act, 1973

This set up the Office of Fair Trading and the post of Director General of Fair Trading. The OFT does not deal with complaints from consumers but suggests new laws on trading and can take action against firms who are regarded as engaging in unfair trading practices. This might include agreements between firms on prices or restrictions on competition. The OFT can also ask the Monopolies and Mergers Commission to investigate take-overs and mergers if it feels that they are against the interest of the public.

Unfair Contract Terms Act, 1980

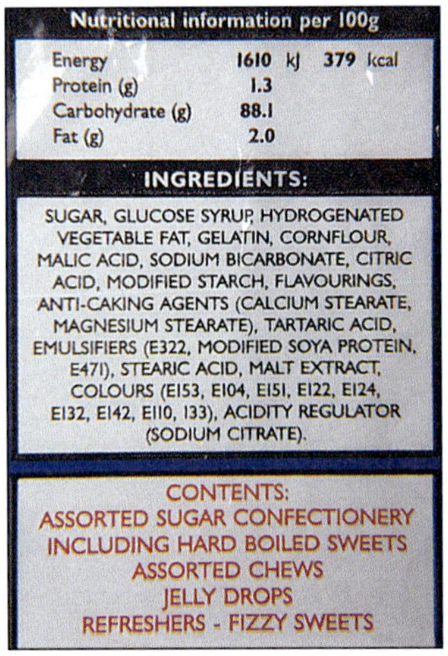

This Act prevents firms from avoiding their responsibilities by writing certain clauses into their contracts. For example, a dry cleaner cannot avoid paying compensation if items are damaged, even though he may have a sign up in his shop which states that he does not accept liability for loss or damage to items during cleaning. All disclaimers must be reasonable to be acceptable.

Food and Drugs Act, 1955

This Act makes it illegal to offer food for sale which is 'unfit for human consumption'.

(*Note* The UK is affected by European legislation governing the quality of food and what needs to be displayed on labels).

How to complain

- The seller is responsible if a good proves to be faulty or not fit for the purpose it is sold for. The customer must take the good back to the shop where it was purchased and not go to the manufacturer.
- If the seller accepts that the good is faulty s/he must offer the customer all of his money back. The customer does not have to accept a replacement good, the offer of a repair, or a credit note.
- If the shop refuses to accept responsibility, the customer may wish to seek help from the *Citizens Advice Bureau*. (See page 216.) The customer may be advised to take the matter up with the firm direct or to contact a trade organisation, if the firm is a member of one.
- If these courses of action fail to bring a satisfactory result, then the customer will need to take the matter to court. If the value of the good is less than £1000 the customer can take the matter to the *Small Claims Court*. This is much cheaper than going to the County Court and the customer can pursue his or her case without the need for a solicitor.

Exercise

Do you know your rights?

In each case below state what your rights are and name the appropriate course of action to be taken. Mention any Acts involved in the case.

1 You buy a pair of jeans in a sale. When you get them home you find that there is a fault in some of the stitching. You take them back to the shop but the manager refuses to give you your money back, pointing to a clear sign which says 'Sale goods not returnable'.
2 You receive some charity Christmas cards through the post. There is a note inside asking you to purchase them or return them to the charity within fourteen days.
3 You are over 18 and have just signed an HP agreement to buy a motorcycle. After signing the agreement in the shop you have second thoughts about it and decide to cancel the agreement. You were given the full facts about how much it would cost you at the time of signing.
4 You buy a jumper at Marks and Spencer. When you get home you find it is the wrong size.

5 You open a tin of tuna fish and find a fly inside.

Independent help for the consumer

The British Standards Institution (BSi)

This awards the Kitemark to goods which are tested and come up to British Standards. These standards lay down such things as the safety factors, quality of materials, and thickness and strength, for a large number of products. (See page 152.)

British Electrotechnical Approvals Board (BEAB)

This is similar to BSI but deals only with domestic electrical equipment such as televisions, fires, hair dryers, and electric blankets. The BEAB label shows that the item has passed the very strict standards laid down in the test. Some items, such as electric blankets, must pass the BEAB test to be sold in the UK.

Citizens Advice Bureau (CABs)

These are independent local advice centres which are staffed partly by volunteers and partly by paid employees. They give free advice on most matters including consumer problems. They will advise on the courses of action available and may take the matter up informally with the shop or firm concerned in the dispute. Some local authorities have a specialist Consumer Advice Centre which concentrates purely on consumer problems.

Trade associations

Many industries have their own trade associations which lay down codes of practice for their members. Examples of these include the Association of British Travel Agents (ABTA) and the Motor Agents Association (MAA). Consumers can make complaints to the trade association if they feel a firm is breaking their code of practice.

The Consumers Association

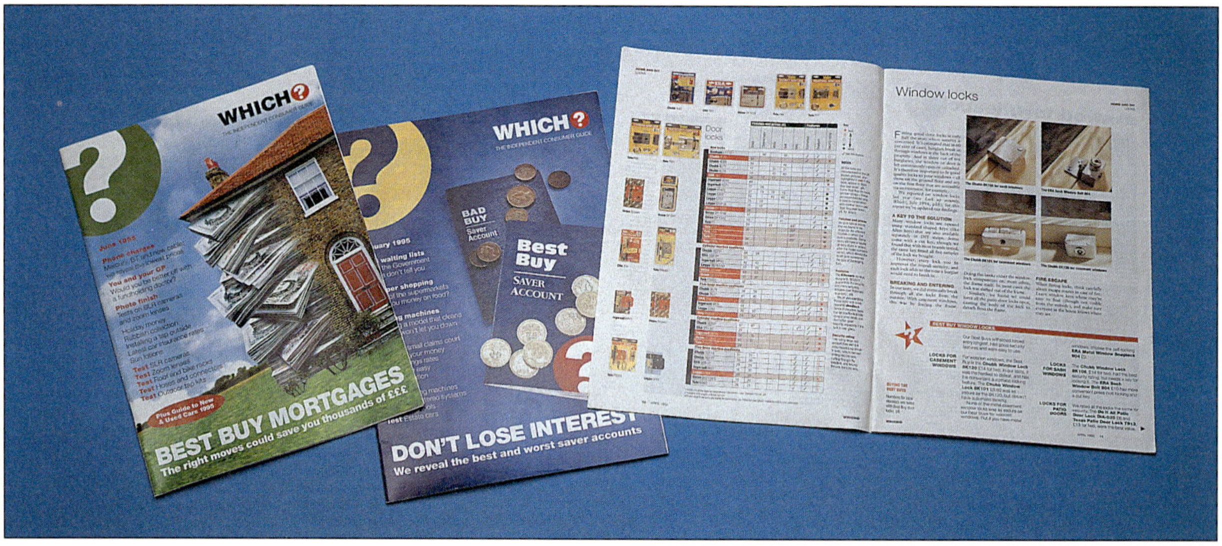

This is a completely private organisation which is financed from members' subscriptions. The Consumers Association publishes *Which?* magazine each month which includes tests on products and recommends 'Best Buys'. The Consumers Association also acts as a pressure group on firms and the Government when it feels that products are unsatisfactory or consumers have been treated unfairly.

The Trading Standards Department and Environmental Health Departments

These are maintained by local authorities to check on such matters as weights and measures, local trade practices, and public health.

Nationalised Industry Consumer Councils

These investigate complaints made by consumers about the nationalised industries. (See page 221.)

Summary of key words and ideas

- Products have a marketing **life-cycle** of research and development, introduction, growth, maturity (saturation), decline, and obsolescence.
- It is normally only in the mature stage of the cycle that total costs of production start to be covered.
- Firms use a variety of methods of **market research** including the use of existing information, as well as surveys and test marketing.
- **Target market** The people that a product is aimed at according to age, sex, and income.
- **Product concept** The idea for a new product and the image which the manufacturers are trying to create for it.
- The **market or equilibrium price** is where demand is equal to supply.
- **Cost-plus pricing** is calculated by adding a mark-up to average cost.
- **Market skimming** is charging a high initial price for a product.
- **Market penetration pricing** is charging a low initial price in order to establish the product.
- **Price discrimination** is charging different prices for the same product to different groups of consumers.
- **Brand loyalty** is encouraging consumers to keep buying the same product.
- **Market segmentation** is promoting a product in different ways to different groups of consumers.
- **Product Image** The view manufacturers and advertisers wish consumers to have of their product.
- **Consumer protection** is necessary to safeguard the buyer from being misled by advertising or sold faulty or dangerous products.
- The **ITC** supervises advertising on television through a code of practice. The **ASA** does the same for all other forms of advertising.
- The consumer is protected by legislation and independent consumer bodies.
- A sale of a good implies a contract between the seller and the buyer.

Test questions

1 Complete the following for the life cycle of a product: Research and Development.........? Growth.........? Maturity (saturation).........? Obsolescence.........?

2 Name four ways in which a firm might try to make its brand of a product appear to be different from that of a rival.

3 Your brand of soap is losing some of its share of the market to a rival. Describe two methods of product promotion you could use to try to regain your share of the market.

4 'Before the launch of their new car, Ford spent two years carefully researching the market. They looked at existing data as well as carrying out their own market research. They felt that it was very important to select the correct image for their new product and that the advertising conveyed the correct message to the consumer.'

a What is meant by the launch of a product?

b Explain how Ford would go about researching the market for a new car.

c Give an example of an image that Ford might want to create for a new car.

d Describe the ways Ford might promote the new car.

5 Describe four different ways in which the consumer is protected.

6 Advertising on television is controlled by a code of practice.

a What body attempts to see that the code of practice is carried out?

b Give an example of an advertisement that might break the code of practice.

7 'When a good is sold there is a contract between the seller and the buyer even though there may be nothing written down.'

a What does a contract mean in this case?

b Name three legal obligations which are placed on the seller.

8 Name three things a person must be told when buying a good on credit.

9 a What does the 'Kitemark' tell the consumer?

b Describe one other label a product might have to help a consumer.

Extension questions

1 Draw a supply and demand diagram for a brand of chocolate bar.

a Mark the equilibrium price.

b Show the effects of (**i**) a rise in the price of a close competitor (**ii**) an increase in the price of cocoa.

2 Mitex have produced a new trainer which is superior to all the rivals. The average costs of production are £25 per pair. The closest rival trainer is priced at £42. Suggest *three* different pricing strategies Mitex might adopt, explaining the advantages and disadvantages of each strategy.

3 'Advertising raises a firm's costs but helps to increase their profits'. Explain what this statement means.

Suggestions for coursework

1 Choose a product bought by your colleagues. Carry out market research to find out why they buy it, what makes them choose a particular brand, etc. On the basis of this information, design three new product concepts. Carry out further market research to select the one which is likely to be the most successful. Prepare for a final launch by refining your product and its advertising.

2 Prepare a quiz on consumer protection and test it on different groups of people by age and sex to find out their knowledge and understanding of their rights. Visit a Citizens Advice Bureau to find out the consumer area where they receive most requests for help.

3 Carry out consumer research on supermarket plastic carrier bags. How much do they cost? How strong/or attractive are they?

4 Record a variety of TV or radio advertisements. Analyse them in terms of when they appeared, length, method of selling etc.

5 Track a new product over a period of time. Show how it was launched, how it continued to be advertised and how its price changes over time and between shops. Evaluate the success of the advertising campaign and the pricing policy.

Section

4 The public sector

unit 16 State and local government enterprise

Aims

At the end of this unit you should understand:

- What is meant by the public sector.
- The importance of the public sector in the UK economy.
- The aims of the public sector and how they differ from the aims of the private sector.
- How the public sector is controlled and managed.
- How the public sector is financed.
- What is meant by privatisation.
- What is meant by social costs.

What is the public sector?

The public sector consists of all those businesses which are directly owned by the State (the Government) or by a local authority (a council). All other businesses are in the private sector.

(*Note* Public limited companies (PLCs), such as Barclays Bank, or Shell Oil, are in the private sector).

Exercise

Place the following business activities into two groups under the headings of *public enterprise* and *private enterprise*:

The importance of the public sector

In the UK, about 40% of all economic activity is produced by the public sector. Approximately 25% of the working population is directly employed by the State or by local authorities and many more people are indirectly employed, (e.g. private building firms constructing council houses). The public sector consists of:

- Services provided by the State (National Health Service, defence, etc.)
- Nationalised industries and public corporations (BBC, Bank of England)
- Local authority services (education, street cleaning, recreational facilities, etc.)

Aims of public enterprise

The main aim of the private sector is to make a profit; nationalised industries are also meant to make a profit, some make very large profits (as with British Gas, before it was sold to the private sector), whilst others, (such as British Steel before it was privatised) made large losses. But profit is not the main aim of the public sector. There are a variety of aims, and these are best seen by looking at the reasons for public sector enterprise.

Reasons for public sector enterprise

- To provide a service where the private sector does not make provision because it is unprofitable, e.g. sewerage, defence, uneconomic railway lines, the care of the sick and the elderly.
- To provide a basic level of service in areas which are regarded as being socially very important, e.g. education, health, fire protection.
- To control more easily an industry where the nature of the good or service means that it is in the hands of one supplier, (known as a monopoly), e.g. the Post Office.
- To assist an industry which is facing severe economic problems. This was the case with industries such as steel and coal which faced a rapid decline after 1945 because of a loss of their markets.

Extension section

The reasons for an industry being in the public sector are often political. In recent years some industries, such as gas, telecommunications, and even rubbish collection, have been put into the private sector. There is considerable argument as to whether they are best in the public or the private sector.

Case study

Should we privatise the National Health Service?

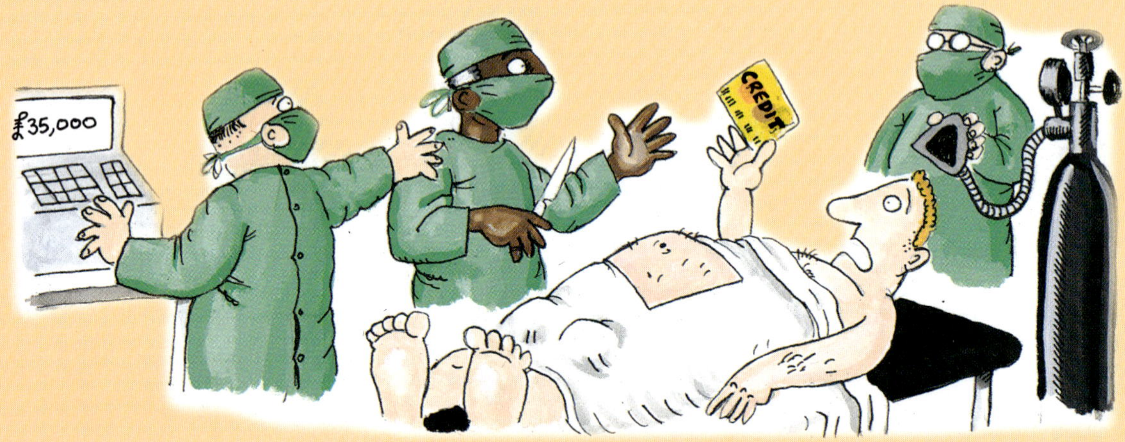

In the US there is very little public enterprise. Many of the jobs done by the public sector in the UK are carried out by the private sector in the US. There is no National Health Service in the US. The patient is charged a fee when s/he visits the doctor and all medical care has to be paid for. A stay in a hospital costs about £300 a day, and that does not include any treatment! A broken limb could cost £5000 or more and major operations could easily cost £50,000. To help pay for this, Americans take out insurance cover. This is expensive and increases with the age of the person and their medical record. As with car insurance, there is a no-claims discount for people with good medical records.

Some people in the UK would like to see a system for health care similar to that of the US. They argue that taxes would be lower and health care would be more efficient, with less waiting time and a better standard of service.

1. Make a list of arguments both for and against having only private medical care.
2. How is the National Health Service paid for in the UK?
3. How is medical care paid for in the US?
4. Do you think a totally private medical system would be cheaper or more expensive than the National Health Service? Explain your answer.
5. Would a private medical system be more efficient than a public one? Explain your answer.
6. Who might benefit and who might suffer if the National Health Service was abolished and replaced by a totally private system?

The idea of social costs

One argument often used to support public enterprise is that of social cost. Social costs are all the costs which a particular decision imposes on society. A decision to build a new stretch of motorway, for example, will not only have private costs, such as the cost of the land and the construction costs, but will also have social costs in terms of the noise and other forms of environmental damage it may inflict on the area.

It is argued that the private sector only takes account of private costs when it is making a decision, whilst the public sector is able to take account of both private and social costs. This is illustrated in the following case study.

Case study

Should the Barton line close?

Barton is a seaside town with a population of 50,000. It is at the end of a railway line linking it to the City of Runswick, 25 miles away. The road link between Barton and Runswick is poor and is less direct than the railway because there is currently no road crossing of the Barr estuary. The rail link currently makes an annual loss of £500,000 and its future is under consideration.

A group of residents, hearing that the line was under threat, formed the 'Save the Barton Line Society'. These were the points they put forward to British Rail in favour of keeping the line open:

- Closure of the line would mean increased journey times by road. Many people commute to Runswick and the increased journey time by road would make this very difficult. This could add to the already high unemployment in the area.
- Many tourists and day trippers come to Barton by rail and closure of the line would mean a decline in the tourist trade and a loss of jobs in the tourist industry.
- The cost of improving the road system would be equal to the current losses on the rail link for at least five years.

1 What are the social costs of closing the rail link?
2 Why would a private company close the line?
3 Why might British Rail keep the line open?

Financing public corporations

Public corporations obtain their finance from four main sources:

- **Grants and loans from the Government** This is financed from taxation and Government borrowing. Money is normally loaned on the basis of it being paid back with interest, but in some cases, where the public sector organisation continues to make large losses, the Government has to 'write off' outstanding loans. Money given or loaned to the public sector must be voted through Parliament.
- **Direct borrowing from the public** Nationalised industries can sell stock or borrow in other ways, from the public and financial institutions. The Government guarantees the interest and repayment.
- **Grants and loans from other public corporations** Some public corporations make large profits and these are used to help finance loss-making corporations or major investment projects.
- **Fees** These are the main source of finance for the BBC.

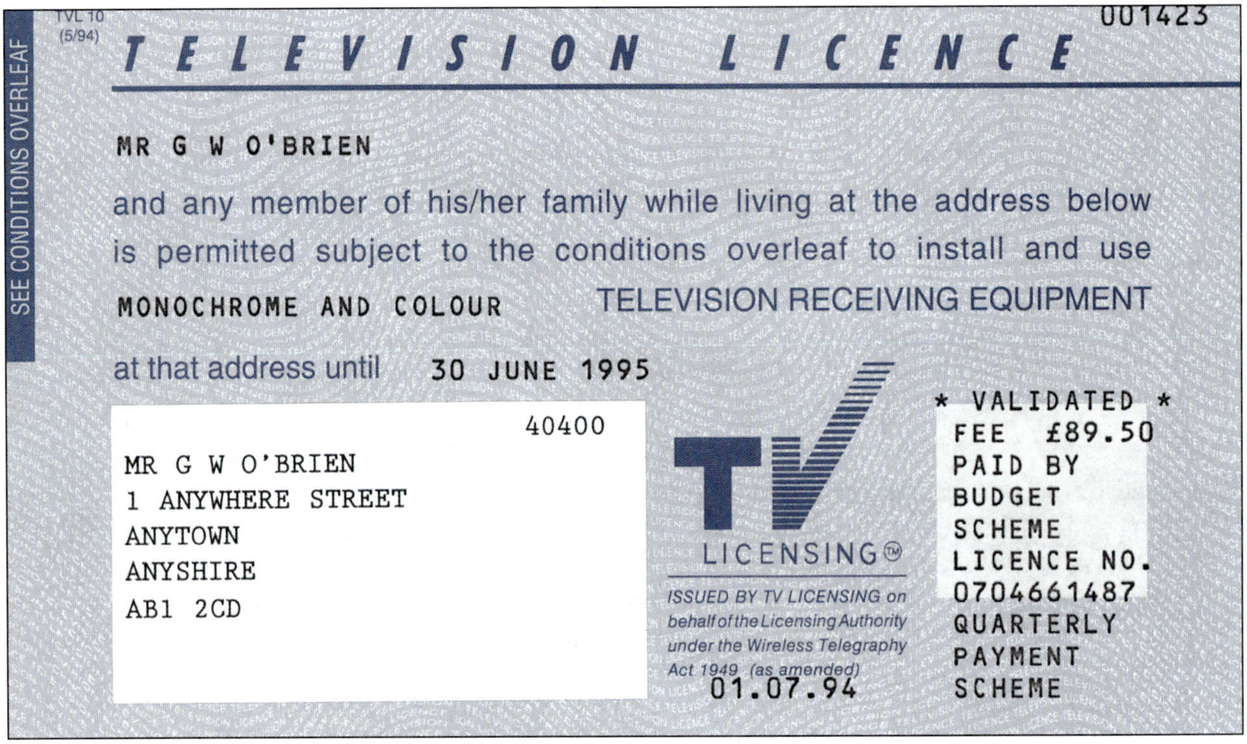
SEE CONDITIONS OVERLEAF

TVL 10
(5/94)

001423

TELEVISION LICENCE

MR G W O'BRIEN

and any member of his/her family while living at the address below is permitted subject to the conditions overleaf to install and use

MONOCHROME AND COLOUR TELEVISION RECEIVING EQUIPMENT

at that address until 30 JUNE 1995

40400

MR G W O'BRIEN
1 ANYWHERE STREET
ANYTOWN
ANYSHIRE
AB1 2CD

TV LICENSING®

ISSUED BY TV LICENSING on behalf of the Licensing Authority under the Wireless Telegraphy Act 1949 (as amended)

01.07.94

* VALIDATED *
FEE £89.50
PAID BY
BUDGET
SCHEME
LICENCE NO.
0704661487
QUARTERLY
PAYMENT
SCHEME

Privatisation

It was the policy of the Conservative Government elected in 1979 to reduce the size of the public sector.

Privatisation is the selling of a public sector enterprise to the private sector. This is normally done by inviting the public to buy shares in the enterprise which is being sold off. This was the case with British Telecom, British Gas, the Trustees Savings Bank, and British Airways.

In all these cases, the shares on offer were considerably over-subscribed – more people wanted to purchase them than there were available for sale. This caused the share price to rise rapidly when dealing opened on the Stock Exchange. Shareholders, in the case of British Telecom and British Gas, were offered vouchers to help pay bills as well as interest on their shares and the chance to make a capital gain.

At the time, the privatisation of British Gas was the largest ever flotation of a company in the UK. Over 4000 million shares were offered for sale at a price of 135p per share. The shares were well over-subscribed when applications closed in December 1986.

The case for privatisation

Privatisation is very much a political issue. The arguments put forward in favour of privatisation include:

- Industry is more efficiently managed in the private sector.
- Sale of public corporations raises money for the Government which would otherwise need to be raised through borrowing or taxation.
- The privatisation of an industry makes it more subject to competition and this helps to make it more efficient.
- Consumers are offered more choice. Telephone lines are rented from British Telecom but calls can be made using Mercury or BT.

The arguments against privatisation

- It is debatable whether the private sector is more efficient than the public sector.
- The corporations which have been sold off were all highly profitable ones and their sale has resulted in a long-term loss of revenue to the Government.
- The sale to the private sector has not increased competition. It is difficult in some industries such as water or gas supplies to introduce choice. Public monopolies have simply become private monopolies over which the Government has less control.

Local authorities

England and Wales are divided into either Counties (such as Kent and Warwickshire) or Metropolitan Districts (such as Greater Manchester). London is divided into boroughs (such as Westminster and Greenwich). Scotland and Northern Ireland have their own systems of local government.

What do local authorities do?

Local authorities must, by law, supply certain services, including education, refuse collection, and fire and police services. These are called *mandatory services*. Other services, such as leisure facilities, are at the discretion of the local authority.

Some of these services, such as refuse collection, must be *'put out to tender'*. This means that private contractors can bid against the local authority to supply the service. The result is that in some areas refuse collection and school meals are supplied by private companies.

A private refuse disposal company

Exercise

1 List all the services which are provided by your local authority.

2 Your local authority has put school meals out to tender. The contract is awarded to a private company who will produce the meals centrally and reheat them in microwave ovens in the schools. The Council will pay the company for any free meals which are provided.

- **a** List the arguments for and against awarding the contract to the private firm.
- **b** Who will gain and who will lose from the decision?

Financing local government services

- *Council Tax* calculated on the value of the property and the number of adults living there. There is a business rate for shops, offices and factories.
- *Block grants* from the Government out of central taxation.
- Borrowing by selling *local authority bonds* which carry a guaranteed fixed rate of interest.
- *Fees* from users (admission charges to leisure centres, market rents, etc.)

Case study

Wessex County Council

The diagram shows how Wessex County Council raised its finance and how this was spent last year.

1 What percentage of their revenue came from property owners?
2 What percentage of their revenue came from central government?
3 What was over half the revenue used to provide?
4 What would be provided by Social Services?
5 The Jones family have three children aged 14, 16, and 18. The eldest is at university. The Jones family live in a three-bedroom, semi-detached house and own a car.

Mr and Mrs Smith are pensioners living on their own in a four-bedroom, detached house. They do not own a car.

a What services provided by Wessex County Council would both households use?
b Which services would be used by the Jones household and not by the Smiths?
c Which services might be used by the Smiths and not by the Jones family?
d Which household would pay more in council tax?
(Explain your answer).
e In what way might the council tax system be considered unfair?

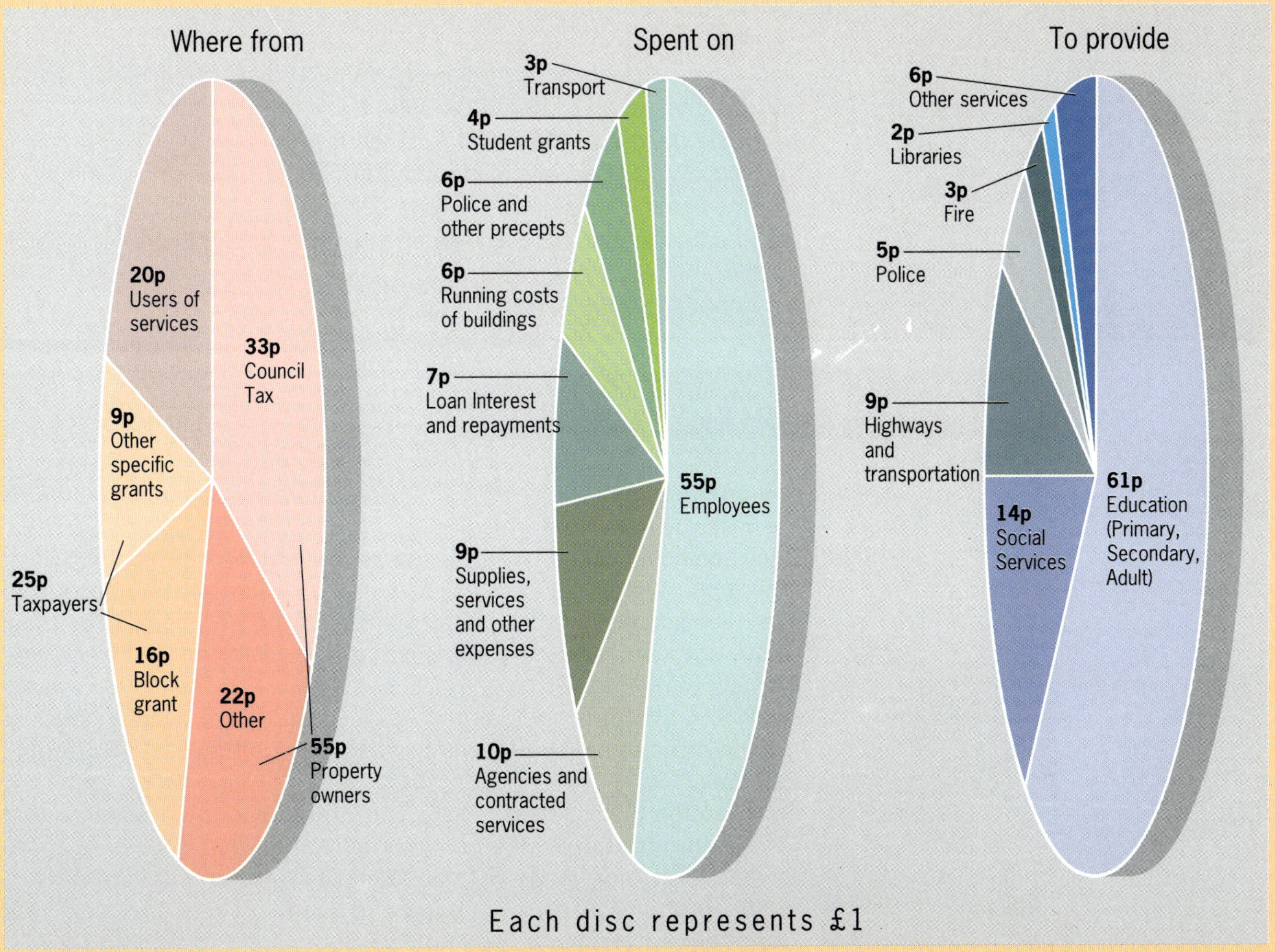

Extension case study

A new hypermarket for Barchester?

Barchester is an old and attractive city with a busy shopping area in its centre. AW Mitchell Associates, a property development company, has applied for permission to build a hypermarket on an area of land now owned by the Council. The area of land is on the outskirts of the town and is currently used for recreational purposes. They have offered either to buy the land or to rent it from the Council.

1 List all the costs and all the benefits of allowing the scheme to go ahead.

2 Say whether each of the following people would be in favour or against the scheme, giving reasons for your decision:
- **a** a shopkeeper in the centre of the city,
- **b** the chairperson of the Barchester Council finance committee,
- **c** the chairperson of the Barchester Council leisure committee,
- **d** the chairperson of the Barchester Council employment committee,
- **e** a householder living in the city.

Summary of key words and ideas

- The **public sector** consists of all those enterprises which are owned by the State or local authorities.
- **Social costs** are the costs imposed on society by a particular decision.
- The public sector has aims other than the maximisation of profit and may take account of social costs when making decisions. The private sector does not normally take account of social costs because profit is its main aim.
- Public corporations and nationalised industries are financed through grants from central government and loans and they are answerable to Parliament.
- **Privatisation** is the sale of public corporations to the private sector.
- **Local authorities** provide a range of services either directly or through private contractors and are financed through central government grants, property taxes, and charges to users.
- The public sector needs to weigh up all the costs, including social costs, and all the benefits in making decisions on particular projects.

Test questions

1 Name any three nationalised industries or public corporations.
2 Give two reasons for State ownership of industry.
3 Name any four industries which used to be in the public sector but are now in the private sector.
4 Describe two ways in which public corporations raise finance.
5 Describe three important ways in which local authorities obtain finance.
6 Name four important services provided by local authorities.
7 What are the two main factors which determine how much council tax is paid on a property?
8 The Betchington City Council is considering what to do with an area of land near the city centre which has recently become vacant. There are two main proposals:
   a a new shopping centre to be developed by a private property company;
   b for the Council to purchase the land and build a leisure centre and a car park.

   List the advantages and disadvantages of each proposal and say which you would vote for, giving the reasons for your decision.

Extension questions

1 Explain why the current system of council tax might be regarded as unfair and suggest an alternative method to replace it.
2 What is meant by social costs? Describe two social costs which might result from the closure of a coal pit.
3 Choose any public corporation and put the case for and against its privatisation.
4 Brunton Town Council has put the contract for maintaining its parks out to tender. A private company has submitted a tender which is less than the cost of the service provided by the Council's own parks department.
   a What is a 'tender'?
   b What are the arguments for and against having the work done by a private contractor?

Suggestions for coursework

1 Every local authority must publish information on how it raises its finance and how it spends it. Obtain copies of this information from two councils and compare their finance and expenditure. Try to explain any major variations between the two authorities.
2 Take any major new development project in your area, e.g. a shopping centre, hypermarket, leisure centre, or industrial estate. Find out as much as you can about it from the Council and local newspapers, e.g. how much it is costing and how it is being financed. Analyse the costs and benefits of the project. If you had the deciding vote on the Council, would you vote for or against the project? Explain the reasoning behind your decision.
3 The water industry was privatised into a number of separate companies owned by shareholders. Obtain the prospectus and financial details of any three water companies and compare them in terms of size, charges, profits, and dividends. Explain any conclusions you reach about the differences between them.

unit 17

The Government and business

Aims

At the end of this unit you should understand:

- How overall Government economic policy affects business.
- How particular Government measures both aid and control business.

Note Many of the ways in which Government aids and controls business are dealt with in detail in earlier units. This unit provides a summary of the large range of Government measures affecting business activity.

Government economic policy and business

The targets

The targets for Government economic policy and how much importance is given to each one depends upon which political party is in power. Most political parties would agree on the following objectives:

- A low rate of inflation (the rate at which the general level of prices is changing over a period of time).
- A low level of unemployment.
- Growth in the general level of income and wealth through a growing economy.
- A surplus of exports over imports. Exports are goods and services sold abroad. Imports are goods and services bought from overseas.

In order to try to achieve its objectives, Government has a number of *measures* at its disposal, including:

- *Changes in taxation*, both direct taxes, such as income tax, and indirect taxes, such as VAT.
- *Increasing or decreasing the amount of public expenditure* on such things as pensions, defence, and social services.
- *Increasing or decreasing the amount of money it borrows*. Government does not raise all the money it requires through taxes. The difference between its revenue from tax and the amount it spends is financed through borrowing (National Savings, Premium Bonds, etc).
- *Interest rates* Government has some influence over the cost of borrowing money. It can also influence the ease with which credit can be obtained.
- *The Exchange Rate* This is the rate at which one currency can be changed for another. The Government has some influence over the rate at which the pound can be changed for other currencies.

Taxation

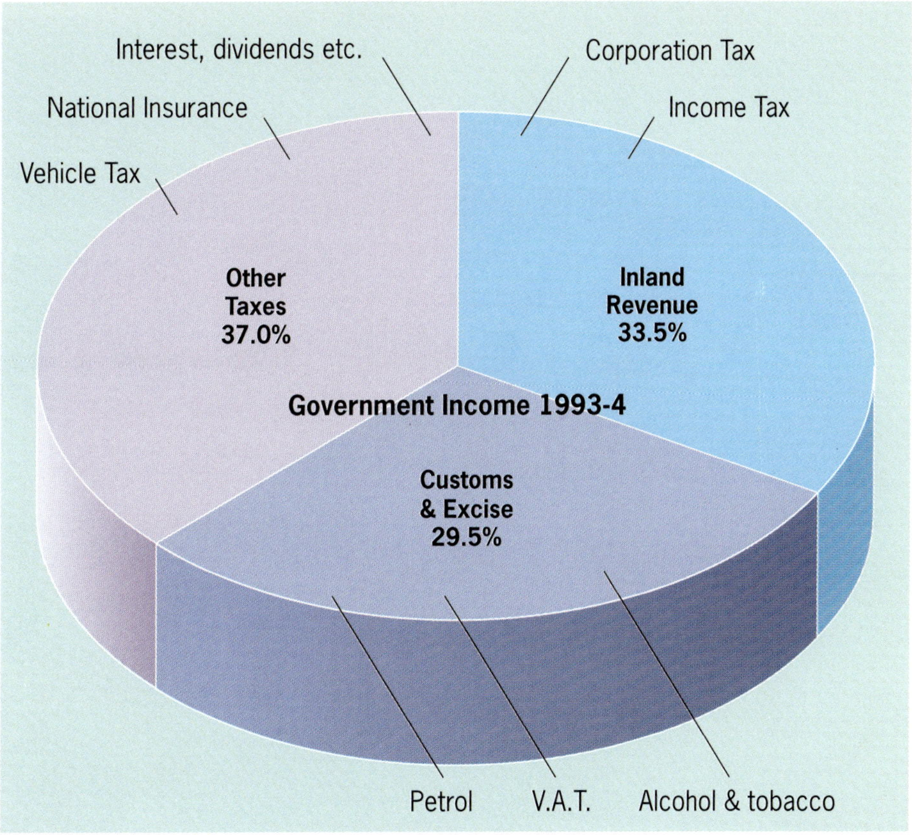

Changes in taxation have both a direct influence and an indirect influence upon business. If Government were to increase the tax on petrol, the price of petrol would rise (unless the oil companies paid all of the tax increase themselves). The direct result of this may be that less petrol is bought. The indirect effects may be that the cost of transport rises and that people have less money to spend in general (assuming that they buy some petrol and that there are no other changes in tax or expenditure). The cost of delivering goods and raw materials will increase and this will be passed on to consumers in the form of higher prices.

Kinds of tax

Income tax is paid to the Inland Revenue and is charged on all earnings, including employment, self-employment, interest, and rents.

Corporation tax is a tax paid by companies on their profits. Companies are allowed to offset tax against any losses they have made.

Value Added Tax (VAT) is a tax paid on most goods and services. It is charged at each stage in production but is passed on to the final consumer.

Customs duties are charged on goods brought into the country.

Excise duties are charged on certain products made in the UK, e.g. beer, cigarettes, whisky, petrol. About 80% of the price of a packet of 20 cigarettes and over 50% of the price of a litre of petrol is taken in tax.

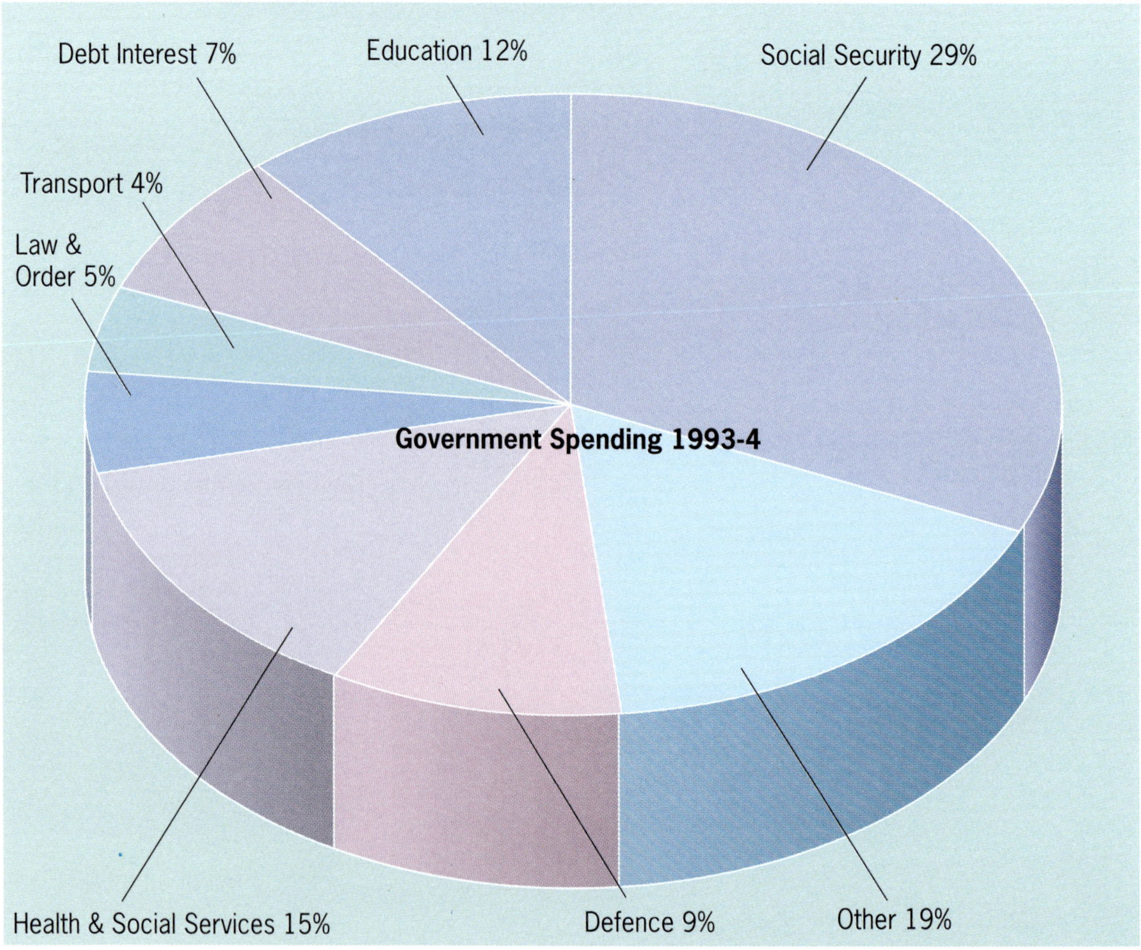

Public expenditure has both direct and indirect effects upon business:

- The level of Government spending influences the amount of money people have to spend in general and this in turn affects the demand for the goods and services produced by firms.
- Government spending may have a direct influence on particular businesses. For example, a decision to increase spending on housing will affect the building industry and those firms supplying building materials.

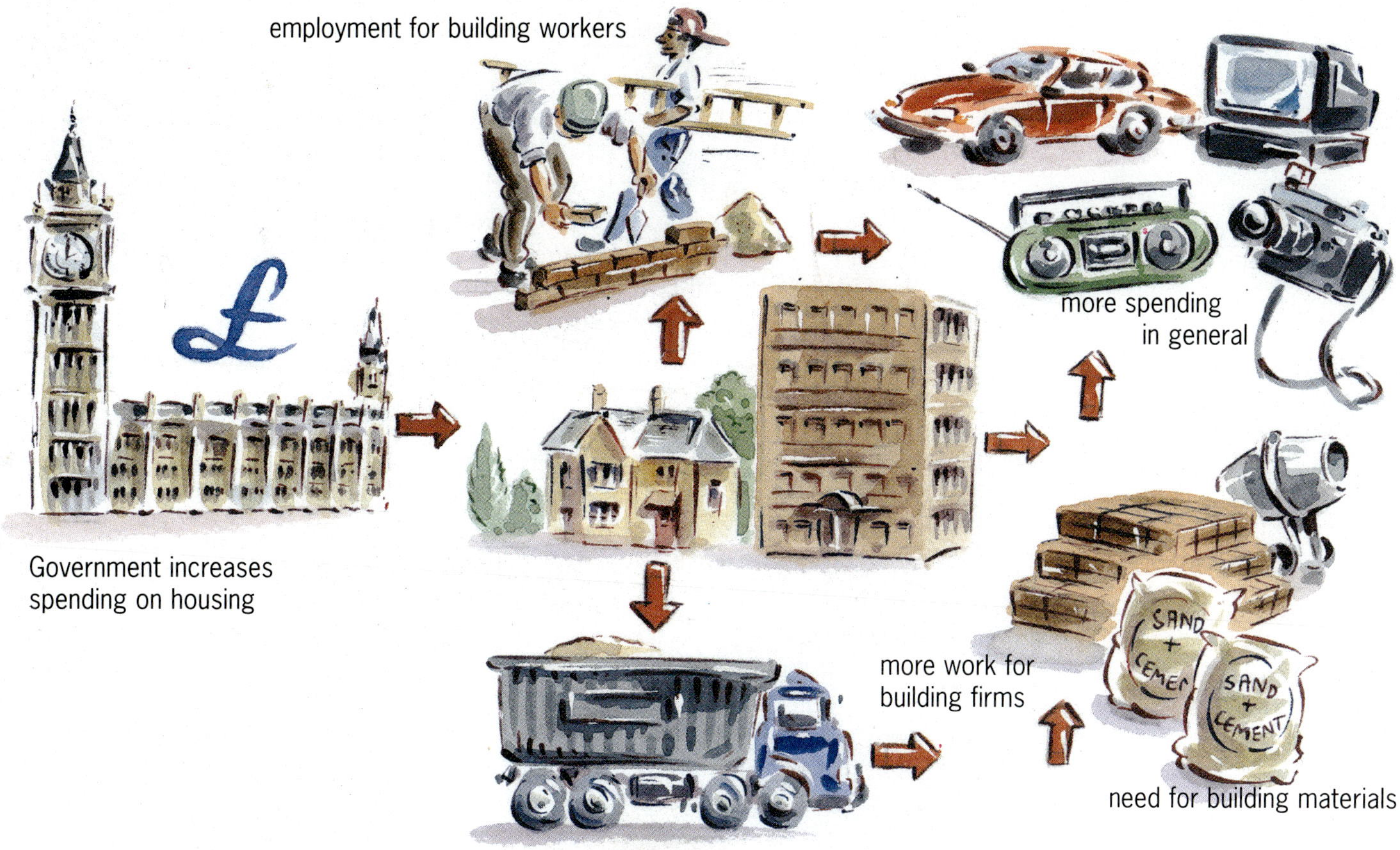

Exercise

For each situation given below, produce a diagram similar to the one above to show the possible effects of the change on businesses:

a The Government increases the excise duty on beer.
b Income tax is reduced and VAT on cars is abolished.
c Public expenditure in general is reduced and there is a particular reduction in spending on defence.
d There is a large increase in spending on books, materials and equipment in primary schools and in overall Government spending.

Interest rates

The rate of interest is the charge for borrowing money for a period of time. There are lots of different rates of interest and the charge will vary for example between bank loans, hire purchase agreements, credit card sales, and building society mortgages. The rates at which banks loan money will also vary depending upon the type of customer and the size of the loan. Large firms, requiring large loans, can often negotiate lower rates of interest than small borrowers. All these rates of interest are linked together and the Government has an influence over them. The rate of interest is very important to businesses.

Government Increases Interest Rates by 1%

Mortgage Rates up by 0.5%

Cost of Borrowing Rises

A rise in the rate of interest will mean:

- The cost of borrowing money for firms will have increased. This increases their total costs and either results in lower profits or price increases.
- Firms will be more reluctant to take on new borrowing and there may be less investment in new equipment and buildings.
- Firms will find it more difficult to expand by borrowing money.
- Consumers will find it more expensive to buy on credit; they will have to pay out more for mortgages and other loans and this will result in a general fall in the demand for goods and services.

The reverse will be true of a fall in interest rates:

- Existing loans will be cheaper, resulting in a fall in total costs.
- Firms may be encouraged to borrow money for new equipment, buildings, and expansion schemes.
- Consumers will find it cheaper to buy on credit, resulting in an increase in demand for goods and services. This effect will be further increased if the mortgage rate falls, allowing people more money to spend on things other than housing.

The exchange rate

What the £ is worth
(March '95)

New York:		
$	**1.5875**	(1.6005)
London:		
$	**1.5859**	(1.6035)
DM	**2.2171**	(2.2201)
FFr	**7.8820**	(7.8980)
SFr	**1.8459**	(1.8398)
Yen	**143.13**	(143.13)
£ Index	**84.6**	(85.0)

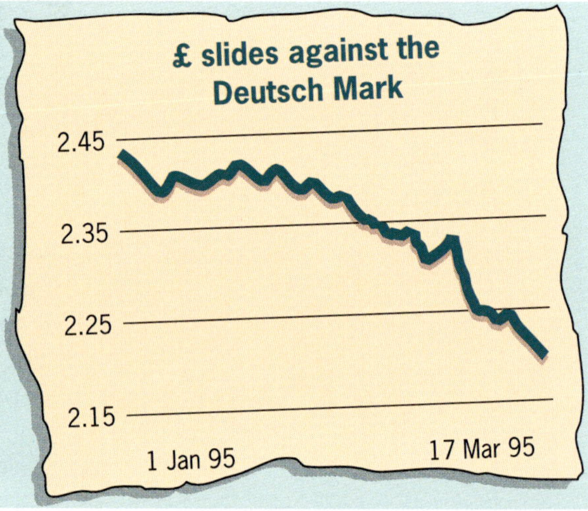

The exchange rate is the rate at which one currency can be changed for another. It is the cost of buying one currency with another. Exchange rates are constantly changing: the pound may be worth $1.35 one day and $1.30 the next. There are many factors which determine exchange rates, but the Government can influence them to some extent if it chooses.

A fall in the exchange rate, i.e. the pound is worth less in terms of dollars, francs, yen, etc, means:

- Exports (goods and services being sold abroad) become cheaper and easier to sell.
- Imports (goods and services coming into the country from abroad) become more expensive.

The reverse is true if the exchange rate rises: exports become more expensive and imports become cheaper.

Case study

The effects of a falling pound on Talbot Textiles

(Is a fall in the pound good or bad for British business?)

After the recent fall in the pound against the dollar and most European currencies, we asked Talbot Textiles' export sales manager, Clare Kenney, whether this was good or bad for Talbot's.

'There is no easy answer to this question. We export to Europe and the USA so our products will be more competitive in those countries. This might help us sell more. But there are also costs to take into account. We import cotton from the US and some machinery from Germany. They're all going to be more expensive in the future. The falling pound does mean that competition from imports won't be so intense in the future – that's a plus factor.'

1 Explain why a fall in the price of its exports is not necessarily an advantage for Talbot Textiles.
2 Why are Talbot's costs likely to increase as a result of a fall in the pound?
3 Why will competition from imports be less intense in the future.

Inflation

Inflation means a rise in the general level of prices over a period of time. Inflation is measured by looking at an average of prices; within that average some prices are likely to be rising more rapidly than others. Inflation affects business in a number of ways:

- If prices are rising more rapidly in the UK than in other countries, it will make UK exports relatively more expensive, and therefore less attractive, and imports will be more attractive to buyers.
- Costs to the firm will rise if the price of materials is rising. The firm will need either to pass these rising costs on to the buyer or suffer a cut in profit.
- Inflation causes considerable uncertainty. If a contract is signed today for a major engineering project to be completed in two years' time, and inflation increases during that period, the firm may find that it is making a loss on the contract because its production costs have risen.
- Some types of business may benefit through inflation. Property prices, for example, often increase more rapidly than the average rate of inflation, so that those businesses concerned with the property market benefit from rapidly rising prices.
- If firms expect the price of certain materials to rise in the future, they may well be tempted to increase the quantity of stock that they are holding, knowing that it will cost them more in six months.

Health and safety

Health and safety at work is governed by the 1974 Act:

- The Act covers all places of work including factories, shops, schools, and farms.
- Employees must appoint a Health and Safety Officer to be responsible for the Act being carried out.
- Employers have a responsibility to look after the health and safety of their employees and to take steps to try to prevent accidents occurring, e.g. having guards on dangerous machinery, providing protective helmets and ear, eye, and breathing protection where the circumstances call for them.
- Employees have a responsibility to themselves and to other employees to take steps to prevent accidents occurring.
- There are specific rules for the handling of dangerous substances, such as asbestos and toxic chemicals.

Exercise

List all the dangers shown in the illustration below.

Case study

DANGER!! SPOT WELDING. WEAR SAFETY GLASSES AT ALL TIMES

Keith West, a young apprentice, who had been at the firm three months, suffered some permanent damage to his sight. With the support of his union, he took Scott Engineering to court to try to claim compensation for his injury.

The Evidence

The firm claimed that there were notices in the welding area stressing the need to wear safety glasses and that there were plenty of pairs of glasses available at the time of the accident.

The union claimed that Mr West had not been told to wear safety glasses at any stage in his induction training. His supervisor had not stressed the need to wear the glasses. A fellow worker had told Mr West, 'Nobody here bothers to wear the glasses. They're uncomfortable and get in the way'. Few of the workers did, in fact, wear the glasses and the Safety Officer had not reported this fact to the management.

1 In what way could the following people be blamed for the accident:
- **a** Keith West,
- **b** the firm,
- **c** the supervisor of Keith West,
- **d** Keith West's fellow workers,
- **e** the Safety Officer?

2 Who do you think is most responsible for the accident? Explain your answer.

Monopolies, mergers, and restrictive practices

The Government attempts to prevent businesses restricting competition or engaging in activities which are unfair to the consumer.

The Monopolies and Mergers Commission has the power to investigate firms that control 25% or more of the market for a particular good or service within the UK. They can also investigate mergers (joining together of firms) and takeovers which will result in the new firm having 25% or more of the market or the acquisition of assets worth £30 million or more. The Monopolies and Mergers Commission can make certain recommendations if it is found that the firm is acting against the public interest.

The Restrictive Practices Court can investigate cases where firms are engaging in activities which might be regarded as being unfair to the consumer. Such restrictive practices might include price rings where a group of firms agree to fix their prices, agreements on tenders (bids) for contracts, and firms agreeing to supply only particular retailers.

The Office of Fair Trading can refer businesses to both the Monopolies and Mergers Commission and to the Restrictive Practices Court.

The *European Union* has the power to investigate firms that are operating restrictive practices within the member countries. This makes it possible to take action against some multinational companies. These are firms with subsidiaries in a number of different countries.

Case study

OFT smashes price ring in road-building tenders

The Office of Fair Trading has uncovered a price fixing ring in the road-building industry. Over 200 firms were yesterday found by the Restrictive Practices Court to have been involved in rigging tenders or fixing prices for the supply of road-making materials including sand, gravel, asphalt and macadam. The customers, who are mainly county councils, may be able to sue the suppliers because of the excess costs they have incurred and because the suppliers have breached the Restrictive Practices Act.

An OFT investigation over several years discovered that prices for materials and haulage were sometimes fixed by local agreement and sometimes suppliers agreed which company would get the job and made sure that company submitted the lowest tender. In some cases minimum orders for materials were also fixed.

The firms involved have had to promise not to operate such agreements in future. If they fail to abide by the promises they will be in contempt of court and liable to fines.

1. Explain how the road-building industry was engaged in restrictive practices.
2. How might the restrictive practices benefit the road-building companies?
3. Why would the restrictive practices by the road-building firms be against the public interest?
4. What action was taken against the road-building firms?

Case study

A Happy Eater all clear for Forte

FORTE'S £190 million acquisition of the Happy Eater restaurants chain and a group of other catering and hotel businesses from Hanson Trust has been given the all clear by the Monopolies and Mergers Commission.

The MMC was called in to investigate the deal in October last year, two months after Forte took control of the former Imperial Group operations.

In addition to the 70 strong Happy Eater chain, the deal gave Forte control of five Welcome Break motorway service areas, making it the largest operator in the business, together with 30 Anchor Hotels and some 85 restaurants and inns.

The Commission was asked to pay particular attention to the implications for competition in the roadside restaurant market where the group already owned the Little Chef chain.

In its report, published yesterday two months ahead of schedule, the Commission concluded unanimously that the merger 'may be expected not to operate against the public interest.'

The Commission – which carried out a survey into motorists' eating habits as part of the investigation – concluded that although the potential for monopolistic behaviour may have increased as a result of the Happy Eater acquisition there are powerful constraints upon it. Its report points out that a high proportion of motorists are as happy to stop at a pub or other type of outlet as at the Little Chef or Happy Eater restaurants.

1 What take-over was under investigation by the Monopolies and Mergers Commission in the article?

2 Why was the proposed take-over giving cause for concern?

3 Why did the Monopolies and Mergers Commission consider that the take-over would not be against the public interest?

How Government aids and controls business: a summary

Business activity	Government measures	
Setting up	**Support** Enterprise schemes. Training schemes. Small firms service. Assisted areas. Grants. Loans. EU support.	See Unit 5
	Restraints Company and Partnership Acts. Registrar of Companies. Planning Restrictions.	See Unit 3
Employment	**Support** Training schemes. Job centres. Information.	See Unit 13
	Restraints Health and Safety at Work Act. Employment Acts. Equal opportunities. Employment contracts. Redundancy payments.	See Units 14 and 17
Employee relations	**Support** ACAS. Trade union legislation.	See Unit 14
	Restraints Unfair dismissals. Industrial tribunals.	
Marketing	**Support** Export credits Guarantee department. Trade fairs. Import restrictions. EU single market.	See Units 15 and 18
	Restraints Monopolies and Mergers Commission. Consumer Protection Acts. Restrictive Practices Act. Advertising Standards Authority. Independent Television Commission. EU regulations.	See Units 15 and 17

Note The effect of the European Union (EU) on business is discussed in Unit 18.

Summary of key words and ideas

- **Inflation** is a rise in the general level of prices over a period of time.
- If inflation is higher in the UK than in other countries it will make it more difficult to sell goods abroad, and imports will appear more attractive.
- The Government uses the level of tax and the level of public spending to influence the economy. An increase in public spending and a decrease in tax will result in increased spending by consumers.
- **Interest** is the cost of borrowing money. An increase in the rate of interest will make it more expensive to borrow and this will tend to reduce credit and hire-purchase spending.
- The **exchange rate** is the rate at which one currency can be changed for another. An increase in the exchange rate will make exports more expensive and imports relatively cheaper. A fall in the exchange rate will make it easier for firms to export, but their import costs will also rise.
- The Government both supports and restrains business activity. It supports it in terms of finance, training schemes, and helping exporting firms. It places restraint upon firms in terms of the conditions of employment, and practices which may be unfair to the consumer.
- The **Monopolies and Mergers Commission** investigates businesses which control 25% or more of the market for a good or service and can recommend action to be taken if it is found that the firm is acting against the public interest.
- The **Restrictive Practices Court** investigates business activities which are regarded as being unfair to the consumer.

Test questions

1 'One main objective of Government economic policy is to have a low rate of inflation'.

a What is meant by inflation?

b Name two other main objectives of Government economic policy besides low inflation.

c What problems could a high level of inflation cause for a business?

2 The Government decides to abolish VAT on household electrical goods made in the UK.

a What is VAT?

b Describe two possible results of this action.

c Why might the Government take this action?

3 The Government announces that it intends to increase its spending on road-building by £300 million.

a Describe two direct effects that this will have upon the road-building industry.

b Describe what the indirect effect of this might be on the whole economy (assuming that the Government does not make any other changes).

4 'Interest Rate rises by 2%'.
   a What is meant by an interest rate?
   b Give two reasons why this might be harmful to businesses.

5 The exchange rate of the pound against the French franc falls from 8 francs to the pound to 7 francs to the pound. How would this fall affect:
   a someone from the UK going on holiday in France,
   b a firm that exports a large part of their output to France,
   c a firm importing components from France?

6 Describe two ways in which the Government attempts to assist people who are unemployed to find another job.

7 Describe four precautions which the Health and Safety Act insists upon in a workshop.

Extension questions

1 The Monopolies and Mergers Commission can recommend measures to be taken against firms which are shown to be 'acting against the public interest'. Describe two ways in which a firm might be considered to be acting against the public interest.

2 The Restrictive Practices Court investigates unfair trade practices such as price rings and agreements on tenders.
   a What is a price ring?
   b Why might a price ring be unfair to the consumer?
   c How would agreements on tenders operate?
   d How could both price rings and tender agreements be beneficial to the firms involved in them?

Suggestions for coursework

1 The Budget is announced each year in March. Collect as many details and reports as possible of the last Budget. Describe the changes which are being made in taxation and spending and say how they might affect businesses. Try to include comments from the CBI, the TUC, and individual businesses.

2 For your school or a local business do a survey to see how the Health and Safety Act is carried out. Try to obtain an interview with the Health and Safety Officer. Say what the main causes of accidents are and what measures are taken to try to prevent them from occurring.

3 Watch out for reports of take-over bids or restrictive practices which have been referred to the Monopolies and Mergers Commission or the Office of Fair Trading. Why has the firm been referred? What was the outcome? Who benefits and who loses out as a result of the decision?

unit 18 Into the Twenty-first Century

Aims

At the end of this unit you should understand:

The factors bringing about change in the business environment;

- The European Union and the Single Market
- Increasing competition
- The 'green' issue
- Technological change

The European Union

The UK joined the European Union (previously known as the EEC) in 1973. The aim of the European Union (EU) is to promote economic and political co-operation in order to increase the wealth of the member countries. The EU has an impact on businesses in the UK:

- Funding of enterprise and research projects
- Support for agriculture
- Controls on monopolies and restrictive trade practices
- Controls on the conditions ofemployment
- Measures to protect the consumer
- Setting minimum environmental standards
- Encouraging trade between member countries

The EU headquarters in Brussels

The single market

The single market was created in 1993. The aim of the single market is to encourage trade and prosperity through the removal of trade barriers between member countries, including:

- Physical barriers (customs checkpoints and documentation)
- Customs duties
- Different regulations governing the quality of goods

The ultimate objective of the EU is to create a market where goods can be traded between member countries as if it were one large country such as the USA. One of the most controversial proposals is to have a single European currency.

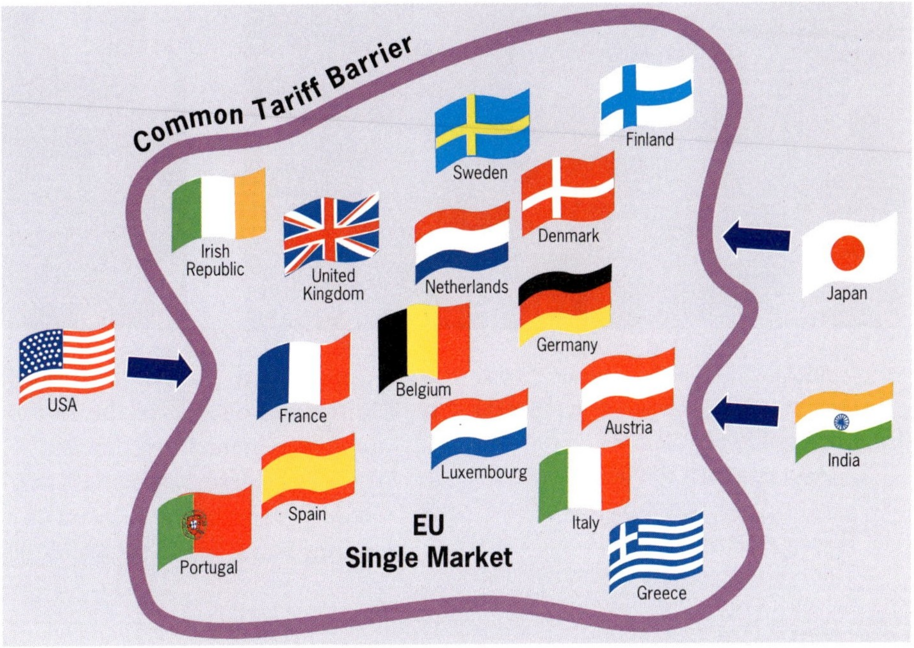

Benefits to business of the single market:

- Exporting of goods and services is made easier because of removal of barriers to trade.
- Importing of raw materials and components is also made easier.
- Greater economies of scale due to a larger market. (See page 96.) The population of the EU is currently about 350 million - substantially larger than the USA.
- Easier to set up factories and branches of a company in other EU countries.

x

Disadvantages to business of the single market

- Greater competition. Businesses cannot be protected by customs duties.
- The need to conform to EU standards for goods which might add to costs.
- Goods coming from countries outside the EU are subject to a common tariff (customs duty). EU countries are not free to negotiate their own tariffs and this may result in higher costs or inferior materials and components being purchased from EU countries.

Effects of the single market

- Increased trade between EU member countries.
- Large companies are becoming increasingly European, often with a European headquarters and a number of factories located in different EU countries. Sometimes factories will specialise to obtain economies of scale. Smith, Kline and Beecham, for example, makes different drugs in each of its European factories.

Above: The British company ICI has factories operating within other EU countries. The two factories shown here are in Belgium and the Netherlands

Below: A Japanese Honda car factory operating in the United Kingdom

- Businesses are subject to greater competition within the EU.
- Companies outside of the EU are establishing factories within the EU in order to benefit from the removal of customs duties. This is particularly true of Japanese companies such as Nissan and Honda.
- Co-operation between firms in the EU, for example Rolls Royce engines being made by Mercedes.

The changing business environment

The increasing pace of change

Technological developments, increasing competition within the EU and the rest of the world, and the quicker movement of goods, all make for an increasing pace of change for businesses. How will this influence firms in the 21st century?

- Businesses will have to adapt rapidly to changing circumstances. The organisation has to be flexible with 'flat' management structures (see page 123) which enable individuals and teams to make decisions quickly. Workers need to be multi-skilled and prepared to re-train in order to cope with new technology.
- The product life cycle (see page 196) will be shorter and businesses have to respond quickly to changing customer needs and requirements. The changeover time for switching production needs to be short, and stock kept to a minimum.
- Quality at low cost will be essential for the business to compete in increasingly competitive markets. Quality assurance (see page 152) needs to be good, waste kept to a minimum, and 'just in time' production methods used (see page 150).
- The firm will need to invest in research, product development, new technologies, and training to compete successfully in world markets.
- Businesses will be linked to each other, their customers and data bases through the 'information super highway' (see page 135). This will keep them up to date with changes and enable them to rapidly communicate decisions to all parts of the organisation.

The 'green' company

The Government and the EU have taken measures to enforce and persuade businesses to take more care with the environment. There is legislation to control firms emitting toxic waste. Consumers are persuaded to switch to lead free petrol by the government putting less tax on it.

Businesses are keen to present an environmentally 'friendly' image to their customers. They have found that this helps to promote the company (see Units 8 and 15). Major oil companies like Shell and BP demonstrate how they replace the natural habitat after they have laid a new pipe line. The water companies emphasise the measures they are taking to help clean up the coastline. The Body Shop only sells cosmetics which have not been tested on animals. Many businesses stress that they use recycled materials in their packaging.

Some businesses will not deal with countries that have repressive governments. Others put considerable amounts of money into supporting community projects and education in the UK and in developing countries.

Do businesses have a genuine concern for the environment or is it simply another form of marketing in order to increase profits? Some would argue that businesses have moral values and that they act in an ethical way. Others would argue that businesses act purely out of self-interest to increase their profits. Probably both arguments are partly true. Companies with a good public image are often the most successful. Some companies have demonstrated that their very success depends on their concern for their employees, their customers, and the environment.

Discussion questions

1 As the managing director of a major UK company making sports equipment, argue the case for or against the UK remaining a member of the EU.

2 In what ways might the single market help to:
a lower costs,
b increase costs for a manufacturing firm?

3 What types of technological change do you think will affect businesses in the 21st century?

4 Why is the pace of change for businesses increasing and how do you think businesses will respond?

5 Do businesses have a genuine concern for the environment or do they act purely out of self-interest?

Index

Note Page numbers in bold refer to entries in the summary sections at the end of each chapter.

Acknowledgements

I wish to personally acknowledge the assistance received from Peter Crane, Colin Swansborough and Hilary Thomson in preparing the text for the first edition and to Kay Hart and Lynne Butler for their help with the new edition.
I would also like to thank my family for their support during the period of writing both editions.
David R. Butler

The publishers would like to thank the following for permission to reproduce photographs and other copyright material:

Abbott Mead Vickers, BBDO Ltd/Pepsi p 204; **The Advertising Archive** p 200, 225; **Advisory Conciliation and Arbitration Service** p 241; **Bank of England** p 145 *right*; **Biffa Waste Services Ltd** p 226; **The Body Shop International Plc** p 207; **The Boots Company Ltd** p 99; **British Electrotechnical Approvals Board** p 215; **British Gas Plc** p 147; **Nicole McMahon** p 225; **The British Petroleum Co Plc** p 248 *left*; **British Standards Institute** p 152; **British Steel plc** p 147; **British Telecommunications plc** p 133 *bottom*; **Cadbury Schweppes plc** p 99; **Commission for Racial Equality** p 193; **The Consumer's Association** p 216; **Domino's Pizza Group** p 89 *top*; **Employment Service** p 162 *left*, 241; **The Environmental Picture Library/D Townend** p 144 *left*, **/Robert Brook** *right*, **/Martin Bond** p 248 *right*; **Equal Opportunities Commission** p 193; **Mary Evans Picture Library Ltd** p 208; **Format Partners Photo Library/Melanie Friend** p 181, **/Judy Harrison** p 185 *bottom*, **/Sheila Gray** p 190; **Forte plc** p 240; **S & R Greenhill** p 48, 81 *top left*, 180 *top right*, 221 *right*; **Robert Harding Picture Library Ltd** p 162 *right*, 191; **Heart of England Training and Enterprise Council** p 172; **Honda (UK) Ltd** p 246 *bottom*; **ICI** p 99, 246 *top*; **Independent Television Commission** p 209, 241; **Rob Judges** p 117 *bottom*; **Legal & General** p 99; **Lewis's, Oxford** p 89 *bottom*; **Lloyds Bank Plc** p 50; **Midlands Electricity plc** p 65; **National Association of Citizens Advice Bureaux** p 216; **The New Work Trust Co Ltd** p 241 **Garry O'Brien** p 26, 37, 89 *middle*, 94, 117 *top*, 118, 119, 153, 155, 156, 160, 184, 185 *top*, 186, 205 *bottom*, 214, 216 *bottom*, 221; **Powerstock Photo Library** p107; **Quarterdeck UK Ltd** p 135; **Rank Organisation plc** p 99; **Rex Features Ltd** p 66, 132, 133 *top*, 148 *bottom*, 177 *right*, 180 *top left* and *bottom*, 221, 244; **J Sainsbury plc** p 103, 111; **Samsung Electronics (UK) Ltd** p 133 *middle*; **Sunseeker International (Boats) Ltd** p 148 *top*; **Thames Valley Enterprise Ltd** p 49; **Trustees Savings Bank Group Plc** p 50; **Nestle Rowntree** p 198; **Tony Stone Images** p 149, 177 *left*, 247; **Unilever** p 99; **Virgin Management Ltd** p 95; **Watson Look Communications Ltd** p 81 *top right*; **Williams Grand Prix Engineering Ltd** p 206;

In some instances we may have failed to contact the copyright holder prior to printing. The publisher apologises for any inadvertent errors or omissions and if contacted will be pleased to rectify these at the earliest opportunity.

Illustrations are by:

Juliet Breese p 78, 163, 164;
Stefan Chabluk p 6, 13, 16, 22, 31, 35, 36, 37, 52, 69, 70, 71, 72, 75, 78, 81, 82, 98, 100, 1201, 105, 108, 109, 117, 118, 119, 123, 151, 155, 156, 171, 184, 185, 197, 201, 202, 203, 227, 231, 232, 245;
Cox Design Partnership p 41, 42, 44, 54, 58, 60, 61, 110, 116, 150, 163, 164, 165, 175, 234;
Paul B Davies p 19, 32, 83, 88, 96, 139, 166, 238;
Mark Dobson p 3, 21, 62, 77, 79, 80, 95, 126, 196, 197;
Simon Fell c/o 2D Agency p 1, 15, 93, 219;
Mickey Finn p 8, 10, 11, 28, 33, 34, 44, 76, 81, 102, 121, 122, 134, 137, 203, 235, 236;
Steve Noon p 17, 51, 598, 67, 72, 83, 168, 169;
Martin Shovel p 17, 42, 43, 45, 84, 129, 176, 215, 220;
Alex Tiani p 31, 127, 131, 152, 213, 214;
Harry Venning p 9, 64, 84, 120, 136, 138, 154, 176, 189, 212, 222, 230, 237;
Gary Wing p 5, 29, 40, 49, 57, 65, 85, 87, 108, 128, 129, 142, 143, 146, 199, 223, 228, 233;

Cover photograph by **Ian Pillinger**

Oxford University Press, Great Clarendon Street, Oxford OX2 6DP

Oxford New York
Athens Auckland Bangkok Bogotá Buenos Aires
Calcutta Cape Town Chennai Dar es Salaam Delhi
Florence Hong Kong Istanbul Karachi Kuala Lumpur
Madrid Melbourne Mexico City Mumbai Nairobi Paris
São Paulo Singapore Taipei Tokyo Toronto Warsaw

and associated companies in
Berlin Ibadan

Oxford is a trade mark of Oxford University Press

First published 1989
Reprinted 1991, 1992, 1993, 1994
New Edition First Published 1996
Reprinted 1997, 1998

ISBN 0 19 832797 8 School edition
ISBN 0 19 832751 X Bookshop edition

Printed in Hong Kong